LANDSCAPE INFRASTRUCTURE
Case Studies by SWA

The Infrastructure Research Initiative at SWA (ed.)

INFRA LAND STRUC SCAPE TURE

Case Studies by SWA

Ying-Yu Hung

Gerdo Aquino

Charles Waldheim

Julia Czerniak

Adriaan Geuze and Matthew Skjonsberg

Alexander Robinson

Birkhäuser
Basel

THE EDITOR OF THIS PUBLICATION, THE INFRASTRUCTURE RESEARCH INITIATIVE AT SWA,
APPRECIATES COMMENTS FROM READERS WHICH SHOULD BE DIRECTED TO THE FOLLOWING
EMAIL ADDRESS: LANDSCAPE-INFRASTRUCTURE@SWAGROUP.COM

GRAPHIC DESIGN CONCEPT AND LAYOUT: YEE DESIGN AND LIZ LAGEDROST, LOS ANGELES
PROJECT COORDINATOR: NATALIE SANDOVAL, LOS ANGELES

EDITORIAL SUPERVISION: RIA STEIN, BERLIN
COPY-EDITOR: MELISSA VAUGHN, BELMONT, MASSACHUSETTS

A CIP CATALOGUE RECORD FOR THIS BOOK IS AVAILABLE FROM THE LIBRARY OF CONGRESS,
WASHINGTON, D.C., USA

BIBLIOGRAPHIC INFORMATION PUBLISHED BY THE GERMAN NATIONAL LIBRARY: THE GERMAN
NATIONAL LIBRARY LISTS THIS PUBLICATION IN THE DEUTSCHE NATIONALBIBLIOGRAFIE;
DETAILED BIBLIOGRAPHIC DATA IS AVAILABLE ON THE INTERNET AT HTTP://DNB.D-NB.DE.

© 2011 BIRKHÄUSER GMBH
P.O. BOX 133, CH-4010 BASEL, SWITZERLAND
PRINTED ON ACID-FREE PAPER PRODUCED FROM CHLORINE-FREE PULP. TCF ∞
PRINTED IN GERMANY

ISBN 978-3-0346-0593-9

WWW.BIRKHAUSER.CH

9 8 7 6 5 4 3 2 1

CON TENTS

PRE
FACE

by Gerdo Aquino

THE ROLE OF PUBLIC INFRASTRUCTURE in our cities and towns is changing. The integration of clean energy, mass-transit alternatives to car traffic, and changing attitudes about water conservation has created a new set of performance criteria for existing and proposed infrastructural corridors. As large, contiguous systems, these corridors are networked across a vast scale of public and private lands, serving the historic purposes of moving vehicles, electricity, water, and oil. The primary aim of this book is to question the ongoing viability of these single-purpose corridors by proposing that a multifunctional approach is more in tune with contemporary society. Two landscape-based systems seem appropriate as programmatic overlays to these infrastructural systems. The first is a ubiquitous pedestrian system. As residential densities increase, so does the need for improved transit and equal access to open space for social and cultural activity. The second is natural systems— water, vegetation, soil, and habitat and their latent potential to operate within a broader, more connected distribution network. Landscape becomes the medium through which to formulate and articulate solutions for the integration of infrastructure with viable programming that can address the pressing issues facing many cities around the world. In effect, landscape plays a more structured role in the development of new infrastructure, raising the question: can landscape itself be considered infrastructure, when acting as a kind of conveyance or distribution network capable of moving people and supporting a variety of living systems?

This book, *Landscape Infrastructure*, drew substantial inspiration from a symposium held at the University of Toronto in 2008, called "Landscape Infrastructures— Emerging Practices, Paradigms and Technologies Reshaping the Contemporary Urban Landscape," in which academics, writers, and practitioners shared their views on this topic and its potential to heighten the polemics of landscape. The symposium posited that landscape infrastructure repositions landscape as a complex, instrumental system of essential services, resources, and processes that underpins contemporary urban economies and acts as a kind of performative hybrid infrastructure that is as much about culture as about engineering. The symposium participants overwhelmingly argued that a fresh point of view is needed to plan and manage cities with outdated infrastructure and that a focus on infrastructure is the key to a more vibrant and functional 21st-century city. The City of Chicago's Green Alley Program of 2007, for example, seeks to transform an unprecedented 3,057 kilometers of poorly drained public alleyway infrastructure into 14.16 square kilometers of permeable surface area to reduce flooding and heat-island effect, while maintaining access for service vehicles and creating a viable medium for plants. What is compelling about this approach to repurposing infrastructure is the potential for a simple landscape gesture (porous paving) to simultaneously yield ecological benefits such as ground water recharge, phytoremediation, habitat creation, and a contiguous recreation framework for people.

The Infrastructure Research Initiative at SWA (I.R.I.S) was created by Ying-Yu Hung and myself as a testing ground for engaging and redefining infrastructure in the context of future growth in our cities and towns. This book seeks to position the future of infrastructure as an integrated alternative for improving mass transit, enhancing public accessibility and ecological performance, while remaining economically sound. Further objectives of the book are to merge relevant topics in hydrology, natural systems, density, transit, pollution, and public health with infrastructure and program. A series of critical essays will explore the potential of landscape infrastructure as a means to further dialogue. Case studies collected by I.R.I.S represent the work of various SWA studios and are offered, not as a definitive collection, but rather as a broad outline positing a set of principles and strategies with which to explore the potential of this topic and the various contexts that can nurture further investigation, research, and analysis. As an integral part of our daily regimen, infrastructure must be reimagined for the advancement of our culture, ourselves, nature, and the lifestyles we hope to sustain now and in the future.

Reading the Recent Work of SWA | CHARLES WALDHEIM

WHAT CAN ONE SAY WHEN CONFRONTED with the recent work of the SWA Group, as presented in this publication? It would do well to clarify the work's origins and attributions —to locate it in relation to SWA's origins, historical iterations, and diverse contemporary identities. This reading would also allow one to situate the work of SWA in the broader design milieu and disciplinary discourse of landscape architecture as a form of urbanism.

This publication and the "Infrastructure Research Initiative" that initiated it are largely the intellectual and practical work of Gerdo Aquino and Ying-Yu Hung in the Los Angeles office of SWA. Aquino and Hung formed a studio of SWA in downtown Los Angeles in October 2004. Given SWA's historic footprint in California, and the proximity of its Laguna Beach office, one would read the formation of this new studio as motivated by something other than simple market share; the formation of the LA studio has at once reinvigorated SWA Group's historic commitments to studio culture and—reinforced the autonomy of its principals. It is possible to view the recent work of the LA studio (we may efficiently refer to the speculative studio within the corporate body as Aquino/Hung et al.) as forming a contemporary alternative to the popular perception of late SWA as a large, multinational, corporate landscape architecture and planning firm. This particular form of a smaller studio within a larger practice is relatively well established, often referred to as a "boutique" design studio operating within the structure of a large corporate design consultancy. The economic and cultural logics supporting this arrangement are not uninteresting and might be fairly generalized as affording a desirable combination of seemingly irreconcilable attributes for a design practice. Among the perceived benefits are financial stability, cash flow, and general name-brand reputation on the business side of the ledger, combined with an agility, flexibility, and openness to new ideas traditionally associated with younger, smaller, and less well-capitalized design shops. Although this formation has many precedents, the work of Aquino/Hung et al. presents specific aspects that deserve attention. SWA, originally formulated as Sasaki Walker Associates in 1957, was conceived around the development of a distinct studio culture of multidisciplinary collaboration, decentralized autonomy, independent decision-making, and design innovation. The formation of the LA studio, and Aquino's direction of it, could then be read in two ways: as an attempt to expand SWA's practice in the context of increasing competition for brand identity, market share, and critical distinction among its peer institutions, and as a vigorous extension to SWA Group's origins in a commitment to autonomous studio structure and decisive design direction. Perhaps it was viewed equally as a means for recruiting and retaining the next generation of design leadership, who would find the downtown LA location reflective of a newfound cosmopolitanism in the practice of landscape architecture and planning. Whatever the motivations, the rhetorical shift associated with the foundation of an LA studio was significant, both in locational and linguistic terms. Among the related rhetorical moves would be the formulation "Infrastructure Research Initiative"—the impetus for this publication. The use of the term "initiative" places Aquino and Hung on the offensive, carefully setting apart this effort from the "collaborative studio" format that SWA had made its calling card. The use of "initiative" further distinguishes

0 100 300 500m

the activities of the LA studio as addressing more broadly the culture, identity, and core values of the SWA Group brand. By describing the activities of the studio as "research" (as opposed to practice, work, or projects), Aquino and Hung aspire to build a space for experimentation, risk-taking, and the production of landscape projects as cultural forms. Aquino/Hung et al., as well as the supportive senior leadership of SWA, may have intended to use the LA studio as a kind of design think-tank. One could also imagine that they hoped to speculate on future forms of cultural production to reposition SWA Group's work as relevant to design and planning professions increasingly focused on design leadership. This is not to say that SWA Group's impressive half century of landscape design and planning work was not without its historic contributions to the disciplinary discourse and professional aspirations of landscape architecture, urban design, or planning. Rather, it seems possible that the SWA Group found that while they had been extraordinarily successful with global relevance and reach, they were increasingly

perceived by some as having grown beyond their origins as a studio-focused, design-driven shop. This brings us to the first rhetorical clue, and the central claim of the work presented here, in the very title of this publication itself: "infrastructure." By choosing infrastructure as the object of study, Aquino/Hung et al. enter contemporary discourse on landscape as a form of urbanism. This is a crafty move, one not without its ironies, particularly given that SWA has historically had more to do with infrastructure as an element of contemporary landscape and urban design than could be summed up in this modest publication. Of course the SWA Group came to prominence at a moment when landscape architecture was fundamentally committed to the design and construction of urban environments as shaped by infrastructure. In describing the activities of the LA studio as research into infrastructure as an element of urban order, Aquino/Hung et al. consciously appropriated one of the most resonant of contemporary topics in landscape research, one that would simultaneously inform a reading of SWA Group's current commitments as well as shed light on a rereading of the firm's history.

One reading of Aquino's aspirations in rebranding SWA through the LA studio is evident in his identification of infrastructure as one dimension of recent interest in landscape as a form of urbanism. The disciplinary discourse and design methods associated with landscape urbanism emerged over the past decade as a critique of the disciplinary and professional commitments of traditional urban design and an alternative to "New Urbanism." The critique launched by landscape urbanism has much to do with urban design's perceived inability to come to terms with the rapid pace of urban change and the essentially horizontal character of contemporary automobile-based urbanization across North America and much of Western Europe. It equally has to do with the inability of traditional urban design strategies to cope with the environmental conditions left in the wake of deindustrialization, with increased calls for an ecologically informed urbanism, and with the ongoing ascendancy of design culture as an aspect of urban development. The established discourse of landscape urbanism is seemingly enjoying a robust middle age, at once no longer sufficiently youthful for the avant-gardist appetites of architectural culture yet growing in significance as its key texts and projects are translated and disseminated globally. The discourse on landscape urbanism, while hardly new in architectural circles, is being absorbed into the global discourse on cities within urban design and planning, nowhere more rapidly than in the East Asian context of urbanization, particularly through international design competitions for new cities in China and South Korea.

It is no coincidence that over this same period of time, landscape architecture has itself enjoyed a relative renaissance within design culture. This well-documented resurgence of what had been described by some as a relatively moribund field of intellectual inquiry has been particularly fruitful for discussions of contemporary urbanism. In addition to its relevance for describing the contemporary urban field, might landscape have potential to resonate with the larger territorial subjects of urban planning? Ironically, the potential for landscape to inform planning comes from its newfound ascendancy within design culture and the deployment of ecology as model or metaphor rather than through the longstanding historical project of ecologically informed regional planning. As this point is a potential source of confusion and is likely to be a topic of debate, this essay offers a provisional reading of how landscape might profitably inform the present and future commitments of urban planning.

Landscape's renewed relevance as model for contemporary urbanization was first highlighted by European architects and urbanists describing North American cities such as Los Angeles (Kenneth Frampton), Houston (Lars Lerup) or Atlanta (Rem Koolhaas). It has come to stand for a profound critique of the perceived failures of urban design to effectively respond to the spatial decentralization, neoliberal economic shifts, and environmental toxicity found in those cities. Equally, it promises an alternative to the reactionary cultural politics of traditional urban form, in which environmental health, social welfare, and cultural aspiration are no longer mutually exclusive. Although landscape architects may not have been the first to make such claims, the discipline has mounted spirited support for its expanded agency as the field diversifies and grows in design literacy.

Meanwhile, over the course of the past decade, the discipline of urban design has been largely preoccupied with traditional urban form, and has been relatively slow to appreciate the import of landscape's newfound cultural relevance. These developments are not unrelated to the rapprochement between the design disciplines; they have been informed by calls for interdisciplinarity with respect to the challenges of the contemporary city as well as in design education.

It is in the context of urban design's unrealized promise that landscape urbanism has emerged in the past decade. Landscape urbanism has come to stand for an alternative within the broad base of urban design historically defined. Incorporating continuity with the aspirations of an ecologically informed planning practice, landscape urbanism has been equally informed by high design culture, contemporary modes of urban development, and the complexity of public-private partnerships. Although it may be true that the urban form proposed by landscape urbanism has not yet fully arrived, it would be equally fair to say that landscape urbanism remains the most promising alternative available to urban design's formation for the coming decades. Landscape urbanism offered a culturally leavened, ecologically literate, and economically viable model for contemporary urbanization as an alternative to urban design's ongoing nostalgia for traditional urban forms. One evidence of this is the number of internationally prominent landscape architects who have been retained as lead designers of large-scale urban development proposals in which landscape offers ecological function, cultural authority, and brand identity. Another would be the fact that SWA Group has invested in Aquino/Hung et al. the task of rebranding their global enterprise along the lines of contemporary interests in landscape as a form of urbanism.

Yet SWA has been engaged in planning projects concerned with urban infrastructure for a long time. This fact has much to do with SWA's origins in a specific moment of design culture, when the new field of urban design was being invented. At that time, the professional practice and academic study of landscape architecture had much to do with the description and delivery of urban form. The invention of urban design as a design discipline effectively happened at a conference in Harvard on that subject in 1956. It coincided more or less precisely with Hideo Sasaki and Peter Walker forming SWA (1957) and with Sasaki's appointment as Chair of Landscape Architecture at Harvard (1958). In this milieu, and in the institutional context of Harvard's Graduate School of Design, one proposal for the development of the Urban Design program at Harvard (founded in 1960) was that it would be administered by the Department of Landscape Architecture.

This intriguing historical possibility was recently documented by Richard Marshall in the Harvard Design Magazine's issue on the history and future of urban design.[1] It would have rehearsed nearly exactly the origins of urban planning at Harvard, which was itself hatched and housed for a time in the Department of Landscape Architecture. In the cultural context and pedagogical profile of landscape architecture at Harvard during the period 1956–1958, urban infrastructure was rightly considered a disciplinary domain associated with landscape architecture. In this regard, one could read Sasaki Walker Associates, SWA, and subsequent iterations of the firm as having stemmed from an ethos based in collaborations across disciplines, in which landscape architects played a central role in the shaping of urban form. In the economic and social contexts of the late 1950s and 1960s, the firm first rose to prominence through servicing a range of design and planning clients, largely in sites of rapid urbanization and growth. This tendency continued with increasing international engagements for corporate clients, private developers, and public-sector actors engaged in urbanization. From the late 1960s through the 1990s, however, design culture and the discipline of landscape architecture shifted dramatically in favor of smaller design offices, increasing disciplinary and professional distinctions between landscape architects, urban designers, and architects; a simultaneous development was the increasing role of civil engineering and land planning professionals in competition for the management of urbanization. During this transition—one that has been described as a shift from a Fordist to a post-Fordist economy—landscape architecture and planning firms transformed themselves from studio-based collaboratives formed around professional identities and often held as partnerships into larger multidisciplinary organizations increasingly organized around integrated project delivery and mirroring the corporate structure of their clients. This transition found many firms moving internationally to insulate themselves and balance the risk of turbulent domestic business cycles. During this time, SWA transitioned to its third generation of leadership and reorganized itself as an employee-owned firm. SWA was poised to deliver urbanization virtually anywhere on the planet, but design culture and the disciplinary construction of landscape architecture had changed radically in favor of "starchitects," brand-name designers, and celebrity landscape architects. By the late 1980s and early 1990s, as economic imperatives and media culture pushed the design disciplines to embrace an explicitly branded form of design authorship associated with design excellence, SWA had successfully smuggled a collaborative, studio-based form of landscape practice into an ever more globalized marketplace for urbanization. They found themselves in demand globally, frequently called upon to synthesize the effects of multidisciplinary design teams including the work of land planners and civil engineers responsible for urban infrastructure. They were not, however, well positioned to market themselves as an idea-driven, research-focused design studio closely associated with the design philosophy (read style) of a singular figure in the field, as were increasing numbers of their competitors. The challenge of generational transition from founders to next-generation leadership has haunted design practice in North America over the past century. By some, the model that SWA committed to in Aquino/Hung et al.—of a boutique design practice operating within a larger firm—has a long lineage. In architectural practice, the equivalent example could be Skidmore, Owings & Merrill in the 1950s and 1960s. In Chicago, Walter Netsch developed a boutique studio practice, bringing his own clients and staff to bear on a range of award-winning design projects under his name but with the benefit of SOM's support infrastructure and brand name. The combined economic and cultural forces on contemporary practice produce a hybrid in which the individual design talent (and all that it promises in marketing or media) is embedded within the larger service firm (and all that it affords in terms of project experience, market capitalization, and support staff).

So the question persists: what can one say when confronted with the recent work of the SWA Group, as presented in this publication? As this brief introduction is far too limited to aspire to anything synthetic or comprehensive, a rereading of three featured projects might be apt. All three display

an appetite for an ecologically leavened urbanization in the context of massive social, economic, and cultural transformations associated with global processes of urbanization.

In their June 2009 entry for the Anning River International Design Competition in Miyi County, Sichuan Province, China, SWA proposed the organization of a new town through a reading of the site's historic ecologies and contemporary hydrologic networks. The project, "Future Historic Ecologies," proposes the introduction of a range of ecological agents including bio-film matrix strips to stimulate the activation of functioning wetland ecologies. These synthetic agitations of the existing river ecology are situated within an historical and interpretive reading of cultural landscape and ecological heritage. These aspects of the Anning River

proposal point to emergent fields of research, particularly the intersections of river hydrology, synthetic habitat construction, and landscape or agricultural ecology as elements of cultural heritage. The scale, ecological potential, and historical literacy of this proposal illustrate the range of commitments and areas of research fostered within the space of SWA's LA studio and the Infrastructure Research Initiative there.

In their entry for the Chongming Island International Design Competition of June 2008, in Shanghai, China, the studio asks two provocative questions: can we farm habitats? Can the city improve nature? Their project "Cultured Ecology; Ecological Culture," implies that these are relevant questions for contemporary urbanists to consider, but the more probative dimension of the proposal revisits the hybridity of historic ecologies with synthetic environments seen in their Anning River project. In Chongming Island, we see this uncanny twinning of cultural heritage (formerly the province of preservation-minded architects) with highly engineered wildlife habitat (formerly the province of restoration-minded landscape architects). This project proposes a third approach between putting back the city or putting back nature—a synthetic hybrid of infrastructures, urban and ecological. This hybridization and multifunctioning of urban infrastructure form recurrent themes in the work of SWA Group's LA studio.

A third example of the Infrastructure Research Initiative's ongoing concerns can be found in their entry for the "Multifunctional Administrative City" (MAC) International Design Competition of 2007, in South Korea. Here, a conceptual inversion was proposed through which the city is fundamentally reconceived as park—a reformulation of the basic arguments on behalf of landscape as urbanism. The proposal can also be read as an historical reinterpretation of the western tradition of urban landscape understood through urban infrastructure. This historical literacy regarding urban type, block structure, and landscape design reveals the studio's deep affection for landscape history as a medium of city-making, whether in the tradition of Olmsted, Alphand, or others.

These three projects from Aquino/Hung's LA studio adapt contemporary tropes of landscape urbanism practice and reshape them to the service of massive ongoing urbanization. They form an interesting hybrid between the contemporary avant-gardist aspirations of much design practice globally and an enlightened rereading of the histories and traditions of regionally informed ecological planning practice. They rehearse much of the discourse around landscape urbanism

MASTER PLAN FOR THE NORTH LAKE REGION OF CHONGMING ISLAND, SHANGHAI, CHINA.

This 2007 design by SWA Group (LA Office/Aquino/ Hung et. al.) addresses global issues of sustainable development, carbon sequestration, and wetland restoration, while providing for the educational and recreational needs of the residents of Shanghai.

from the past decade or more while formatting themselves to the repetitive standardization of the international design competition. Although North American discourse on urbanism and landscape has tended to maintain a distinction between larger corporate service firms and design-driven boutiques, the list of competitors to these urban design competitions reveals the strong structural symmetries between the celebrity design firms and their corporate counterparts.

First, virtually all competitors represent flexible teams built from a range of international consulting practices. The design firm built around the identity of a single architect or landscape architect and the firm built on a collective corporate identity are converging rapidly on a model of collaboration. Second, it is no longer a safe assumption that the firm identified through a single principal designer is less well-capitalized than its corporate cousin, nor can one make easy assumptions regarding their forms of ownership or profitability. Third, the celebrities and their corporate counterparts are often engaged in joint ventures, partnerships, and buyouts. The design fields in general, and large multidisciplinary urbanism firms in particular, are trending toward a state that has existed in advertising for many years in which a stable economy is found between a few large, global brands that act as holding (and trading) companies for a countless number of boutique design shops.

It is no coincidence that Aquino/Hung et al. identified the discourse around landscape urbanism generally, and infrastructure more specifically, as an entry point into contemporary readings of landscape as a cultural form. Over the past decade, an adjectivally modified form of urbanism

(be it landscape, ecological, or other) has emerged as the most robust and fully formed critique of urban design and planning's failure to produce meaningful, socially just, and environmentally healthful cities. The structural conditions necessitating an environmentally modified urbanism emerged precisely at the moment when European models of urban density, centrality, and legibility of urban form appear rather remote and when most of us live and work in environments more suburban than urban, more vegetal than architectonic, more infrastructural than enclosed. In these spaces, the work of the SWA Group's LA office and its Infrastructure Research Initiative proposes infrastructure as a medium of design informing both landscape and urbanism. Although the LA studio may have begun as an initiative by Aquino/Hung to correlate design and research practice with the City of Los Angeles, while attempting to recruit and retain the next generation of design leadership, it has recently come to portend the future direction of the firm more broadly: Aquino has been named SWA's new president. The scalability of his accomplishments from an insurgent studio in downtown LA to the global scale of SWA Group at large remains to be proven; this publication is timely, revealing both the objects and subjects of contemporary design culture as it continues to transform in relation to urbanization driven by mobile international capital.

NOTES

1   Richard Marshall, "The Elusiveness of Urban Design: The Perpetual Problems of Definition and Role," *Harvard Design Magazine*, no. 24, Spring/Summer 2006, pp. 21–32.

Landscape Infrastructure:

SYSTEMS OF CONTINGENCY, FLEXIBILITY, AND ADAPTABILITY

YING-YU HUNG

LANDSCAPE ARCHITECTURE IS A DISCIPLINE of diverse interests, scales, and territories. In this regard, the field of landscape architecture is vague and requires clarification. Landscape architecture as a profession in the United States, however, is traditionally recognized as engaging two general areas: landscape planning to integrate sensitively natural resources and development, and landscape design as a cultural and economic construct serving people's needs. These two broadly defined areas are at times addressed separately due to scale and site complexities, leading to a fragmented point of view of "landscape."

Over the last 20 years, new trends in landscape architecture have sought to define the practice from a more holistic vantage point, one that is not limited by what we create but that reflects an integral part of our philosophy—our way of life. This new worldview stems from our realization that we, as a society, have contributed to the deterioration of our environment. Landscape architects and urbanists can help reverse the process, cognizant that even with our best intentions, the landscape we create may yield unpredictable results, and that the aspect of "change" is the underlying factor in everything we do.

This philosophical understanding suggests a new way to think about landscape architecture, a way that furthers the dialogue between ecological process and design. To that end, landscape architecture is crossing disciplines; the physical framework from which landscape architecture operates has no boundaries, and the purposes it serves are becoming more infrastructural, sociopolitical, economic, and environmental. In addition, the practice of landscape architecture today is more closely aligned with architecture, urban

design, and planning than ever before. Many successful infrastructural projects often involve landscape architects' full participation with engineers and scientists from the outset. Among many leading practitioners, the convergence of these practices shares a common outlook: the global landscape is mosaic-based, where edges are permeable and the boundaries between cities and countryside are in flux. Within this "mosaic" landscape, there exists a complex set of networks or systems that are highly interconnected and interdependent. The systems cannot be approached in isolation, as even the smallest intervention affects the larger whole. Landscape architecture today offers the means to analyze, synthesize, and provide an organizational framework toward an integrated urban design strategy. At the same time, the landscape architect possesses the unique ability to address a project at multiple scales—to think big and small at the same time, to give form and beauty and create identity and memory in a place.

IDENTIFYING THE TREND: LANDSCAPE URBANISM

"Landscape urbanism" is a term coined 12 years ago by Charles Waldheim, who stated that "landscape has become a lens through which the contemporary city is represented and a medium through which it is constructed."[1] Further, Waldheim contends that landscape architecture has in fact replaced architecture and urban design as the primary discipline that establishes the framework for contemporary city-making. The premise that architecture and urban design have become commodities used to further the economic needs of the city through branding and rebranding has put these professions at risk of becoming irrelevant. In contrast,

landscape architecture seeks to take on the context itself, the infrastructure and the "spaces in between" within urban environments, to instill purpose, legibility, and cohesiveness, so that the city as a whole is healthy and robust.

The tenets of landscape urbanism as described by Waldheim clarify a series of conditions that commonly exist in our practice of landscape architecture today.

1. *The practice of landscape architecture involves the acceptance that ecological and social processes in an urban environment cannot be determined. Modest investment and control at strategic moments during the design process may yield greater richness and complexity in the end.*

2. *As a means to educate the public about the role of nature in the urban context, ecology has largely assumed a performative role as a public spectacle that can be easily understood and appreciated by any person. The same could be said about landscape architecture as environmental art, a medium through which artists and designers reveal the ephemeral forces of nature by visually recording these subtle changes over time.*

3. *By leveraging the public's basic interest in ecology ("ecological literacy"), the landscape architect today is able to create a new development paradigm that is ecologically viable, culturally relevant to the identity of the place, and financially profitable.*

4. *Translating the principles of landscape urbanism into physical form increasingly relies on the use of parametric processes, in which a set of variables or parameters is given to a design problem. By manipulating the variables (which may be ecologically driven), alternative solutions are generated, such as varying degrees of building density, or configurations of building massing yielding optimized open-space networks.*[2]

Waldheim's elucidation of these critical points on landscape urbanism prompted a renewed focus in the profession and reaffirmed the significance of landscape architecture. It is clear that the role of landscape architecture begins at a pre-policy level and where public and private interests establish rapport for a common cause. This common cause forms a physical blueprint for which subsequent policies are adopted into planning guidelines for future projects. SWA's Anning River master plan project in the province of Sichuan, China, best illustrates this process. This 330-hectare project was conceived in a competition to solicit nontraditional strategies toward integrated ecological planning. As the selected winner, the project identified valuable features that would be part of a future infrastructural framework, including 56 hectares of agricultural land, irrigation canals, and a hydro-electric power plant (as an education tool for public outreach). The project further developed innovative technologies to clean the murky water of the Anning River, using bioremediation to make clean water available for passive recreation, wetlands, and forests, to increase biodiversity. This strong ecological planning approach gives the government the tools to apply for public funding, to give the city a unique identity, and to set up control guidelines for future developments.

BROWNWOOD MARSH RESTORATION, BAYTOWN, TEXAS.

The boundary between nature and human habitation is constantly in flux, where human action may easily tip the balance as in the case of a new housing subdivision in Galveston Bay, Texas. The industrial ground water withdrawal caused more than 15 feet of subsidence, bringing the entire development down to sea level. As part of the Superfund project, SWA and Couch Environmental converted the neighborhood into a 60-acre saltwater marsh, creating a rich habitat for wildlife, including 275 bird species, fish, and crustaceans.

IN FOCUS: LANDSCAPE INFRASTRUCTURE

Within the framework of landscape urbanism, infrastructure offers the next step for further inquiry as a city's development and economic future is in direct proportion to its ability to collect, exchange, distribute goods and services, resources, knowledge, and people across vast territories. A city with a well-capitalized infrastructural system provides for an efficient, fluid operation hence maximizing its productive power and regional influence. Funded by powerful public and private ventures, North American cities developed from the 18th to the 20th century were outfitted by a robust system of railways, highway networks, ports, and terminals. The fierce competition for resources, technology, and commerce in the 21st-century global economy necessitates a close reexamination of America's infrastructural viability, to evaluate systems' current capacity, ability to meet expectations, and to repurpose these systems as potential future resources.

The U.S. Interstate Highway System is an example: it was initially developed for national defense purposes—distributing ammunition and wartime vessels and dispatching military personnel efficiently throughout the country. Over the last 50

BALLONA CREEK,
LOS ANGELES, CALIFORNIA.

A channelized waterway isolated from the rest of the urban context by chain link fences. On one side of the channel is a 14.5-kilometer-long bike path which connects the City of Los Angeles to Marina Del Rey.

years, this road system has been re-appropriated for civilian use, carrying 40 percent of all highway traffic, 75 percent of heavy truck traffic, and 90 percent of tourist traffic.[3] Due to overcapacity and lack of funding for improvements and maintenance, the infrastructure is in disrepair. This situation requires that we reevaluate the 75,440 kilometers of contiguous freeway system, to explore alternative means for transportation that are more energy-efficient and to recalibrate the current system into a multimodal strategy, as an ecological conveyance and a resource and energy redistribution mechanism throughout the United States.

WHAT IS INFRASTRUCTURE?

Infrastructure, classically defined, is "the basic facilities, services, and installations needed for the functioning of a community or society, such as transportation and communications systems, water and power lines, and public institutions including schools, post offices, and prisons."[4] This essay focuses on land-based infrastructure and not public institutions and building facilities, simply because the practice of landscape architecture is inseparable from the realm of transport and utility infrastructure.

Our current infrastructural system has several defining characteristics. First, the system is often hidden from view, its logic and functional attributes are not immediately apparent, which breeds unhappy surprises and mounting frustration when the system fails.[5] A case in point was the burst water mains in Los Angeles (part of the city's aging water system), resulting in massive flooding, damaged vehicles and housing, and water outage.[6] Second, the design and engineering of infrastructure was historically conceived in isolation, independent of the overall urban vision. An uncoordinated infrastructural system often leads to conflicts and incompatibility between the infrastructure and its context, resulting in compromise measures such as mitigation, camouflage, and sometimes deactivation of the system, as opposed to the creation of urban parks and plazas that are places of celebration and civic pride.[7] Last, the U.S. as a society, has traditionally placed a high value on the design of monofunctional infrastructural systems, engineered to maximize efficiency at a given time to fulfill a single purpose, but failing to provide a consistent level of efficiency throughout their lifespans. Such a singular approach produces serious impacts on the way infrastructure contributes to urban life. Parking lots, transportation corridors, transit hubs, and channelized waterways are left idle between peak hours, creating voids and barriers in the city. The "rivers" of Los Angeles are channelized waterways, including the 14.5-kilometer-long Ballona Creek corridor, which has an average peak flow of 107 cubic meters per second.[8] During a particularly heavy winter storm in 2010, the entire channel was emptied within two hours, with the discharge directed into the Santa Monica Bay.

These infrastructural systems operate in the background; people know that they exist, but would rather forget about them. We are reminded of their existence when health and safety are at risk, such as in the case of BP's oil spill in the Gulf of Mexico and the 2010 deadly coal mine explosion in West Virginia.[9] When such disasters make headlines, we are suddenly awakened to the cold reality of how infrastructure can threaten our lives, strip us of our livelihoods and diminish our enjoyment of life. As the interaction between countries has become more fluid and the perceived geographical distances between places have been significantly reduced due to immediacy of digital technology and ease of transcontinental flights, the infrastructure as we know it has ventured into uncharted territories—we are at risk of losing our ability to control and manage what we have created.

WHAT IS LANDSCAPE INFRASTRUCTURE?

The recent writings and discourse held among major universities and the professional community at large point toward the undeniable fact that "once married with architecture, mobility, and landscape, infrastructure can more meaningfully integrate territories, reduce marginalization and segregation, and stimulate new forms of interaction. It can then truly become 'landscape.'"[10] The integration of the infrastructural system within the landscape framework requires one to redefine the old system within a new set of paradigms, one that is more aligned to natural systems of ecology.

First, the nature of infrastructure today is successional,[11] where modes of infrastructure may quickly become obsolete, redistributed, and reinvented, subjected by global geopolitical and economic forces. The contingency of today's infrastructure necessitates the system to be designed for flexibility and adaptability.[12]

Second, traditional infrastructure was conceived as a centralized, single-purpose system; the trend for today's infrastructure system is to become decentralized, where the need to address, for instance, stormwater runoff, energy, farming, or transportation are resolved at a local level.[13] Aside from performing its intended functions, the multifunctional variations of these vital systems can be a catalyst for urban revitalization through open-space augmentation, habitat creation, community revitalization, and transformation of urban blight into urban destination.

Last, infrastructure such as roads "are required to perform multiple functions: they must fulfill the requirements of public space and must be connected to other functioning urban systems of public transit, pedestrian movement, water management, economic development, public facilities, and ecological systems."[14] The multifunctional aspect of infrastructure also speaks to the importance of diversification as a general principle in city-making, leading to an optimized condition in which the city and its infrastructure are one and the same—where infrastructure informs how the city is organized and built. A classic example is the Back Bay Fens in Boston, designed and engineered by Frederick Law Olmsted. The site was formerly a saltwater marshland tainted with untreated raw sewage from the city's growing settlement. Land-reclamation projects in the 1820s began a series of dedicated efforts to improve water quality, control floods, and allow a tidal ecosystem to be reestablished. Today the Back Bay Fens is part of the 445-hectare chain of parks, parkways, and waterways forming the Emerald Necklace, bringing improved air quality, urban runoff retention and remediation, wildlife habitats, trails, sports venues, and a 107-hectare arboretum to Boston residents.

In addition to the temporal, decentralized, and multifunctional characteristics that define landscape infrastructure, landscape infrastructure is further comprised of a set of attributes relating to form, function, and time, outlined below, all of which have a cumulative effect benefiting the greater whole. A landscape infrastructure project may contain all of the attributes described, with one more dominant than another given varying degrees of scale, scope, and influence.

1. **Performance.** *As a nonisolated system, landscape infrastructure has the ability to adhere to a set of requirements and achieve measurable results.*

Infrastructure has traditionally been engineered to meet a set of expectations, while the benefits of landscape have often been undervalued due to its inability to produce quantifiable results. By adopting the infrastructure model, the performance of a functioning urban ecosystem can be evaluated and adjusted to achieve maximum results. Chicago, for example, has the world's largest surface area of green roofs for an urban center.[15] The performative nature of green roofs could be quantified through the system's ability to reduce heat gain, collect stormwater, and provide urban wildlife habitat.

LEFT:
Service alleyway in downtown Los Angeles at Broadway and 5th Street.

CENTER AND RIGHT:
Biddy Mason Park in downtown Los Angeles, a pocket park and alleyway between Broadway and Spring Street near the historic Bradbury building. This urban respite is one of the "Art Walk" sites, with interpretive art and sculptural fountains celebrating Los Angeles's multicultural history.

2. Aggregate. *Landscape infrastructure is often seen as piecemeal objects. When consolidated, the collective whole has the ability to remediate and sometimes even reverse negative impact.*

As a car-obsessed country, the United States builds its infrastructure around cars—a complex web of roads and tunnels, car dealers, parking structures, gas stations, and car-wash facilities. Tremendous resources and government incentives have been put toward research of fuel-efficient cars, alternative fuels, waterless car washing, and green parking lot design. These seemingly uncoordinated efforts, if implemented within a given time frame, could help reverse the negative impacts of global warming.

3. Network. *Infrastructure is a connective tissue that brings together disparate elements, instilling cohesion and purpose. The sheer scale and vast resources spent on network infrastructure present tremendous opportunities to leverage unrealized potential in the urban environment.*

U.S. cities that depend on freeways and automobiles as the primary means of transporting goods and services are increasingly being retrofitted with public transit. The transit corridors function as a giant network linking neighborhoods. Neighborhoods and local businesses along the transit nodes grow and benefit from greater exposure to the public, making them more identifiable and valuable.

Los Angeles has 822 kilometers of freeways, 82 kilometers of channelized waterways, 11,265 kilometers of power lines, 10,299 kilometers of streets, and much more infrastructure hidden all over the city that has not been accounted for.[16] The latest survey conducted by the City Council shows that infrastructure improvements rank at the top of the list to improve Los Angeles's neighborhoods. The city's alleyways are narrow corridors nestled between city blocks, typically designed for service-oriented vehicular circulation: parking, loading zone for delivery trucks, and solid waste collection. All together, the alleyways in Los Angeles account for more than 1,448 kilometers of pavement and cover about 777

BUFFALO BAYOU PROMENADE, HOUSTON, TEXAS.

Aerial view oriented westward toward the bayou with I-45 Interchange in the foreground and uptown Houston beyond. The bayou functions as an ecological, recreational corridor, as well as a detention basin that holds excess flood waters caused by frequent hurricane events.

hectares—about half the size of Los Angeles's Griffith Park and twice the size of New York's Central Park. These alleyways could be retrofitted with bioswales, exploratory bicycle trails, and pedestrian greenways and pocket parks, in addition to being service corridors. As a collective system, the alleyway infrastructure, when operated at a city scale, can reduce stormwater runoff, increase tree coverage, and offer health benefits through outdoor exercise.[17]

4. Increment. *The incremental nature of infrastructural projects bears directly on a city's ability to sustain growth through a measured period of time.*

Most public infrastructure projects are realized and put in full operation over many decades, mostly because of the astronomical cost, the availability of public funds, and the political forces at play. In the San Francisco Bay Area, the Bay Area Rapid Transit (BART) system was introduced in 1946, but the extensions to the three Bay Area counties were not completed until the mid-1990s, including the connection to the San Francisco International Airport. Further extension to Silicon Valley and South Bay remains to be realized.[18] Similarly, the protection of our natural resources such as national parks and significant urban parks takes forethought and unwavering determination, and the benefits are cross-generational. Central Park in New York City was envisioned by Andrew Jackson Downing and William Cullen Bryant as a way to address the ills of society: crowded streets, poor immigrants, and crime. For a rapidly growing city such as New York in the 1830s, it was necessary that the park be large enough to anticipate the needs of its populace. As a significant landscape infrastructural project, the completion of the 341-hectare park in 1860 brought forth unanticipated benefits to the local economy through tourism, increases in property and land values, and increased revenues for the government.

In February 2009, the U.S. Congress passed the American Recovery and Reinvestment Act of 2009 in an effort to stimulate the economy, in its deepest recession since the Great Depression. The stimulus package provides $787 billion in appropriations for crisis investments, including $80.9 billion for infrastructure investment (including roads, bridges, railways, sewers, high-performance green buildings, wastewater treatment infrastructure improvements, drinking water infrastructure improvements, electric vehicle development),

$15 billion for supplemental investments (including Bureau of Reclamation, National Park Service, Forest Service, National Wildlife Refuges), and $45.2 billion for energy (renewable energy, smart grid, electric vehicle technologies, and brown-field land remediation).[19]

To counter the effects of the global financial crisis, China also approved a multibillion-dollar package for infrastructure projects. China's Eleventh Five-Year Plan (2006–2010) focuses on infrastructure investments in central and western regions, including road networks, railways, power grids, and irrigation systems, as the rising middle class in these areas demands an improved standard of living on par with the rest of the country. The ongoing South-to-North Water Diversion project, a daunting feat of mega-engineering delivering water from the water-abundant southern provinces to the water-scarce Beijing region, offers the greatest potential for landscape infrastructure.[20]

We live in a historic moment in which many lawmakers and government officials share a vision for sustainable global development. For individuals who convert their diesel cars to biofuel, urban farmers who replace lawns with organic veg-etable gardens and chicken coops, and academics who teach that the most efficient way toward carbon sequestration lies in the preservation of our forest habitats, bogs, and wetlands, the future of landscape infrastructure projects is in plain view.[21] Our cities need this kind of infrastructural approach that extends beyond perceived boundaries and connects various sites to other sites, people to places, communities to communities, people to people, nature to city, and city to nature. With the rapid growth of our metropolises and the shortage of available open space, however, it has been dis-covered that infrastructure is an untapped resource with the capacity to effect positive change. Through the employment of ecological and social principles, the urban infrastructural systems can play a multifaceted role that actively contributes to the betterment of urban life.

NOTES

1   Charles Waldheim, "A Reference Manifesto," *The Landscape Urbanism Reader*, ed. Charles Waldheim, New York: Princeton Architectural Press, 2006, p. 15.

2   Charles Waldheim, "Planning, Ecology and the Emergence of Landscape," lecture, University of Southern California, February 2009.

3   Rodney E. Slater, "The National Highway System: A Commitment to America's Future," *Public Roads*, Spring 1996, vol. 59, no. 4. http://www.fhwa.dot.gov/publications/publicroads/96spring/p96sp2.cfm (accessed June 2, 2010).

4   "Infrastructure" *Webster's Unabridged Dictionary*, 3rd ed., New York: Random House, 2009.

5   Kazys Varnelis, "Invisible City-Telecommunication," *The Infrastructural City: Networked Ecologies in Los Angeles*, Barcelona/New York: Actar, 2009, p. 126.

6   Jessica Garrison, "Two More L.A. Water Mains Burst Overnight, Bringing More Questions," *Los Angeles Times*, September 16, 2009. http://latimesblogs.latimes.com/lanow/2009/09/2-more-la-water-main-burst-overnight-bringing-more-questions.html (accessed June 2, 2010).

7   Gary L. Strang, "Infrastructure as Landscape," *Places*, vol. 10, no. 3.

8   Kenneth Schiff and Martha Sutula, "Organophosphorus Pesticides in Stormwater Runoff from Southern California," *Southern California Coastal Water Research Project*, www.sccwrp.org, November 9, 2004 (accessed June 2, 2010).

9   John Schwartz, "With Criminal Charges, Costs to BP Could Soar," *New York Times*, June 16, 2010. http://nytimes.com (accessed June 2, 2010).

10   Kelly Shannon and Marcel Smets, *The Landscape of Contemporary Infrastructure*, Rotterdam: NAi Publishers, 2010, p. 9.

11   Richard T. T. Forman, *Land Mosaics: The Ecology of Landscapes and Regions*, Cambridge: Cambridge University Press, 1995, p. 63.

12   Clare Lyster, "Landscape of Exchange: Re-Articulating Site," *The Landscape Urbanism Reader*, ed. Charles Waldheim, New York: Princeton Architectural Press, 2006, p. 226.

13   Pierre Bélanger "Landscape As Infrastructure," *Landscape Journal*, vol. 28, no. 1, 2009, p. 87.

14   Elizabeth Mossop, "Landscape of Infrastructure," *The Landscape Urbanism Reader*, ed. Charles Waldheim, New York: Princeton Architectural Press, 2006, p. 163.

15   *City of Chicago Green Roof Program*, 2007. http://www.cityofchicago.org/city/en/depts/doe/supp_info/green_roof_grantsprograms.html (accessed June 2, 2010).

16   *Los Angeles Department of Water and Power, 2004–2005 Annual Report*, City of Los Angeles Transportation Profile 2009, Department of Public Works, County of Los Angeles.

17   *The Green Alley Handbook*, Department of Transportation, City of Chicago, 2006.

18   "A History of BART," Bay Area Rapid Transit. http://www.bart.gov/about/history/index.aspx (accessed June 2, 2010).

19   *American Recovery and Reinvestment Act of 2009*. http://www.recovery.gov (accessed June 2, 2010).

20   "South-to-North Water Diversion Project, China," *Water-technology.net*, http://www.water-technology.net/projects/south_north/ (accessed June 2, 2010).

21   "Old-Growth Forests as Global Carbon Sinks," *Nature*, September 11, 2008, pp. 213–215. http://www.nature.com/nature/journal/v455/n7210/full/nature07276.html (accessed June 2, 2010).

Jon Kusler, "Wetland, Climate Change and Carbon Sequestering," U.S. Environmental Protection Agency, 2005. http://www.aswm.org/propub/11_carbon_6_26_06.pdf (accessed June 2, 2010).

Foregrounding | JULIA CZERNIAK

THE WORD LANDSCAPE, WHEN PLACED in front of other disciplines—think landscape *urbanism*, landscape *ecology*, even landscape *architecture*—qualifies, modifies, and usurps them, simultaneously strengthening landscape's disciplinary base and expanding its range of operations. This is true also of landscape *infrastructure*, which promises to align social and ecological concerns with instrumental and logistical systems in ways that seem almost, well, natural. As designer and theorist Richard Weller argues, "*landscape is infrastructure*... because the landscape is the medium through which all ecological transactions must pass."[1] Cultural geographer J. B. Jackson famously defined landscape "as infrastructure or background for our collective existence."[2] Jackson's conception of infrastructure as background is understandable. Infrastructure comes before the growth of cities, enabling and then sustaining development. It is also the last thing left after cities decline, when its systems are no longer needed to service shrinking communities. Yet numerous bold design attempts to reverse this status, from architect and urbanist Darren Petrucci's "amenity infrastructure" which hybridizes the programs of service and civic space, to SWA's and lighting designers L'observatoire International's luminous treatment of elevated freeways in Houston (featured in this publication), prompt the question: what could be gained by foregrounding infrastructure?[3]

Foreground suggests a prominent or important position. In perspectival images, it is the portion of a scene nearest to the viewer. In literary theory, foregrounding is the practice of emphasizing certain words or images over others that surround them.[4] For the design disciplines, foregrounding suggests a strategy for making infrastructure more visibly useful.

NEAR WEST SIDE NEIGHBORHOOD, SYRACUSE, NEW YORK.

Diagram showing proposed plan interventions, three of which are discussed here (pink dots).

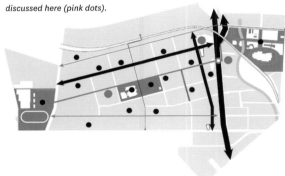

How can designers give equal status to work that *should* be done—visual improvements with civic and social purpose—and work that *must* be done—stormwater control, roadway reapportioning and paving, and erosion control planting?[5] How can we rethink everyday infrastructural improvements to make better neighborhoods in speedy, incremental, and small-scale ways—what graphic designer and design critic Michael Bierut refers to as "more Jane Jacobs-style fast-prototyping to complement ... slow moving Burhamesque big plans"?[6]

UPSTATE: A Center for Design, Research and Real Estate at the Syracuse University School of Architecture, is exploring infrastructure as an asset-based and economical means to restore urbanity in the Near West Side, a neighborhood in Syracuse, New York, which, like many others in shrinking cities internationally, has devolved so radically due to

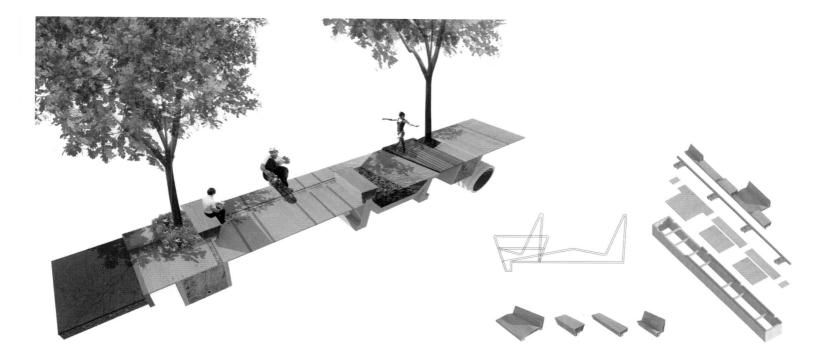

economic, demographic, and physical change that it could now be considered "formerly urban."[7] Syracuse is an apt context for this exploration not simply for its challenging social and spatial context but because of the monies in place for infrastructural improvements in the next few years.

SMALL PACKAGES:
HYBRIDIZING GREEN INFRASTRUCTURE

Best practices for ground-level water-control strategies, including designs for biofilter curb extensions, stormwater swales, and raingardens, can significantly improve the ecological health of cities by recharging aquifers and reducing the volume of water in combined sewer systems that, when overtaxed, force untreated sewage into streams. What is missing from these often cited and easily funded design strategies are civic concerns.

Wyoming Street is a typical local street in the Near West Side that will play a greater role in the future of the neighborhood by becoming the major cultural street, edged by publicly programmed renovated warehouses on one side and housing on the other. Our design approach aims to hybridize the urban ambitions of an avenue with ecological performance. "Avenue" here is used in its traditional sense, as a straight road edged by a line of trees. Drawing on its French source *venir* ("to come")—which emphasizes the *arrival* at a landscape or architectural feature—we anchor the street on both ends with features that both manage and highlight stormwater. On the north end of the street are cast-in-place concrete containments that double as tree pits and infiltration sites. Surface runnels scored into the pavement system lead to a water feature constituted by gathered and recycled

rain. A simple extension of the basin's concrete pour serves as the foundation for seating made of molded plywood, configured to facilitate relaxing, watching, and sleeping and thus to integrate activity with the engineered system. A civic use is combined with an ecological purpose in a small package that can be repeated along the street in response to desire and resources.

NONPARKS: TRANSFORMING
LOW-FUNCTIONING ARTERIALS

If the civic and ecological performance of Wyoming Street's infrastructure is enhanced through the packaging of design elements, then West Street—all eight lanes—is similarly upgraded but through quick and temporary alterations. West Street first served as an industrial corridor for the production of salt in the 1830s.[8] Eventually, in the 1960s, as part of a national trend in regional transit systems, it became an arterial loop around downtown, although the planned traffic flow for which it was designed never materialized. Now West Street is a barrier separating Near West Side residents

NEAR WEST SIDE.
Temporary lane re-purposing for bike lanes to test road shrinkage and to slow traffic.

from downtown. To reduce this separation and produce a new sense of connection, the UPSTATE team proposes to expand West Street's median by temporarily repurposing one travel lane in each direction. This strategy to produce inexpensive nonpark public space is inspired by the New York City Department of Transportation's creation of pedestrian malls in Times Square by simply closing roads and providing chairs, and the new public space added to Madison Square by reorganizing traffic and articulating pavement surfaces with potted plants, furnishings, and bike lanes.[9] Similarly, but with paint instead of plants, the temporary holding strategy for Syracuse will test lane closure, slow traffic, shrink roads, and connect the Near West Side to downtown. We also propose longer-term planting that counters the convention of the tree-lined boulevard: thick green bands grounded by a wide crosswalk that spans the arterial will reach out to neighborhood public schools.

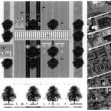

Image of new neighborhood connector across West Street.

Whereas growing West Street's median is temporary, its productivity is extended by planting. About 640 linear meters of West Street provide 5,060 square meters of underutilized urban space for the development of a continuous productive urban landscape of flax, jute, and kenaf. Maintenance and harvesting of these biofiber crops, which are used in paper, textiles, fiberboard, and biocomposite materials, will employ a local workforce. A Syracuse-based company, e2e, has developed a manufacturing process that integrates these three materials in architectural wallboard. Another local company uses flax as an integral component of their linoleum manufacturing process.[10]

STREETSCAPES: FOREGROUNDING BACKGROUND

These examples suggest ways to bring new life and use to underutilized and single-purposed infrastructure. Additionally, much opportunity lies in the unconventional adaptation of the seemingly universal lexicon of the street—trees, sidewalks, pavement surfaces, utility poles, fire hydrants, lights, and curbs—to make them newly visible and recuperate their public value. It is hard to imagine street trees as in any way controversial. For most residents, they are an image of nature in the city and are valued for cleaning the air, controlling heat, providing shade, and indexing the changing seasons. For a few, however, a street tree conjures up images of illicit activities, with trunks and limbs used as platforms for drug exchange through tieing and taping up the illegal merchandise there. And for some, a tree's visible lack of maintenance —weed-filled grates, broken limbs, and signs of stress—is a reminder of a larger pattern of municipal neglect.

In Syracuse, Otisco Street is a typical residential street linking two public schools and connecting across West Street to downtown. Two newly constructed green and affordable homes sit along that street, the product of a recent international competition.[11] Our first-phase intervention has the simple goal of changing perceptions of the street, making it a desirable, livable, "must-see" place that is a working infrastructure and a vivid urban landscape where residents can experience the perfume of linden trees on a June evening, the crunch of autumn leaves, or the sound of cicadas in the summer heat. Newly planted trees are reinforced, literally and conceptually, by a pattern of bright yellow stakes glossed with a phosphorescent surface that glows at night.[12] Their geometry echoes the tree spacing down the street, and their color is mirrored in rings of recycled glass. This street treatment is reinforced by a strategy for an adjacent vacant lot, where inflatable loops provide temporary color, density, and alternative use. This tactic of gathering (of people, sun, and water) is joined by others for land-holding: re-creating (sports courts, object play); joining (desire paths, bird habitat); sprouting (biomass, supergraphics).

These incremental and modest installations foreground infrastructure as landscape and create more city, and urbanity, with less building.

NEAR WEST SIDE.

Images of streetscape during day and night (above left and right). View across a temporary park, one possible holding strategy for a vacant lot (left and right).

NOTES

1   Richard Weller, "An Art of Instrumentality: Thinking through Landscape Urbanism," *The Landscape Urbanism Reader*, ed. Charles Waldheim, New York: Princeton Architectural Press, 2006, pp. 69–86, author's emphasis.

2   The full citation reads: "In the contemporary world it is by recognizing this similarity of purpose that we will eventually formulate a new definition of landscape: a composition of man-made or man-modified spaces to serve as infrastructure or background for our collective existence; and if background seems inappropriately modest we should remember that in our modern use of the word it means that which underscores not only our identity and presence, but also our history." The similarity of purpose to which he refers is the profession of landscape architecture and civil engineering. See J. B. Jackson, "The Word Itself," *Discovering the Vernacular Landscape*, New Haven: Yale University Press, 1984, pp. 1–8.

3   "Stripscape" and "Comfort Zone" are projects by Darren Petrucci: Architecture-Infrastructure-Research (A-I-R).

4   See Helen Artisan Dry, "Foregrounding: An Assessment," *Language in Context*, Arlington: University of Texas Press, 1992, pp. 435–450.

5   This could be similar to the way that contemporary large parks are an *overlay* amenity to the *underlay* of infrastructural improvements such as landfills and flood-control projects. This underlay/overlay terminology is used by Hargreaves Associates when describing their design for Guadalupe River Park, a large linear park in San José, California.

6   Michael Bierut, "When Design Gets in the Way," posted June 19, 2009, *Design Observer* http://observatory.designobserver.com

7   UPSTATE is Julia Czerniak, Joseph Sisko, Jacob Brown, Trevor Lee; Brett Seamans, Stephen Klimek (summer) . The institute, founded in 2004 by Mark Robbins, initiates, facilitates, and showcases projects that apply innovative design research to economic, environmental, political, and social challenges faced by urban communities.

8   For a complete history of West Street, see Paul Salvatore Mercurio, *The West Street Corridor Master Plan: Creating a Balanced Right-of-Way*, SUNY College of Environmental Science and Forestry, Capstone Project, Spring 2006.

9   *World Class Streets: Remaking New York City's Public Realm*, a publication of the New York City Department of Transportation.

10   Thanks to Trevor Lee for his research on Continuously Productive Urban Landscapes (CPUL) and their applicability to Syracuse.

11   The TED house by Onion Flats and the R-house by ARO and Della Valle Bernheimer were two winners of the 2009 "From the Ground Up: Innovative Green Homes" competition, a project of UPSTATE sponsored by the Syracuse University School of Architecture, the Syracuse Center of Excellence, and Home HeadQuarters, Inc. Additional support for construction was provided by the Syracuse University Office of Community Engagement and Economic Development.

12   Linnaea Tillet, of Tillet Lighting, is conducting experiments on such lighting strategies grounded on the use of "luminous surfaces" in lieu of conventional lighting fixtures.

Second Nature:
NEW TERRITORIES FOR THE EXILED

ADRIAAN GEUZE AND
MATTHEW SKJONSBERG

CITY-NATURE SYMBIOSIS

A vibrant city needs three things: good social interaction, good infrastructure, and nature. The great 19th-century parks fulfilled the promise of an urban nature—of a sublime illusion of paradise—and were conceived of largely as an antidote to the ills of industrial-era cities. Today cities are still built over rural landscapes, and shallow interpretations of 19th-century parks are injected afterward. It is time to speculate about a more intelligent approach that results in a new sustainable symbiosis between city and nature.

It is a fact that *Homines sapiens* have, for all intents and purposes, colonized the earth. Mankind's presence is not a modest one. Every corner of the earth has been occupied, laid out, measured, or marked in some way. The idea of virgin nature is more metaphor than reality—a metaphor best represented by the fabled garden paradise from which *Homo sapiens*' ancient forebears were exiled.

Despite the fact that virtually every development site borders on an existing city or infrastructure, and that billboards or industry are visible in every panorama, contemporary planning and modern architecture have stubbornly continued to cherish the illusion of a nature that is authentic. In an increasingly urbanized world, it is interesting that landscape urbanism or "landscape-as-infrastructure" movements seek to define a new theoretical framework for the relation between city and nature. One obvious contribution to this set of ideas would be the evolution of a "second nature" as a promising new strategy for urbanism.

PARKS AND GREEN FOR THE CITY

The urban park was a 19th-century concept, its invention necessary to provide relief to the urban victims of the new, untamed metropolis. Unlike the grand boulevards with which Haussmann carved monumental green arteries into the existing urban fabric, and the early urban parks that designers fitted into the grid, the later parks actually determine the unbuilt city. The large Paris parks of the late 19th century, Bois de Boulogne and Bois de Vincennes, and Olmsted's big North American parks, were the original models of the principle through which landscape guides urban development. Long before the layout of the metropolis had been defined, these parks created a framework for the urban expansion to follow. Greenery delineated the new edges of the neighborhoods to be built, and the green investment was immediately repaid by increased land value. Planning, real estate development, and the poetic presence of nature were combined. Properly regarded, these were the purest forms of landscape urbanism—or landscape-as-infrastructure.

This Olmstedian principle seems still to be the ideal of landscape urbanism, although in practice hardly any critical attention is paid to some of its weaker aspects. Why is it so easily taken for granted that the green of parks will bring a better world?

First, the steadily increasing area of suburban green structures is of a dubiously hybrid character: they are often loud statements of overdesigned park architecture expressing a desire for liveliness, and for the cultural significance of beloved 19th-century city parks; but on the other hand, they attempt to create an idealistic wilderness. Realization

Evolutionary Sequence (left to right). Establishing an infrastructural framework: the creation of new land with dredge material reclaimed from the delta; dunescape shaped by the wind, then stabilized with the planting of buckthorn; transitional landscape and early urban structure; the inhabited dunescape, inclusive of new urban ecologies.

BUCKTHORN CITY.

Landscape of Drifting Sands: Instead of an all defining urban layout, Buckthorn City is a man-made landscape of dunes, buckthorn vegetation, and water for the development of new urban ecologies. The artificial dune is left to be shaped by the wind for some years, its eventual form determined by the interaction of the elements. At a decisive moment buckthorn is planted, whose roots stabilize the dunescape.

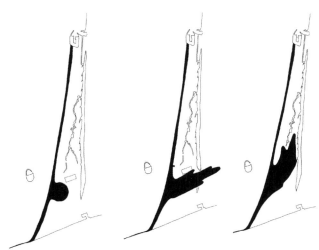

Accelerating Future Colonization: Actively establishing new ecologies capable of absorbing subsequent urbanization frees existing rural and wilderness districts from the pressure of urban development. Buckthorn City also protects the existing coastline from increased storm surges and sea-level rise due to climate change, amplifies ecological diversity in the sea and on the land, and guides the growth of the city.

of these plans often results in a strange nonworld of cultivated innocence. The essential characteristics a park needs to survive, so exhaustively described by Jane Jacobs, are almost always lacking. According to her analysis, for parks and greenery to succeed, a good context is fundamental. Many city dwellers see peripheral green zones as valuable green background, but also as potentially dangerous, and as places to be avoided. There is simply too little activity and no mixing of user groups. Park designers have not succeeded in giving these parks the allure of nature and wilderness.

Second, landscape architecture is fundamentally linked to nature, to mother earth. But the perception of "nature" is a cultural phenomenon, quite different from one country to another. The elemental forces of nature have also, through prosperity or privation, shaped behavioral second natures—yielding national identities, religions, livelihoods, and even wars. From these basic conditions cultures are formed, each with its particular perceptions of nature. When you talk with different nationalities about nature, you are confronted by deeply rooted feelings and cultural convictions, all of which are assumed to be a matter of "common sense."

Finally, the pretension often is that parks are the result of ideology and craftsmanship, and are therefore inherently unique and valuable. However, landscape architecture, in contrast to architecture, is concerned almost exclusively with the public realm—parks, boulevards, riverfronts, streetscapes, and so on. To reach decisions and establish finances, we must work with politicians, local citizens, and bureaucracies with diverse legal systems. Landscape architecture will always focus on outreach, public opinion, interaction, public policy, implementation, and compromise. The discipline cannot avoid responding to sociopolitical contexts.

Economists have an acronym to identify the forces driving development: PESTEL (politics, economics, sociology, technology, environment, and law). It is critically important that contemporary planning initiatives explicitly take these factors into account. Clearly such diverse issues as governance and legislation, high- and low-tech implementation strategies, grassroots advocacy, and megaprojects all are attendant on public policy. So in practice landscape architects and park designers work in a realm between illusion and public policy, and our work is inevitably the most banal and compromised among the design disciplines. At the end of the day, are the built realities anywhere close to the dreamt-of parks and artist's impressions?

RURAL FOOTPRINT

The performative capacity of peripheral parks is overestimated. It is now framed by the notion that the city is benign. This inherited logic of progress has had alarming outcomes in the present era. The reality is that the city is a voracious consumer of resources—cities eat cultural and rural landscapes. Urban eats rural, and rural eats wilderness. Why do we back away from our responsibility to break this pattern?

The recent and ongoing erasure of entire regional landscapes can be observed worldwide, from the east coast of the United States, to the Dutch polders, to Southeast Asia. Much of this area is consumed not by genuine urbanization but by sprawling commercial districts that sap the financial and cultural strength of the city and contribute nothing in return.

The ancient city had little relationship to nature other than a certain proximity to natural resources and strategic considerations of accessibility and defense. In the industrial era we ignored nature; humanity efficiently cleared forests, built motorways, and defeated the sea. In the modern era we did that on a global scale, consuming space and producing waste, and we've lived to regret it. Today, it's about protecting nature. Back to the earth, the cycle of life, our conscience—but this is a rearguard action without a future. The real future in this debate will not be found in a political or philosophical dialogue about what we are protecting or how we are going to "sustain" it, as important as this dialogue is. Society is craving a much more pragmatic solution. Why not actively deliver new ecologies?

In this generation, society has become definitively urban, largely abandoning the rural realm to use or exploitation by commercial interests—often insidiously branded as "green" (i.e., industries deriving ethanol from corn, or electricity obtained by the destruction of irreplaceable geothermal landscapes, etc.). Does our generation erase the rural deliberately or by neglect? Current enthusiasm for urbanism has made rural the blind spot of our era; it takes generations of continuity to inhabit the landscape productively, and that productive inhabitation is now seriously threatened across the face of the earth. It is worth noting that by now every institution offering degrees in architecture or planning has established an "institute of urban design" of some kind. By comparison, we would be hard pressed to find any institution offering programs with comparable emphasis on rural design: correlating technical and research data with sensory and experiential ones, as well as meaningfully and imaginatively deriving formal and procedural implications for projects of diverse scales, and strategically considering their implementation. The mass abandonment of rural regions for urban ones by populations worldwide and the subsequent industrial exploitation of the natural resources left behind potentially threaten society's ability to respond to either crisis or opportunity.

No need to list the advanced historic civilizations that fell, never to recover, at least partially because of their having developed a similar blind spot. And in the current urban context often the superficial presence of greenery appears as stage setting to fill an intuitive void—the absence of nature—but, lacking the genuine substance of productive performance, such gestures ring hollow and do disservice to the optimism of any progressive society.

As we acknowledge the need to reduce civilization's carbon footprint, we must also recognize that every urban block has a displaced and proportionally vast rural footprint, whether active or dormant, near or far. The implicit rural footprint of urbanization provides it with needed natural resources, agriculture, and recreation, and the cultural legacy of these rural regions is certainly of equal significance to that of the urban artifact. With the immense growth of urban populations worldwide, are there options for the metropolis other than devastating the rural landscape? In this regard the generative potential of second nature can be found in its inclusiveness of the rural and urban as polarities of the same civilizing force.

That cities require rural resources is clear. That rural areas benefit from proximity to cities can be readily asserted. But there are contingencies to account for and, all things considered (i.e. experiential qualities, economics, ethics, etc.), these resource exchanges will be effective when balanced through the creation of a methodology relating spatial anatomy, infrastructural proximity, and legislative initiatives—that is, through the elicitive modeling of regional force ecologies (i.e. interests and resources) to identify and "design with" phenomena supporting versatile infrastructures. Acknowledgment of this prompts us to explore the practice of a rural/urban metabolism, to use the biological analogy.

In such a practice, key urban/rural resource exchanges and their capital, nature, and space-producing potentials are considered.[1] Civil, social, and infrastructural forms are related while exploring the opportunities and impacts of legislative, political, and economic interventions. Planners and landscape designers are thus equipped to respond to the challenge of formalizing the city and its systems in ways that acknowledge, understand, and yield to the natural systems that coalesce into "wilderness."

THE PROSPECTS OF SECOND NATURE

The contemporary metropolis is a large organization with a far-reaching and extremely complex metabolism. Apart from infrastructure, this urban jungle is hardly amenable to planning. Transformations are based mainly on small local interventions, and the recycling of old industrial and harbor sites is currently the important trend in urban innovation.

Can large-scale expansion be given direction by establishing a green structure to begin with, as was done with the regional parks Olmsted helped to realize? Is it a viable strategy to make the landscape in advance of the city, even if the layout and functions of the city cannot be defined? The answer is yes. Large-scale re-creation of disused sites and decayed landscapes into new nature is the obvious thing to do. This is a proven and easily applicable concept of genuine relevance for contemporary cities. Further, it is possible, by anticipating local biotopes, water management, and the larger ecological systems, to reintroduce, without

Actively Establishing New Ecologies: 3,400 hectares of forests, grasslands, buckthorn fields, freshwater creeks, and dunes provide a setting for subsequent urban development. This second nature can absorb urbanization, even surpassing the original nature in accommodating Homo sapiens, *while keeping the natural systems intact.*

disproportional investment, an integrative *tabula rasa*—a performative second nature—in which ecological relations, water management, and microclimate become part of the engineering of the city. With interesting features like topography, water, or botany, this orchestrated nature can even surpass the original nature in accommodating *Homo sapiens*. Rather than sentimentally leaving traces of industrial occupation, imagine abandoned military bases, airports or railway sites, polluted industrial coastal areas, all proactively converted into a new wilderness—not by *laissez-faire* wait-and-see but by the strategic implementation of a clever design that dramatizes the new nature. After a short period of groundwork, planting, and new cultivation, irrepressible pioneering vegetation will lay the basis for an ecological structure that will then slowly grow into a climax of habitats with an array of distinct biotopes and microclimates. In principle, the city dweller—a permanent hostage to the 100 percent predetermined use of space—craves these sorts of undefined spaces that have no specified function but are nevertheless useful because they are accessible. Woods, wild open areas, swamps, or dune-style landscapes are the ideal textures close to the city. In 25 years or more, the

potential will be there to once again reclaim and inhabit this second nature, as fields whose use had previously been to lay fallow.

In *De Natura Deorum* ('The Nature of the Gods', ca. 45 BC, which Voltaire called "perhaps the best book of all antiquity") Cicero wrote:

> *...we sow cereals and plant trees; we irrigate our lands to fertilize them. We fortify river-banks, and straighten or divert the courses of rivers. In short, by the work of our hands we strive to create a sort of second nature within the world of nature.*[2]

Cicero's idea of "second nature" clearly encompasses infrastructure, agriculture, and the landscapes incidental to their creation. "First nature"—wilderness—is seen by Cicero to be the realm of the gods, but it is also the raw material and context for second nature.

Jacopo Bonfadio wrote to a fellow humanist in 1541 that gardens make a "third nature, which I would not know how to name."[3] John Dixon Hunt asserts that Cicero's formulation would have been in the mind of Bonfadio, and identifies second nature as even more broadly encompassing the cultural landscape (agriculture, urban development, roads, etc.)[4]—that is, inclusively, the nature we shape, intentionally or otherwise, through the activity of civilization. Seen in this light, it can be said that Cicero's idea of second nature constitutes everything outside of wilderness.

The connotations of behavioral second nature—our individualized, learned, socialized human nature—are equally important. With our built environment, we are normalizing our behavioral second nature. One might say, for instance, that in a society that actively recycles the act of recycling becomes second nature. But without the infrastructure to support recycling, that learned behavior is quickly unlearned.

Our redefinition of the term "second nature" takes both Cicero's use and behavioral connotations into account, but differs in that for us "second nature" specifically describes a designed nature created in adjacency to existing urbanization, capable of absorbing future city growth into itself while maintaining the continuity of ecological systems.

As in an historic process of colonization, the urbanization front will once again be rolled out across this second nature. The special landscape features and ecological characteristics will be absorbed directly into the city. This principle of second nature is not based, as in Olmsted's time, on a hermetic green structure, but rather on a nature having outgrown human hands, being full of character, and forming a magnetic field for an as yet unknown colonization. Unlike the historic pioneers and clear-cutters who could indulge the habit of expropriating or erasing the nature they encountered, a different opportunism will prevail. Topography, water, and vegetation will be utilized in all kinds of ways, generating an urban ambiance with an array of integral spatial qualities, microclimates, stormwater management, leisure, and the innumerable incidental benefits engendered by ecological and social vitality available to all.

SECOND NATURE FOR SECOND COLONIZATION

The ambition of second nature is the radically humane reformulation of the relationship between the urban and rural, amplifying civilization's cultural legacy—that new civilizations to come might not have dropped too many stitches nor have unraveled what could still be useful to *Homo sapiens* in making a homeland of exile. We believe that the principle of second nature will lead to the creation of a new open-ended sustainable urban design approach based on performative integration with the deep patterns of nature itself, particularly in the long-occupied areas where most existing metropolises are situated. In contrast to primitive clear-cutting and industrial-era colonization, contemporary democracies and information societies will adopt a gentler, more reciprocal, and more responsible attitude toward nature.

A good place to start is to disavow the destruction of wilderness from this day forward and to create new ecologies—a second nature that reconciles the urban and rural to the benefit of both. Why would we choose to carry on with the 19th-century cliché of the city as an untamable monster? After all, despite our possession of advanced technology, thanks to civilization's continuity of knowledge we still have the farm and the park—and the ideal city, however incomplete, ought to be inclusive of the humanity epitomized by them both.

NOTES

1   Neil Smith, *Uneven Development*, Athens: University of Georgia Press, 2008, p. 239.

2   Marcus Tullius Cicero, *The Nature of the Gods*, New York: Oxford University Press, 2008, p.102.

3   Jacopo Bonfadio, *Lettere del Cinquecento*, Turin: Utet, 1967, p. 501 (translation by author).

4   John Dixon Hunt, *Greater Perfection: The Practice of Garden Theory*, London: Thames & Hudson, 2000, p. 33.

Modulating Infrastructural Flows to Create Open Space

ALEXANDER ROBINSON

IF WE ASSUME THAT THE POTENTIAL OF LAND for public open space can be measured by its proximity to the maximum number of people, size, and lack of permanent occupation, then the circulatory infrastructures of cities—freeways, streets, railways, urban rivers, and power corridors—present our greatest open-space opportunities.[1] In aging North American cities, where these systems are nearly impossible to expand or shift, they often operate at crippling-high capacities and are usually perceived equally as urban stressors and as essential infrastructures.[2] Freeways in particular exemplify this situation and a growing body of testimonials supports the transformative potential of replacing sections of freeway with open space, either by burying the roadways in tunnels or removing it entirely.[3] Pedestrian colonization of these linear infrastructures occupies the headlines of popular media, testament to its value and effect.[4]

As is apparent to most urban dwellers, however, very little of this hugely valuable space is made into open space. The fact that these challenging spaces are even considered is evidence of the lack of viable alternatives. Although the civic enthusiasm has long faded for many of these infrastructures, they are still critical urban necessities that are very large and difficult to replace or tear down.[5] In cases where they have been colonized, the infrastructures have been defunct, dismantled, or buried at a now almost unthinkable cost.[6]

Although the binary spatial strategies that hide or remove infrastructure are likely to remain successful in terms of quality of open space, they are not the only solution, or the most effective. Burying infrastructure such as freeways is not only usually prohibitively expensive, but it also inhibits the infrastructure from adapting. Not only are most large-scale urban infrastructures here to stay, they are constantly expanding in capacity and services.[7]

How much performance (how much public utility) can we effectively place within these spaces? Specifically, can public open space become an additional performance parameter within these specialized and fixed territories? Can the host of strategies being developed to improve infrastructural performance in-situ be adapted to the creation of open space?

Techniques have been applied to many different infrastructures to accommodate increased use, mitigation strategies for freeway congestion being the most popular example. Common strategies include access modification, specialized lanes, rush-hour restrictions, metering, contraflow lane reversal, and an intelligent transportation system to incorporate these tools for maximum effect. In some cases, traffic systems incorporate special strategies for enabling the movement of emergency vehicles and facilitating evacuation.

These strategies focus on typical infrastructure performance parameters (e.g. increasing traffic capacity), yet their approach is interesting for its emphasis on modification of flows by multiple means and at varied scales and dimensions. In terms of open space, this approach is relevant in several ways.

First, the dynamic modulation of flow substitutes for adding space. Material flow and space are inextricably linked, yet capacity is added by addressing other dimensions. Could dynamic infrastructural flow modulations create opportunities for open space?

Second, modulation of infrastructural flows focuses on strategic performance benchmarks or even uses (e.g. emergency access). For example, in urban river restorations, the flow of stormwater is adjusted to reach water quality benchmarks and to achieve aesthetic goals, such as having green embankments. Can modulation of existing infrastructure flows meet critical open-space benchmarks while maintaining infrastructure performances, thus avoiding the impracticability of a spatially segregated solution?

Third, users adjust to these infrastructural modulations. Most of the congestion mitigation strategies, while increasing capacities, only temporarily reduce congestion, due a pattern often described as "triple convergence." Users alternatively shift into this increased capacity from other times, routes, or modes of travel. Could users adjust (or be adjusted) to open space that is itself potentially dynamic or modulated?

The simple answer is yes. The 1996 environmental restoration of the Besòs River in Barcelona in Spain applied dynamic flow modulation strategies to successfully extract open space from a periodically at-capacity infrastructural corridor. The Storm Surge Warning System times user access to periodic dangerous stormwater flows. Additionally, rubber dams capture regular flows for improved aesthetics and rapidly deflate during rain events, effectively "flattening" the park for maximum flood-protection performance.

In the Rio Besòs restoration, the design focuses on the relationship of flow and open-space qualities. In almost all large urban infrastructural conditions, the flow through the system—whether of vehicles, stormwater, or electricity—renders a space poorly suited to also serve typical open-space functions.

In many cases, the unsuitability of this operational infrastructural space is first determined by a potentially lethal flow, such as fast-moving vehicles or stormwater. Even if the entire space is not dangerous, its flows often produce a host of side effects, aesthetically and physiologically undesirable to open space (e.g. particulate pollution, electrical radiation, noise, foul water quality, etc.) that make any remaining or adjacent space unsuitable. Finally, these infrastructural spaces are not generally viewed as aesthetically appealing and often retain the image or residues of their unattractive flows. The Rio Besòs, for instance, was previously devoid

of vegetation, lethal during storm events (as it is now), and considered the most polluted river in Europe.[8]

However, other qualities of infrastructural flows suggest that modulation may well be a suitable strategy for creating open space. The unattractive aspects of the infrastructure flows are proportionate to their magnitude (e.g. less traffic produces less noise and pollution). Furthermore, these flows are usually highly dynamic and periodic—a quality that, as demonstrated with congestion mitigation or rubber dams, can be intelligently manipulated in-situ. Finally, the magnitude and quality (and side effects) of infrastructural flows are products of larger factors of urban infrastructure, lifestyle, policies, and socio-economic currents, all of which can shift.

To assess the potential of modulation to create open spaces within infrastructure, we need to consider the attributes that define open space. The question of what transforms an ugly, lethal, or asthma-inducing infrastructural space into an acceptable form of public open space is complex. Yet the specific nature of modulation, especially at the scale of infrastructure, requires not just a clear set of attributes but measured thresholds. How clean or green a space, exactly, does modulation need to produce?

SPACE/TIME MODULATION.

The Rio Besòs Storm Surge Warning System modulates human access based on multiple information sources, including weather forecasts. Rubber dams modulate low-flow conditions for improved aesthetic quality (e.g., increased water surface) without conflicting with flood protection performances. Other elements, such as power transmission lines, have been customized for the flow conditions.

Compared to the performance parameters of infrastructural flows, human-based assessments of suitability range greatly, from physiological and legal thresholds of physical safety, air quality, and even sound pollution to subjective issues of aesthetics, program, permanence, and environmental justice.

Whatever thresholds may be developed, given the performative demands of infrastructural space, modulation of flows and application of resources are not likely to achieve a bucolic image or program of open space but rather an assemblage of particular attractive qualities; modulation produces an open space that is itself a modulated version of typical open-space qualities. In many cases, the modulation of infrastructural flows alone may only be able to achieve certain human thresholds, and additional intervention will be necessary to modulate other qualities to acceptable levels.

For example, in the Rio Besòs, the access system modulates the threat to humans of lethal storm flows. Modifying the flow of the river to a completely safe condition would be foolish; by modulating human access the space is made suitable with a minimal investment. Temporary modulations of the flow of the water with the rubber dams produce a more aesthetic public space without disrupting the corridor's primary infrastructural performance of flood protection.

The combined strategies of modulating infrastructural flows and open-space interfaces to extract public open space from infrastructure represent an interesting, if still largely abstract approach to improving public space availability. More specifically, I propose three modulation strategies.

QUANTITY/QUALITY

Many of the large circulatory infrastructures of the city typically run at or above capacity and produce a variety of environmental stressors given the quantity and quality of flows accepted into their spaces. The quantity (and to some degree quality) of these flows is often set by the capacities that the infrastructures provide. A city that provides absolute flood control invites developers to develop flood-prone areas and increase impervious surfaces for further runoff. However, the flows themselves, especially those human in origin, are dynamic, and quantities will shift as urbanity shifts.

A reduction of the quantity of flows is a difficult proposition. Highly efficient decentralized systems, such as stormwater infiltration wells, sewage-treatment systems, and solar or geothermal power, may relieve centralized systems enough to reduce infrastructural capacity, but city engineers often perceive any surplus as useful for worst-case scenarios.[9]

Historically, quantity was either adjusted or regulated within the feedback loop of infrastructure capacities (e.g. combined sewer overflow mitigation) or other contributing feedback loops (e.g. high gas prices and traffic). As congestion mitigation has demonstrated (particularly rush hour metering), the design and implementation of feedback loops appears to be the best strategy for modulating infrastructural quantities in-situ.[10] Future feedback loops could be designed to achieve open-space benchmarks or relieve infrastructural space, though perhaps not as explicitly as the off-shore power plant proposal for San Diego, where lower power consumption allowed the system to surface and provide open space.[11] Dynamic exhibits could educate the public by monitoring flows and providing feedback by measuring the distance to critical open-space thresholds.[12]

The quality of flows, particularly significant for stormwater and vehicles, have significant health and environmental impacts and are subsequently already highly regulated. Future technological innovations that modulate particular

QUANTITY/QUALITY MODULATION.

Methane-powered buses in Los Angeles have improved the cohabitation of bicyclists and buses in dedicated lanes.

stressors could do much to attain open-space benchmarks. Hybrid vehicles produce significantly less pollution and sound, and air pollution from all vehicles has been vastly reduced.[13] Strict storm sewer dumping regulation followed by stormwater mitigation requirements are greatly improving the open-space attractiveness of urban waterways.

Imagine, for instance, an enhanced hybrid vehicle, nearly silent and emission-free, that could be segregated in a lane equipped with additional sensory-mitigation technologies to reach a suitable threshold to share or be adjacent with open-space programs. Or perhaps, more likely, strategic citywide improvement to stormwater quality could allow federally endangered fisheries to populate urban waterways, prompting protections and improvements that would benefit its transformation to open space.

SPACE/TIME

Most infrastructural flows are periodic. The suitability of a space for open space is in part determined by the scale and quality of the periodicity, which ranges widely. Open space within this context may be timed, not entirely unlike the way public parks are often closed at night, except that the "timing" consideration is the magnitude and frequency of dynamic urban flow. Where flow is irregular or unpredictable, especially if dangerous, such spaces are generally determined to be off-limits. In cases such as arid flood-protection corridors, large infrastructural spaces that may reach lethal flow capacities only for a fraction of the year, the space is used even when access is restricted. The number of swiftwater rescues (more than a 100) that occur each year in the Los Angeles River is a testament to the failure of managing such an attraction with a binary approach.[14]

Modulating human access to infrastructural flows is likely to produce the greatest immediate results. With the rapid advance of information technology that not only tracks infrastructural flows but also optimizes them, such systems could identify timed open-space opportunities between flows and notify users of conditions. Flexible, timed spaces are already common on freeways and roads that contain contraflow or reversible lanes or where timed meters control access.[15] Given the scale and proximity of many of these spaces, users would likely adapt to this kind of periodic open space.[16]

Alternatively, systems such as the Storm Surge Warning System at the Rio Besòs, could identify moments of unsuitability that may be impossible for an average user to detect. For instance, are there particular times of the day when electrical corridors are safer for use?[17] With the speed and lethality of flows in many of these systems, the systems would also need to be predictive to ensure that the slowest-moving user is not left behind. The design of such non-vehicular user messaging systems could be integrated into landscape features and does not need to mimic current automobile traffic message systems.

Although larger compositional modulations may produce significant results, more likely are smaller, directed modulations to reach certain suitability thresholds. In many situations a minor modulation of infrastructural flows for safety considerations could make the difference between unsuitability and suitability. Occasional drastic modulations, as for special events such as marathons, could produce a highly valued set of timed and specially programmed spaces.

Inherent to this idea of timing public space between or amid infrastructure flows is the issue of how the physical space can be designed to effectively accommodate both

SPACE/TIME MODULATION.

Basic open-space elements are designed to yield in the face of extreme and dynamic flow conditions. An example is the folding handrail on Los Angeles River.

LOS ANGELES RIVER, RESEDA, SAN FERNANDO VALLEY.

The current morphology of an upper reach of the Los Angeles River is unsuitable as open space by any regular standard. What modulations can bridge between the flow accommodation requirements of the channel and minimum open-space suitability?

uses. Within the highly volatile conditions of major urban infrastructures, especially freeways and waterways, even the most innocuous public-space amenity can jeopardize high-magnitude infrastructure flows. For this reason open-space amenities within these conditions must be adapted to coexist and not conflict with extreme conditions; in some cases, they may need to be dynamic objects.

Recently installed guardrails along bikepaths that enter the flood channel of the Los Angeles River are designed to fold over during flood events to avoid catching debris—their pedestrian safety function thus periodically overridden by more pressing flood concerns. After baseline safety needs are met, what other elements can be adapted for these extreme conditions that infrastructure flows present? Perhaps these elements could be combined with systems such as controlled-access devices or other technologies to reduce particular stressors and support programs well suited to these unusual forms of open space.

SPATIAL COMPOSITION

The modulation of flows to reach benchmarks via spatial reconfiguration is the most powerful and costly strategy. Burying infrastructures to create open space is a simple and effective demonstration of this. Given the large costs, most future spatial reconfigurations will have to offer improvements besides the creation of open space, such as the provision of public transportation infrastructure.[18] Proving the utility and potential of integrating open space is the responsibility of landscape architecture.

The most common spatial strategy is the widening or expansion of infrastructural flow corridors, often with the

sacrifice of other amenities, such as safety medians or planted areas.[19] This strategy generally runs counter to the potential of open space and is limited within developed cities. In some cases, however, the expansion of the capacity of a flow can create spatial opportunities. The widening and modification of the Rio Besòs corridor allowed for more flexibility by embedding more performance, including open space, subsurface wetland, and a power corridor.

Increasingly common within infrastructural corridors is the specialized segregation of flows to achieve certain benchmarks. Freeways such as the LA Harbor Freeway have added specialized long flyover lanes that exclusively carry high-occupancy vehicles, while urban waterway improvements projects, such as the restoration of Cheongyecheon River in Seoul, segregate noisome flows into subsurface conduits to enable bucolic flow conditions. Wildlife corridors built over or under major freeways are heavily fortified to simulate a natural undisturbed condition necessary for maintaining genetically diverse populations.

Coupling flow segregation with the previous two strategies could minimize the resource investment in complex spatial structures. Ultimately the design problem is whether a certain quantity, quality, and period of flows, infrastructural and human, can be segregated to create suitable open space.

Modulation thresholds might be both very specific in terms of suitability (such as safety) and require flexibility or creative interface design in the form, function, and look of open space. There will always be users for available space within the urban context, but when does the "average" user adapt to exceptional conditions? Furthermore, how does the condition change users and alter their perception of urbanism or nature?

The purpose of this discussion is to consider whether a framework of strategies based on infrastructural flows and their modulation could produce further design innovation and progress in capturing more urban open space. It is a common fallacy to assume either the suitability of sharing these infrastructural spaces with human use or the inevitability of spatially segregated solutions.

As global warming countermeasures and sustainability research continues to champion the relatively small footprint of high-density urban conditions, the perceived value of providing significant urban open space will only increase.[20] This framework seeks to offer a more nuanced approach to capturing infrastructural space that may result in a more flexible and feasible set of potentials, including resource-efficient ways of adapting the inherent flux of infrastructures into landscape infrastructures.

NOTES

1 The area occupied by the Los Angeles River flood-control corridor over the 50 kilometers within the City of Los Angeles represents 304 contiguous hectares of potential open space. This is comparable to the 341 hectares occupied by Central Park in Los Angeles. While capturing some portion of this space for open space may seem insignificant relative to the estimated 12,141 hectares of open space in Los Angeles City, the centrality of the LA River and other major infrastructure spaces could create a huge improvement in terms of accessible open space. *LA River Revitalization Master Plan*, Los Angeles Bureau of Engineering et al., April 2007.

2 Brian D. Taylor, "Public Perceptions, Fiscal realities, and Freeway Planning: The California Case," *Journal of the American Planning Association* 61, no. 1 (Winter 1995): p. 43–59.

3 The High Line Section One in New York City was built on a defunct elevated freight railway line. Cheongyecheon River Restoration in Seoul required the removal of an elevated freeway. Boston's Big Dig cost an estimated $22 billion (see footnote 6).

4 Diane Cardwell, "For High Line Visitors, Park Is a Railway Out of Manhattan," *The New York Times—Breaking News, World News & Multimedia*. http://www.nytimes.com/2009/07/22/nyregion/22highline.html?_r=1&ref=high_line_nyc (accessed June 24, 2010).

5 Hugo Martin, "Will More Freeways Bring More Traffic?" *Los Angeles Times*, 10 April 2002, sec. B, p. 1.

6 "Wouldn't it be cheaper to raise the city than depress the artery?", Congressman Barney Frank supposedly said at the beginning of the project. "...the Big Dig will have cost nearly $15 billion—more than the Panama Canal, the Hoover Dam or Interstate 95, the 3088 kilometer highway between Maine and Florida." See Dan McNichol, "Big Dig Nearing Light of Costly Tunnel's End," *The New York Times*. http://www.nytimes.com/2004/07/25/news/hub-guide-getting-around-big-dig-nearing-light-of-costly-tunnel-s-end.html (accessed June 24, 2010).

7 The 402 kilometer Tehachapi Power Corridor near Los Angeles improves and expands existing power corridors to help deliver policy-mandated renewable energy from the Techachapi wind farms. Tiffany Hsu, "Southern California Edison completes first part of Tehachapi renewable energy transmission project," *Los Angeles Times*. http://latimesblogs.latimes.com/money_co/2010/05/southern-california-edison-completes-first-part-of-tehachapi-renewable-energy-transmission-project.html (accessed June 24, 2010).

8 Liat Margolis and Alexander Robinson, *Living Systems: Innovative Materials and Technologies for Landscape Architecture*, Basel: Birkhäuser, 2007, pp. 130–131.

9 During the master planning process for the Los Angeles River, discussion with city engineers revealed an unwillingness to rely on private property stormwater BMPs (Best Management Practices, such as rain barrels, rain gardens, green roofs, etc.) to reduce peak flows and flood events. Long-term maintenance was an issue and moreover, many did not believe that even if implemented citywide, such measures would significantly reduce flows in a major rain event—one that could threaten public safety.

10 *Reducing Traffic Congestion in Los Angeles*, Research brief. Santa Monica: RAND, 2008.

11 Alexander Trevi, "Wave Garden by Yusuke Obuchi," *Pruned*. http://pruned.blogspot.com/2005/06/wave-garden-by-yusuke-obuchi.html (accessed June 24, 2010).

12 See Fiber Optic Marsh, Liat Margolis and Alexander Robinson, *Living Systems*, op. cit., pp. 132–133.

13 "Historical Data," *South Coast AQMD*. http://www.aqmd.gov/smog/historicaldata.htm (accessed June 24, 2010).

14 There are more than 100 swiftwater rescue calls a year in the City of Los Angeles. Cf. Nancy J. Rigg, "Swiftwater Rescue Protects Rescuers and Gives Victims a Fighting Chance to Survive," *Swiftwater Rescue News*, 11 March 2010. http://swiftwaterrescuenews.wordpress.com/2010/03/11/giving-flood-victims-a-fighting-chance-to-survive-3/ (accessed May 31, 2010).

15 Southern Expressway in Adelaide, South Australia, is the world's longest reversible freeway. "Southern Expressway." http://en.wikipedia.org/wiki/Southern_Expressway (accessed June 24, 2010).

16 Surfers and other ocean users, in particular, employ advanced technologies and services to determine when conditions are suitable for their sport, such as off-shore buoys, webcams, and prediction models.

17 The only established connection between magnetic fields associated with transmission corridors and health is in high-magnitude conditions. "Fact Sheet N°322: Electromagnetic Fields and Public Health," *World Health Organization*, July 2007. http://www.who.int/mediacentre/factsheets/fs322/en/index.html (accessed May 31, 2010).

18 A recent 1.6-kilometer-long sound wall in Los Angeles cost $5 million, below the usual estimate of $6.25 million per kilometer. Sound walls are the most common infrastructural improvement focused on a particular human threshold, and their budgets are often associated with freeway expansions rather than rectifying existing conditions. Nathan McIntire, "Sound wall along 210 freeway in Arcadia gets mixed reviews from residents," *SGVTribune.com*, May 14, 2010. http://www.sgvtribune.com/ci_15087562 (accessed June 25, 2010). "Soundwall Program," Metro—Los Angeles County Metropolitan Transportation Authority. http://www.metro.net/projects/soundwalls (accessed June 25, 2010). See also: "A New Infrastructure: Transit Solutions for Los Angeles," the open ideas competition sponsored by the SCIFI (Southern California Institute of Future Initiatives) program at the Southern California Institute of Architecture (SCI-Arc) and *The Architect's Newspaper* in 2009.

19 Daisy Nguyen, "Historic preservationists protest improvements to LA's oldest freeway," *San José Mercury News*, May 16, 2010. http://www.mercurynews.com/breaking-news/ci_15098329?&nclick_check=1 (accessed June 25, 2010).

20 David Owen, *Green Metropolis: Why Living Smaller, Living Closer, and Driving Less are Keys to Sustainability*, New York: Riverhead Books, 2009.

01

PER FORM ANCE

As a nonisolated system, landscape infrastructure has the ability to adhere to a set of requirements and achieve measurable results.

One of a dozen private companies operate and manage the Tehachapi wind farm near Los Angeles with around 5,000 wind turbines. Producing 800 million kilowatt-hours of electricity, the turbines provide enough power to meet the residential needs of 350,000 people every year. Pictured here is a typical monitoring station optimizing the performance of over 300 separate turbines by analyzing wind patterns and velocity 24 hours a day.

BUFFALO BAYOU PROMENADE

Entangled Ecological Infrastructure

The Buffalo Bayou is an 84-kilometer-long languid river meandering its way to the Gulf of Mexico via the relatively flat coastal plain of Houston, Texas. Buffalo Bayou is also the principal drainage system for much of Houston, balancing built environment with a diverse urban ecosystem of native riparian plants, bottomland hardwood forests, and a range of flora and fauna and marine life. The bayou has been significant in the development of Houston. According to Houston historian, Louis Aulbach, for centuries, before explorers descended on the Gulf of Mexico, native Indians, such as the Bidais and Akokisa, camped and traded along the lush banks of the bayou and prowled its clear clay-bottomed waters. In the late 1800s the bayou became a robust corridor of culture, social activities, shipping, and transportation. By the turn of the 19th century the area experienced sprawling real estate developments along the embankments of the Buffalo Bayou concentrated in what is now downtown Houston. With the escalating development, boat traffic and transportation along the bayou increased so dramatically it was designated the "National Commercial Highway of the Republic."

Over the years the corridor densified, and while Houston prospered as an emerging city, the bayou languished. Haphazard engineering of the waterway, increased urban runoff from impervious surface area; the severing of critical ecological systems within the watershed and the proliferation of freeways (symbolized by the heroic I-45 interchange over the Buffalo Bayou) signaled a distinct change in the programmatic use and ecological relevance of the Buffalo Bayou, especially within the middle to lower reaches of the watershed. Significantly, in the larger regional context of Houston, the Buffalo Bayou was one of the few bayous left in central Houston to resist being reconstructed with concrete in the 1960s and 1970s.

Traditionally, development had turned its back on this portion of the bayou. Towering freeway structures criss-crossed the corridor, blocking out sunlight and spilling concentrated sheets of water off their sides during rainstorms. The waters of the bayou brought with them debris, trash, and silt that were constantly being deposited along the bank. Pedestrians who ventured into this segment found themselves more than 9.1 meters below the grade of surrounding streets, out of view and with few access points. Excessively steep banks were subjected to severe erosion. Invasive plantings were overgrown and created unsafe walking conditions.

The situation of the bayou in Houston's inner city became so dire that in the mid-1980s advocates of the Buffalo Bayou, who desired to see the return of a natural systems corridor, prompted new initiatives through which to transform a section of the corridor as a precedent that other sections of the corridor might follow. Recognizing these challenges, the landscape architects and engineers employed a series of site-specific design solutions to reposition the corridor back into the public realm. The driving force behind this project was the Buffalo Bayou Partnership (BBP), created in 1986 as a coalition of civic, environmental, governmental, and business representatives.

It was decided that a 1.6-kilometer section of the Buffalo Bayou, located in downtown Houston and overlaid by the I-45 interchange, would be the focus of this initial investigation (spearheaded by the Buffalo Bayou Partnership in conjunction with SWA) of how to structure a transformation based on principles of urban design, ecology, recreation-based programming, fluvial geomorphology, and hydrologic flood engineering. The project, called the Buffalo Bayou Promenade, would convert a neglected, trash-soaked eyesore, challenged by an entangled infrastructure of freeways and bridges, into a multifaceted urban park—adding 9.3 hectares of park land to Houston's inner city. It integrates the natural and historic Buffalo Bayou into the fabric of the city. This project is one of the first that celebrates the urban bayou rather than abandoning it. Re-engineered sloping of the banks and a series of stairs and ramps reconnect Houstonians to their native bayou.

Invasive plant species such as bluestem grass (*Dichanthiem annulatum*), Japanese honeysuckle (*Lonicera japonica*) and bushkiller (*Cayratia japonica*) had overtaken many of the embankments along the bayou. These aggressive monocultures were removed, and replaced with a variety of native and naturalized, flood-resistant riparian vegetation and trees, helping to reestablish wildlife habitat in the area. By incorporating diversity, the planting plan recreates a living green tissue into the ecologically degraded bayou. Groves of native trees were used to soften the harsh urban infrastructure, buffer noise, and mitigate the scale of the freeways. Areas under existing trees and freeway structures and along banks were planted with ferns, ruellia, and other robust native plants to provide a lush, green ground plane that would resist erosion and could be maintained easily. The critical role of planting as an aesthetic erosion-control measure and element of habitat creation has nurtured a waterway that is now home to an established presence of ducks, herons, turtles, and fish.

The plantings operate as a system for stabilization and provide a framework for incorporating future designed elements along the bayou. The 1.6-kilometer built stretch of promenade includes pedestrian and bike paths, which connect into a surrounding network of trails, totaling 32 kilometers. Strategic points along both sides of the Buffalo Bayou Promenade allow for easy access to the greater bayou for different types of water-based recreation. Elements within the constructed project, including public art, were designed to account for the natural periodic flooding of the bayou, providing park visitors with varied experiences throughout the year.

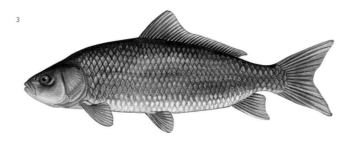

1
Houston, Texas, 1891. Bird's eye perspective of Houston's evolving fabric in the context of the Buffalo Bayou. View looking south, present-day downtown Houston centered in the perspective.

2
Picnicking along the banks of the Buffalo Bayou, Houston, 1920. This image shows the recreational potential of the bayou for boating, sight-seeing, travel, sunning, sitting, and strolling.

3
The smallmouth buffalo (*Ictiobus bubalus*) also known as buffalo fish, can reach a length of more than 1.2 meters and weigh as much as 30 kilograms. It thrives in sluggish areas of large rivers and shallow lakes from Pennsylvania and West Virginia to Alabama and Texas, and it is the number-one commercially caught fresh-water fish. It is believed that the name Buffalo Bayou either originated from this particular species of fish still found in the shallow waters, or that it was named for the bison that once roamed the area.

4

The Buffalo Bayou watershed covers an area of the City of Houston that is roughly 267 square kilometers and is almost entirely urbanized, sustaining a population of 410,658. The Buffalo Bayou Promenade project is approximately 1.6 kilometers long and is situated in the downtown core of Houston.

5a + b

Existing conditions of the downtown section of Buffalo Bayou in the mid-to-late 1990s. These photos document the impact of seasonal storm flows within the bayou's fluvial and coastal mudflat marsh origins. Visually, the eroding clay, silt, and fine-sand banks are devoid of riparian plant growth that would have normally protected the banks.

The absence of plant material and the neglected appearance of the corridor, conjoined with the derelict spaces underneath the freeway infrastructure, created unsafe conditions for pedestrians and cyclists.

BUFFALO BAYOU PROMENADE

6

The diagram illustrates the proposed landscape system, following the Buffalo Bayou
as is moves in an easterly flow through
downtown Houston on its way to Galveston
Bay. The first phase of the Promenade
project is a 1.6-kilometer section forming
the northern edge of the downtown core.
The complex network of elevated freeways

provided SWA with a vertical dimension to
consider when strategizing the location
and form of pathways, planting, outdoor
programs, lighting, art, pedestrian access,
and bicycle circulation.

7

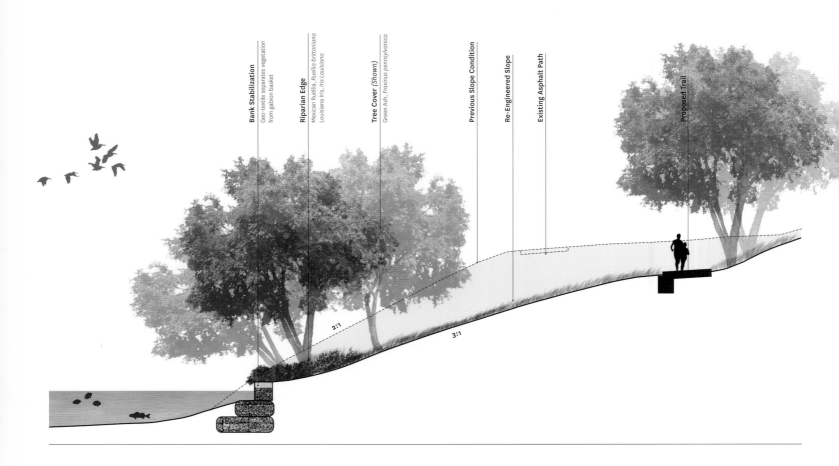

Bank Stabilization
Geo-textile separates vegetation
from gabion basket

Riparian Edge
Mexican Ruellia, *Ruellia brittoniana*
Louisiana Iris, *Iris Louisiana*

Tree Cover (Shown)
Green Ash, *Fraxinus pennsylvanica*

Previous Slope Condition

Re-Engineered Slope

Existing Asphalt Path

Proposed Trail

2:1

3:1

7

Composite section illustrating existing and proposed conditions. The existing 50-percent exposed slopes were prone to erosion and were not capable of sustaining vigorous plant life or supporting recreation. This condition was exacerbated by seasonal flooding which would further scour the banks and accelerate erosion. The landscape architects at SWA proposed a contiguous gabion wall system, riparian planting, and a re-engineered 33-percent slope to maintain hydrologic flows and strengthen opportunities for open-space recreation, access, and circulation.

UNDERWATER GABION

8

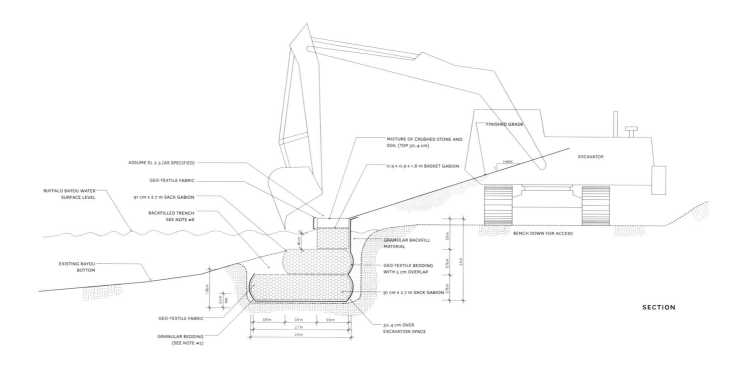

FINISHED GRADE

MIXTURE OF CRUSHED STONE AND
SOIL (TOP 30.4 cm)

ASSUME EL 2.5 (AS SPECIFIED)

0.9 x 0.9 x 1.8 m BASKET GABION

3 MAX

EXCAVATOR

GEO-TEXTILE FABRIC

BUFFALO BAYOU WATER
SURFACE LEVEL

91 cm x 2.7 m SACK GABION

BACKFILLED TRENCH
SEE NOTE #8

GRANULAR BACKFILL
MATERIAL

BENCH DOWN FOR ACCESS

EXISTING BAYOU
BOTTOM

GEO-TEXTILE BEDDING
WITH 5 cm OVERLAP

91 cm x 2.7 m SACK GABION

GEO-TEXTILE FABRIC

GRANULAR BEDDING
(SEE NOTE #2)

0.9 m   0.9 m   0.9 m
2.7 m
2.9 m

30.4 cm OVER
EXCAVATION SPACE

SECTION

Construction Considerations

- Excavate and level existing slope to accomodate heavy equipment and lessen movement of soil.

- Install geo-textile fabric and coat with granular bedding to prevent geo-textile from floating.

- Install the first course of prefabricated and prefilled 97 cm diameter x 2.7 m long sack of gabions. Fill shall be 1.2 x 2.4 m stone, as specified.

- Stack the prefabricated and prefilled second-course 91 cm diameter x 2.7 m long sack gabions on the first course as shown. Stagger the second course gabions to that they lie between adjacent gabions on first course. Additional courses shall be laid in like manner.

- After placing the second-course gabions at the desired elevation, specified granular backfill shall be installed at the backface of the bulkhead, between the bank and the geo-textile fabric, to the top of the second course.

- Top 0.9 x 0.9 m gabion baskets will be set to proper alignment and filled in place with 1.2 x 2.4 m granular fill as specified. The top 30.4 cm shall be a mixture of crushed stone and soil with geo-textile fabric lining on the bottom and front face.

- Finish backfill to top of 0.9 x 0.9 x 1.8 m basket gabion. Grade the backside slope as shown on the contract drawing (3:1 max.)

- Backfill bayou side of excavation at the gabion bulkheads with excavated bayou bottom material.

- All welded-wire top brackets shall meet ASTM A975 and be metal-coated with PVC coating.

- All double-twisted mesh wire sacks shall meet ASTM A975 and be metal-coated with PVC coating.

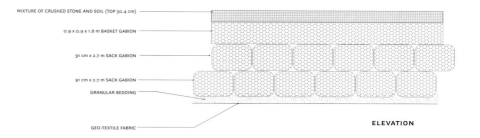

MIXTURE OF CRUSHED STONE AND SOIL (TOP 30.4 cm)

0.9 x 0.9 x 1.8 m BASKET GABION

91 cm x 2.7 m SACK GABION

91 cm x 2.7 m SACK GABION

GRANULAR BEDDING

GEO-TEXTILE FABRIC

ELEVATION

8

Construction detail of the contiguous underwater gabion system used along the banks of the Buffalo Bayou Promenade. The stepped design provides water egress at any point while allowing floating storm debris to pass through. Additionally, hydrologic modeling was reviewed by the Harris County Flood Control District to ensure that floodwater conveyance would not be compromised by these improvements. Work was then approved by the U.S. Army Corps of Engineers prior to construction. Alternative methods were studied, and it was determined that the gabion approach was the most responsive to issues of water velocity, permeability, stabilization, plant growth, materiality, opening up views, and aesthetics.

DIAGRAMMATIC SITE PLAN

9

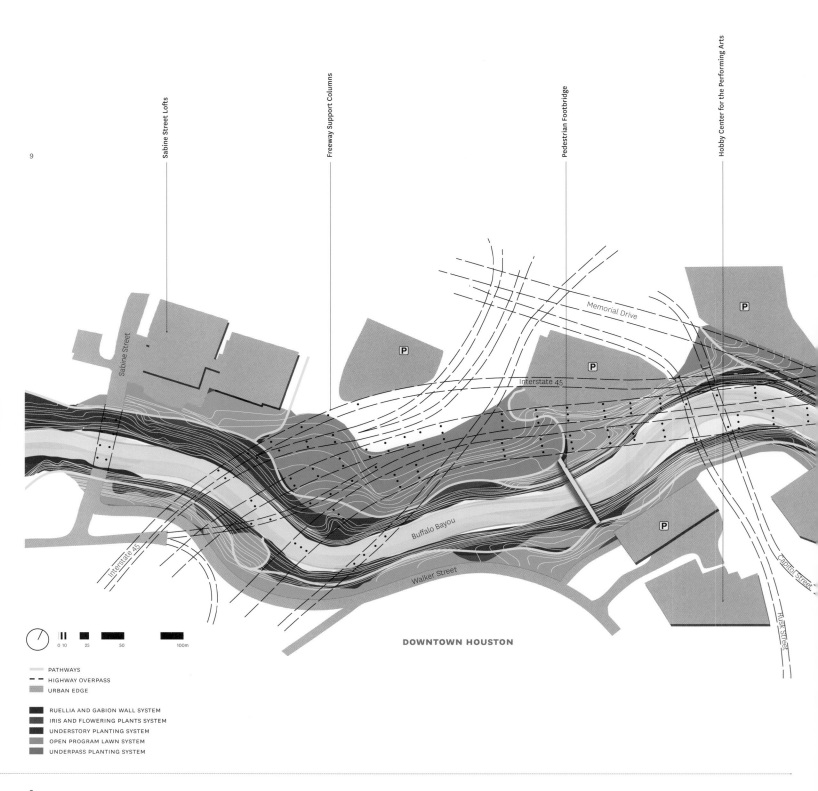

Sabine Street Lofts

Freeway Support Columns

Pedestrian Footbridge

Hobby Center for the Performing Arts

Sabine Street

Memorial Drive

P

P

Interstate 45

P

Buffalo Bayou

Interstate 45

Walker Street

P

Capitol Street

Rusk Street

DOWNTOWN HOUSTON

0 10   25   50   100m

PATHWAYS
HIGHWAY OVERPASS
URBAN EDGE

RUELLIA AND GABION WALL SYSTEM
IRIS AND FLOWERING PLANTS SYSTEM
UNDERSTORY PLANTING SYSTEM
OPEN PROGRAM LAWN SYSTEM
UNDERPASS PLANTING SYSTEM

9
Site plan of the Buffalo Bayou Promenade.
The confluence of the river with the overhead geometries of the freeway, create
opportunities for light and shade, as well
as scale and variety for programming and
pedestrian experience.

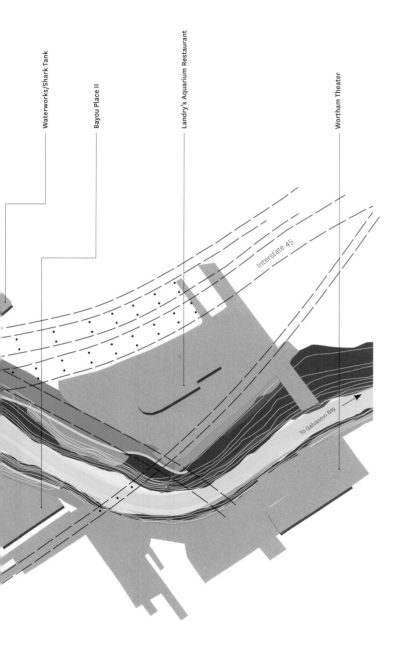

Waterworks/Shark Tank

Bayou Place II

Landry's Aquarium Restaurant

Wortham Theater

Interstate 45

To Galvaston Bay

 omit

10a

10b

10c

11

10a – 10c
32.2 kilometers of contiguous trails to run, walk, and bike are being planned and implemented along both sides of the bayou. Residents, visitors, and tourists are rediscovering the bayou as on outlet for recreation and a healthy lifestyle.

11
Promenading along the upper embankment of the bayou has become a popular activity for pedestrians in search of destinations, activities, events, or just people-watching. On this particular day, the City of Houston was organizing a free outdoor concert on the bayou.

RUELLIA

12

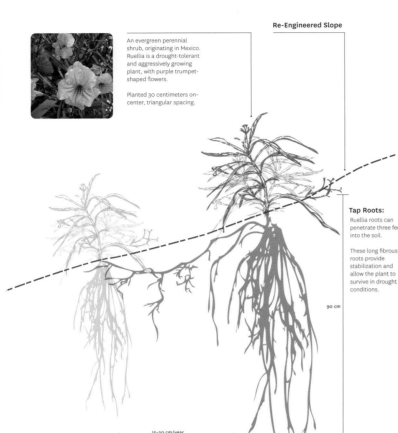

An evergreen perennial shrub, originating in Mexico. Ruellia is a drought-tolerant and aggressively growing plant, with purple trumpet-shaped flowers.

Planted 30 centimeters on-center, triangular spacing.

Re-Engineered Slope

Tap Roots:
Ruellia roots can penetrate three feet into the soil.

These long fibrous roots provide stabilization and allow the plant to survive in drought conditions.

90 cm

15–30 cm/year

Root Rhizomes:
Ruellia reproduce and grow through underground stems known as rhizomes. These extensions of the plant produce roots and shoots from below-ground nodes. Horizontal growth from a single plant can extend up to 30 centimeters each year.

The horizontality of this growth provides additional soil stabilization .

13

14

15

12
Native and naturalized riparian plants such as the Mexican petunia (*Ruellia brittoniana*, varieties "Katie" "Blue Shade" and "Mexican"), Louisiana iris (Iris "Louisiana"), local ferns, and others were chosen for their deep-rooted ability to control erosion and sustain the future hydrologic actions of the bayou.

13
The natural channel and the soil along its banks have been stabilized through the use of gabions and the anchoring of 12,700 metric tons of rock and recycled concrete. The open gabion cages allow for tree roots and riparian ground covers to form a natural edge while providing a porous foundation for the riparian benthic community. Weeds and other invasive plants have been replaced by a revegetated embankment program comprised of 287,000 plants (including native perennials, ground cover, and 641 trees). This photograph shows the planting of green ash (*Fraxinus pennsylvanica*), a native riparian tree, along the river's edge, creating a shade canopy over the water, cooling water and enhancing habitat.

14
Species of fern proliferate under the shady areas of the elevated freeway structures, providing both an erosion-control measure and potential habitat for native wildlife.

BUFFALO BAYOU WILDLIFE

The adult loggerhead turtle can grow up to 159 kilograms. These turtles inhabit both oceans and coastal waterways.

Blue herons on the site are territorial and use the bayou for nesting and foraging.

Gulf coast toad
Bufo Valliceps

Eastern narrow-mouthed toad
Gastrophryne Carolinensis

Cricket frog
Acris Crepitans

Green tree frog
Hyula Cinerea Cinerea

Houston toad
Bufo Houstonensis

Upland chorus frog
Pseudacris Triseriata Feriarum

Leopard frog
Rana Pipiens

Bullfrog
Rana Catesbeiana

Green anole
Anolis Carolinensus

Ground slink
Lygosoma Laterale

Southern prairie slink
Eumeces Septenrionalis Obtusirostris

Texas horned lizard
Phrynosoma Cornutum

Western slender glass lizard
Ophisaurus Attenuatus Attenuatus

Six-lined racerunner
Cnemidophorus Sexlineatus

Northern fence lizard
Sceloporus Undulates Hyacinthinus

Mockingbird
Mimus Sp.

Mexican free-tailed bat
Tadarida Brasiliensis

Rafinesque's big-eared bat
Corynorhinus Rafinesquii

White-tailed hawk
Buteo Albicaudatus

Brown-headed cowbird
Molothrus Ater

Belted kingfisher
Megaceryle Alcyon

Bank swallow
Ripana Sp.

Alligator gar
Lepisosteus Spatula

Armored catfish
Hypostomus Sp.

Blue catfish
Ictalurus Furcatus

Blue talapia
Talapia Aurea

Bullhead minnow
Pimephalus Vigilax

Common carp
Cyprinus Carpio

Creek chubsucker
Erimyzon Oblongus

Flathead catfish
Pylodictis Olivarius

Bigmouth buffalo fish
Ictiobus Cyprinellus

Gizzard shad
Dorosoma Cepedianum

Green sunfish
Lepomis Cyanelius

Inland silverside
Menidia Berylina

Mexican free-tailed bats prey on insects in the bayou. Their colonies are some of the largest congregations of mammals.

Largemouth bass
Micropterus Salmoides

Longear sunfish
Lepomis Megaiotis

Longnose gar
Lepisosteus Osseus

Mosquito fish
Gambusia Affinis

Rio Grande cichlid
Cichlosaoma Cyanoguttatum

Smallmouth buffalo fish
Ictiobus Babalus

Rough green snake
Haldea Stiatula

Timber rattlesnake
Crotalus Horridus

Yellow-bellied racer
Oluber Constrictor Flaviventris

Eastern coachwhip
Masticophis Flagellum Flagellum

Eastern hognose snake
Heterodon Platyrhinos

Diamond-backed water snake
Natrix Rhombifera Rhombifera

Texas brown snake
Storeria Dekayi Texana

Prairie king snake
Lampropeltis Calligaster Calligaster

Mississippi ringneck snake
Diadophis Puncatatus Stictogenys

Southern copperhead
Agkistrodon Contortrix Contortrix

Texas coral snake
Micrurus Fulvius Tenere

American alligator
Alligator Mississipiensis

Common snapper
Chelydra Serpentine Serpentina

Loggerhead turtle
Caretta Caretta

Mississippi mud turtle
Kinosternon Subrubrum Hippocrepis

Western chicken turtle
Deirochelys Reticularia Miaria

Red-eared turtle
Pseudemys Scripta Elegans

Three-toed box turtle
Errapene Carolina Triungula

Alligator snapping turtle
Macroclelys Temminckii

Atlantic hawkbill sea turtle
Eretmochlys Imbricata

Green sea turtle
Chelonia Mydas

Leatherback sea turtle
Dermochelys Coriacea

Great egret
Casmerodius Albus

American peregrine falcon
Falco Peregrinus Anatum

Artic peregrine falcon
Falco Peregrinus Tundrius

Attwater greater prairie chicken
Tympanuchus Cupido Attwateri

Bald eagle
Haliaeetus Leucocephalus

Brown pelican
Pelecanus Occidentalis

Piping plover
Charadrius Melodus

Whooping crane
Grus Americana

Wood stork
Mycteria Americana

Great blue heron
Ardea Herodias

Striped mullet
Mugil Cephalus

Opossum
Didelphis Marsupialis

Short-tailed shrew
CrypTotis Parva

Striped skunk
Mephistis Mephistis

House mouse
Mus Musculus

Raccoon
Procyon Lotor

Fox squirrel
Sciurus Niger

Hispid cotton rat
Sigmoodon Hispidus

Eastern cottontail
Sylvilagus Floridanus

Nine-banded armadillo
Dasypus Noveminctus

The bigmouth buffalo fish is a bottom feeder, living on the many microinvertebrates that can be found within the bayou waterways.

15
Aquatic and terrestrial ecosystems at the water's edge are enhanced by the overhead woody canopy that provides shade and regulates water temperatures. Seasonal leaf fall adds to the nutrient-cycling soil and moisture. The aquatic system provides diversity and interspersion of habitat niches and corridors for migration and dispersal of wildlife, particularly migratory birds.

16
Buffalo Bayou sustains habitat for blue herons, loggerhead turtles, hawks, and a few migratory birds such as purple martins, warblers, and wood ducks. A variety of fish can also be found in the bayou including the smallmouth buffalo fish. The bayou is also home to one of the only handful of nonmigratory bat populations in the world, the Mexican free-tailed bat. In Houston, bat watching has become a popular outdoor activity where, at dusk, one can observe more than 150,000 bats flocking into the sky.

17

18

17
Aerial view of the I-45 interchange over the
Buffalo Bayou Promenade. The overlay of
the highway, the bayou, and recreational
systems reflects a sense of spatial efficiency
and challenges conventional expectations of
single-use infrastructure.

18
A new pedestrian and bicycle bridge links
the northern greenway (Allen Parkway) with
Houston's central business district. People
had previously avoided going from one to
the other because of concerns over safety.
The new pedestrian bridge is expected to

help catalyze a future growth area for the
Arts District while creating an iconic destination in which to experience and view
the bayou.

19
This stretch of urban park land provides new connections that not only bring people to the bayou but allow them to travel from north and south by foot and bicycle.

20
The Buffalo Bayou Partnership has developed a vibrant calendar of events for the Buffalo Bayou Promenade corridor. Activities such as the annual Bayou Bash (a musical and food extravaganza) and the Regatta (a competitive canoeing event that draws as many as 800 participants in three separate competitive divisions) have galvanized the bayou's potential as a regional recreation amenity within the City of Houston.

23a

21

22a

23b

22b

21

This commissioned artwork, a poetic interpretation of a canoe frame, is positioned at each park portal, providing visitors with a symbolic link between the city's Arts District and its historic bayou.

22a + b

Accessibility is assisted and given identity by galvanized steel railings conceived and implemented by local artists.

23a + b

Images of recent flooding at Buffalo Bayou: sediment, debris, and vegetation left behind after the flood water recedes.

25

26

24 (previous spread)
The success of the park was in large part measured by its ability to function as a safe pedestrian environment at night. The landscape architect, SWA, and L'Observatoire International Lighting Designers conceived of three orders of lighting to illuminate the park: 1) a primary trail-lighting system,

2) a system of lights to wash hidden spaces, and 3) an art-driven lighting component (as seen in these photographs), where a theatrical lighting system, including LEDs, casts a surreal glow onto the concrete freeway supports as day turns to night. Monthly phases of the moon were

interpreted as a wash of blue light when the new moon occurs, which then gradually shift to white as the full moon emerges.

25
The first-order trail fixtures contain lamps engineered to withstand periodic submersion and possible vandalism.

26
High-intensity light fixtures were concealed within the structural recesses of the freeway infrastructure to create a more ambient lighting effect.

27
Evening view looking south toward the
Buffalo Bayou Promenade and downtown
Houston beyond.

ANNING RIVER NEW SOUTH TOWN

Future Historic Ecologies

The farming industry in China sustains 1.2 billion people and contributes up to 20 percent of the nation's gross domestic product. Growing populations and improved technology has increased agricultural demand, resulting in an intensification of labor, increased use of chemical fertilizers, and reliance on irrigation. In response, China has embarked on an agricultural reform program to revitalize these sectors through new developments, investments in improved irrigation and water management, and through environmentally sustainable production practices. The city of Miyi County sits within the Anning River Valley in the southwestern portion of the Sichuan Province. The river valley is part of the second largest alluvial plain in the region, covering an area of 34,700 square kilometers. The rich soils of the plain support over 200,000 hectares of agriculture, with 76 percent of the 3.4 million residents of the valley relying on farming for their livelihood. The government of Miyi County supports initiatives for improved agricultural practices and seeks to transform its primarily farm-based municipality of approximately 200,000 residents into a unique and exemplary resort town—with tourism, recreation, and commercial/residential centers—which maintains agriculture as part of its economy and identity.

A 200-hectare site, which lies south of the historic district of Miyi County and straddles the Anning River, was selected for a master planning proposal that would serve as a new ecological resort district for the city. This new district is able to accommodate a population of 95,000 with large commercial and cultural facilities located at the north end of the site, and residential homes located along the east bank of the river. Open space along the river is created by the manipulation and enhancement of a set of complex hydrological systems. "Future Historic Ecologies" was the name given to the project in reference to the conceptual design process, in which each of the existing hydrological systems was evaluated in terms of its historic function, current performance, and potential to be leveraged into serving the new district as a regional tourist destination. These existing systems consist of the Anning River levees, a new hydro-electric dam, mountain stormwater runoff channels, agricultural canals, and the surrounding floodplain. As a network they present the opportunity to define a new set of performative parameters that will become the basis for hydrological infrastructure, which engages residents and functions in water filtration and flood control.

At present the Anning River is polluted and unsuitable for most water programs; the mountain stormwater channels are intermittent and often flush out large concentrations of sediment, while agricultural canals carry chemicals and fertilizers that also dump into the river. A solution to these issues was developed through two different approaches: one that retrofits the historic system for future use, and the other which creates new or parallel systems for specific performative goals. The retrofitted hydrological infrastructures include the Anning River and existing mountain channels and agricultural canals. Each of these elements is carefully modified to suit new program requirements. For instance, the concrete levee walls of the river are altered to accommodate vegetation that can resist flood-force flows, while a rubber dam within the waterway maintains minimum water levels during dry seasons, as well as offering an aesthetically pleasing reflecting surface year round. Both the mountain channels and agricultural canals are structurally

improved and planted with green buffers to help improve water quality. The new hydrological system is composed of a series of water bodies parallel to the river that function as a large scale "treatment train." Polluted river water is diverted into the system at the North Lake where artificially constructed floating wetlands absorb pollutants and begin to improve water quality. Water then flows through the designed "central park" where the meandering flow helps to collect sediment and continue the filtration process. Further south, a wetland park contains and treats the water before it reaches its final destination in the South Lake—a large swimmable water body with fully cleansed water, able to support ecological habitat and human recreation. Thus the system is organized along a gradient from partially treated to fully treated water, and from a technological, artificial, and formal approach to a more naturalistic and interactive one.

Resort and local amenities are integrated into the larger hydrological strategy. The North Lake is designed as an extension of Miyi County and is surrounded by community buildings. The South Lake, with clean water, naturalistic islands, and rustic architecture serves as a resort. The east side of the river is family-focused, with a new recreational complex adjacent to the residential homes. A boardwalk running along the river levee is lined with local shops and connects the North and South Lake. The iconic Phoenix Tower building, near the center of the site, sits along the boardwalk and serves as a bridge to the South Lake, while anchoring the entire development. A large portion of the waterfront is maintained for agricultural use, but with variety of program including educational centers, farmhouse restaurants, pathways, and model organic farms.

1a – 1c
The cultural landscape of the region is characterized by its rich agricultural heritage, a result of the area's natural system of dramatic mountains, large rivers, and alluvial valleys. The master plan proposes a mutually beneficial relationship between traditional land uses and future developments.

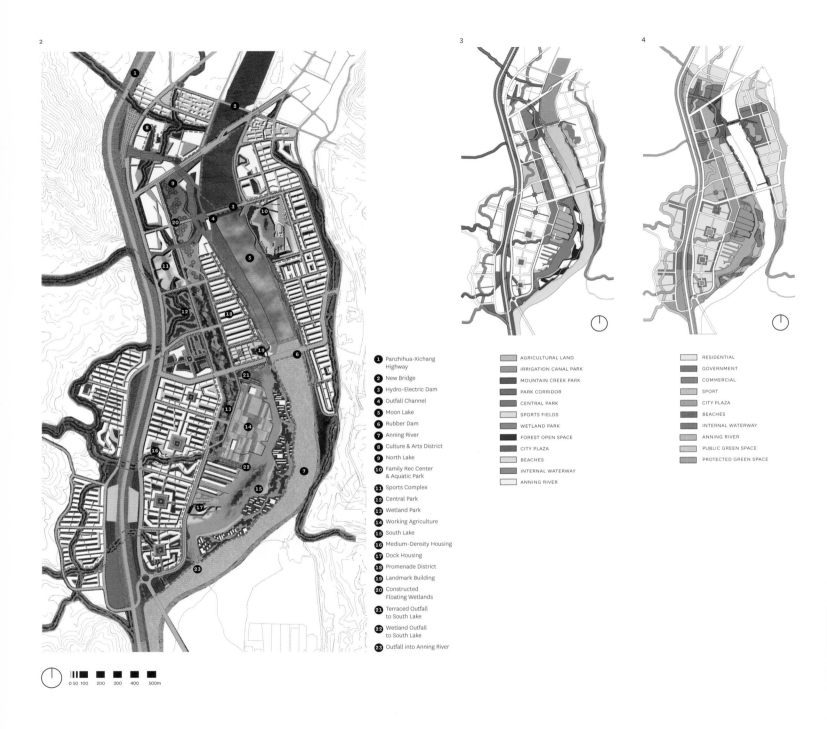

2

3

4

1 Panzhihua-Xichang Highway
2 New Bridge
3 Hydro-Electric Dam
4 Outfall Channel
5 Moon Lake
6 Rubber Dam
7 Anning River
8 Culture & Arts District
9 North Lake
10 Family Rec Center & Aquatic Park
11 Sports Complex
12 Central Park
13 Wetland Park
14 Working Agriculture
15 South Lake
16 Medium-Density Housing
17 Dock Housing
18 Promenade District
19 Landmark Building
20 Constructed Floating Wetlands
21 Terraced Outfall to South Lake
22 Wetland Outfall to South Lake
23 Outfall into Anning River

0 50 100 200 300 400 500m

AGRICULTURAL LAND
IRRIGATION CANAL PARK
MOUNTAIN CREEK PARK
PARK CORRIDOR
CENTRAL PARK
SPORTS FIELDS
WETLAND PARK
FOREST OPEN SPACE
CITY PLAZA
BEACHES
INTERNAL WATERWAY
ANNING RIVER

RESIDENTIAL
GOVERNMENT
COMMERCIAL
SPORT
CITY PLAZA
BEACHES
INTERNAL WATERWAY
ANNING RIVER
PUBLIC GREEN SPACE
PROTECTED GREEN SPACE

2

The master plan for the 200-hectare site provides housing and amenities for a projected 95,000 residents as well as attractions and facilities for tourists and regional visitors. At the core of the design is a highly programmed water treatment system that runs parallel to the existing Anning River.

3

The master plan employs a wide range of open-space types to accommodate both the local community and tourists, while taking full advantage of the programmatic potential of the improved hydrological system.

4

Land use is arranged according to a number of factors, including water program, proximity to the existing town, and access to open space. Special features include the preservation of a large parcel of waterfront agriculture and a new linear water treatment system.

5

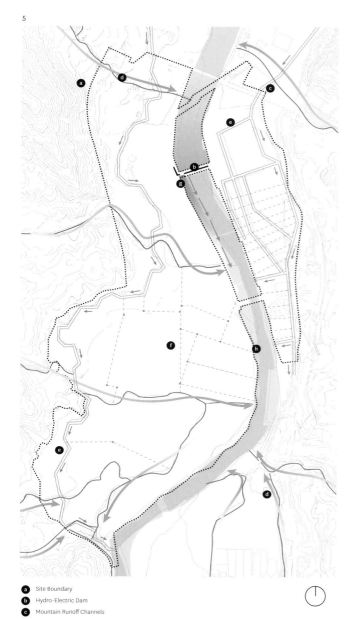

- **a** Site Boundary
- **b** Hydro-Electric Dam
- **c** Mountain Runoff Channels
- **d** Flow of Mountain Runoff
- **e** Main Irrigation Channels
- **f** Secondary Irrigation Channels
- **g** Outfall Channel
- **h** Anning River

6

7

5

The existing hydrology is complex and challenging. At the core is the Anning River, a turbid and powerful river fed by intermittent mountain streams. Running parallel to the river and following its contours are irrigation canals for agriculture and aquaculture.

6

A hydro-electric dam (shown with gates partially open) will divert water from the upper Anning River to the outfall channel. The warm water (created as electricity is produced) flows through the outfall channel, cooling down before it reenters the lower Anning River.

7

View of the treatment system at North Lake, where water is diverted from the Anning River and begins the filtration process, passing through a series of floating wetland islands. The entire filtration system becomes a central landscape feature for the new district.

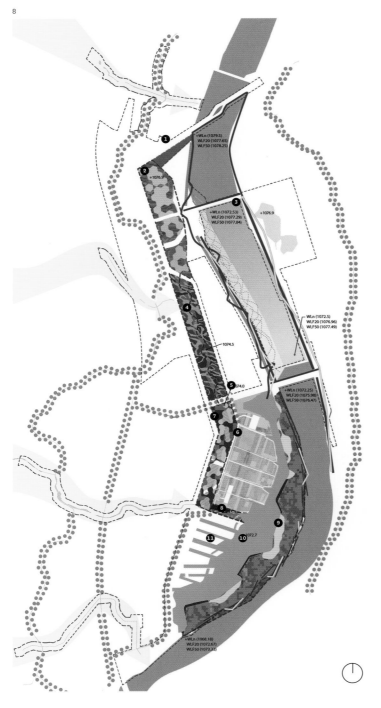

8

+WLn (1079.5)
WLF20 (1077.65)
WLF50 (1078.25)

+1076.9

+WLn (1072.53)
WLF20 (1077.29)
WLF50 (1077.84)

+1076.9

WLn (1072.5)
WLF20 (1076.96)
WLF50 (1077.49)

1074.5

1074.0

+WLn (1072.25)
WLF20 (1075.98)
WLF50 (1076.47)

1072.7

+WLn (1068.18)
WLF20 (1072.67)
WLF50 (1073.33)

1. Sculptural Diversion [Hybrid]
2. Pattern Art Ecological Lake
3. Cultural/Infra-Front Boardwalk
4. Water Meander
5. Agricultural Amphitheater
6. Accessible Terraced Agriculture
7. Natural-Pattern Wetlands
8. Mountain Stream Outlet
9. South Boardwalk/Fragmented Levee
10. Drift Island [Hybrid]
11. Eden Lake

TRANSITIONAL INFRASTRUCTURES

Elements bind the existing infrastructures with synchronous infrastructures.

Sculptural Diversion [Hybrid]

Water Infra Sediment Treatment Train

Design quality begins as a hard edge (the dam) and transitions to the formal lake and ecologies.

Access is provided by embedded walkways.

Drift Island [Hybrid]

Water Infra Edges Providing Graded Access to Waterfront

Island appears to be an accumulated drift, held together by a series of hard edges, and interrupted by beaches in between.

Heavy forest hides signs of development.

Access boardwalk on both sides of the beach.

SYNCHRONOUS INFRASTRUCTURES

Diversion enables ideal synchronicity between infrastructure, ecologies, and cultural elements.

Pattern Art Ecology Lake

Water Infra Sediment Settling

Formal patterns of wetland vegetation and treatment areas.

Walkways on two levels provide access.

Water Meander

Water Infra Sediment Treatment Train, Check Dams, Wetlands

Water slowly trickles, meanders, and cascades down through falls and check dams, providing integration of water and people movement.

Edge is graded to allow access under bridges, and for people to walk alongside the water cleansing technology.

Agricultural Amphitheater

Natural-Pattern Wetlands

Water Infra Sediment Treatment Train, Water Quality Polishing, Natural Habitat

Design quality is a mix of natural forms, new ecologies, and large wetland areas.

Area is accessible through boardwalks, which lead inside bird viewing platforms.

Mountain Stream Outlet

Water Infra Sediment Settling/Treatment Areas

Design quality is wild, organic, and sculptural; building off of the Natural-Pattern Wetlands.

Walkways allow for bird watching.

Eden Lake

Water Infra Minimal, Outlet to Anning River.

Edges maximize human and water interaction.

Islands in the center build wildlife.

Access to beaches, watercraft rentals/docks, and boardwalks.

8

Due to the scale and ambition of the project, the master plan contains a complex and diverse set of water infrastructures and strategies. The project proposed two main types: synchronous, in which program and (new/ideal) infrastructure are fully integrated, and retrofitted, in which (existing) infrastructure is improved upon. Transitional infrastructure links the synchronous with the retrofitted features.

RETROFITTED INFRASTRUCTURES

Existing infrastructure must be retrofitted with new cultural infrastructure. These retrofits weave through and interact with site systems.

Cultural/Infra-Front Boardwalk

Water Infra Levee Wall, Outfall Channel (moving warm water), Rubber Dam (still water)

Design quality of the levee wall is clad in stone and riprap. The boardwalk undulates and floats over the levee to reflect a "cultural front," not just an infrastructural front. Views of the dam and other cultural moments provide breaks from the levee's linearity. The minimal structure of the boardwalk allows for greater vegetation growth and distinct moments of overhang.

Access walkways float over the outfall channel in places with arbors and shade.

Accessible Terraced Agriculture

Water Infra Irrigation Canals

Minimal intervention highlights the formal structure of the agriculture.

Access via levees provides additional views. Access bridges cross over irrigation canals.

South Boardwalk/ Fragmented Levee

Water Infra Stepped Levee Introducing Riverside Pocket Ecologies.

Materiality of the levee and boardwalk changes and becomes fragmented. The levee "splits" apart to become small stepped gabion walls. Pieces of the boardwalk connect to the walls and continue access through the site.

A low path runs below flood level, among the gabions, while a high path runs above.

9

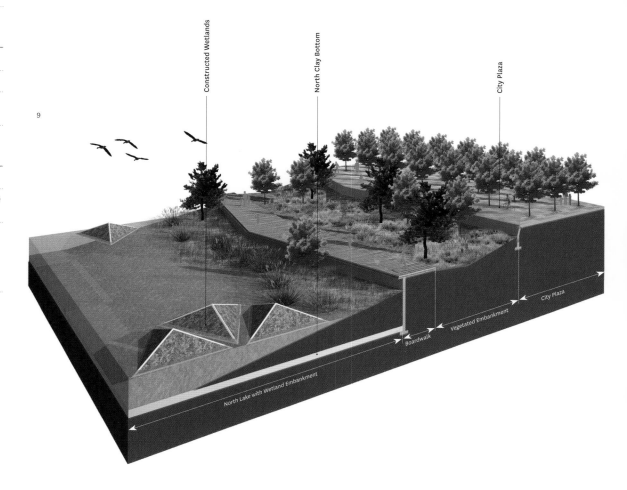

9
Prototypical water treatment system and open-space concept. At the North Lake, biological treatment islands are arranged as "flower" pads and aid in an early stage of water treatment.

10

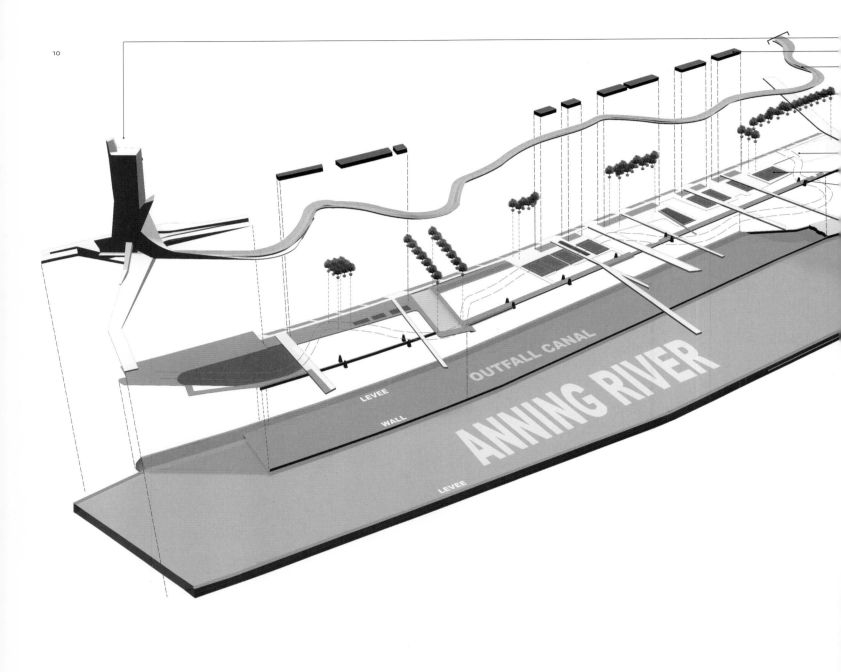

ANNING RIVER

OUTFALL CANAL

LEVEE

WALL

LEVEE

10

Axonometric drawing showing how the
existing hydrological infrastructure along
the Anning River is retrofitted into central
programmatic elements. Here, the dam
outfall wall becomes a support structure
for a suspended boardwalk containing park
programs, a local commercial area, and an
arbor/water feature.

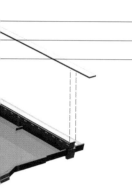

Landmark Building

Commercial Buildings

Canal Pergola

Planter with Trees

Footprint of Canal Pergola

Sports Field

Interpretive Pylon at Walk on
Top of Wall at Outfall Canal

11

12

11
The iconic Phoenix Tower lies at the center
of the New South Town and includes a
public amphitheater, retail space, and
educational exhibits.

12
Bird's eye view of the new development. The
South Lake in the foreground (which will
be swimmable) is spectacularly flanked by
agricultural areas, lake housing, a natural
ecological and wooded resort island, and
the Phoenix Tower.

SECTIONS OF LEVEE SYSTEM

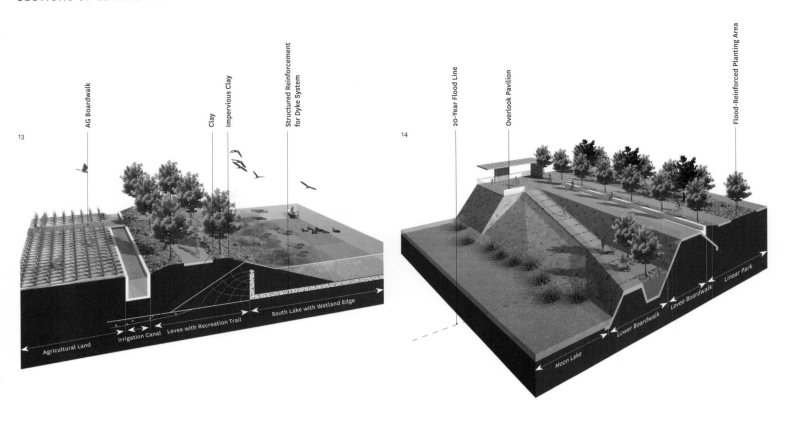

13

AG Boardwalk

Clay

Impervious Clay

Structured Reinforcement for Dyke System

20-Year Flood Line

Overlook Pavilion

Flood-Reinforced Planting Area

14

Agricultural Land

Irrigation Canal

Levee with Recreation Trail

South Lake with Wetland Edge

Moon Lake

Lower Boardwalk

Levee Boardwalk

Linear Park

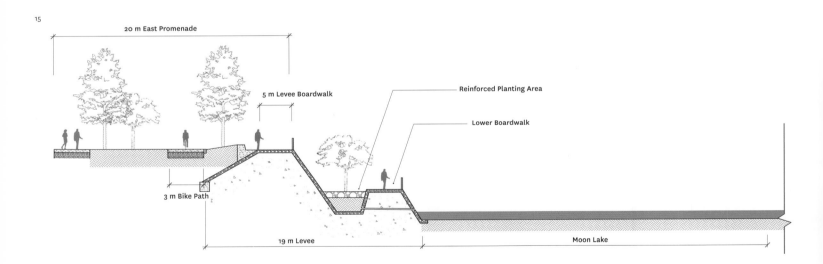

15

20 m East Promenade

5 m Levee Boardwalk

Reinforced Planting Area

Lower Boardwalk

3 m Bike Path

19 m Levee

Moon Lake

13

The preserved agriculture creates an important cultural landscape that continues to be productive, but also contains a rich assortment of paths, interpretive facilities, and landscape types. Clay is used to form an impervious barrier within the waterways.

Water from the Anning River is kept separate from water in the lakes due to the engineered clay wall and reinforced structural dyke system.

14

The modified river levee includes a series of overlooks with paths that lead down below the 20-year flood line and bring visitors close to the water. Reinforced planting beds help stabilize levees and allow for vegetation on this lower path.

15

Detailed section of the east boardwalk and adjacent Moon Lake. The drawing illustrates levee construction and the integration of infrastructural systems.

16a

16b

17

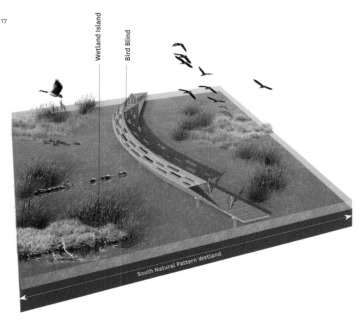

Wetland Island

Bird Blind

South Natural Pattern Wetland

16a + b
People are encouraged to use and interact with the project. The system of water becomes an amenity for local residents while also serving to clean water and provide new habitat.

17
Throughout the site, the boardwalk changes in response to specific hydrological and ecological conditions. Seen here, where the grade of the water is near that of the roads, the boardwalk navigates users away from traffic while providing integrated cover for observing wildlife.

CALIFORNIA ACADEMY OF SCIENCES

High-Performance

Roofs are perhaps the most underutilized spaces in the urban context given their limited accessibility and inflexible programming potential. Yet beyond their obvious building functions, urban roofs present a unique opportunity to address the effects of climate change in our cities. Individually, green roofs are proven to effectively harvest stormwater and insulate buildings. As a collective system, many green roofs can act as a kind of high-performance green infrastructure network that can reduce heat-island effect, improve air quality (including removal of particulate matter), improve water quality, and create wildlife habitat. Significant advances in green-roof technologies have emerged in recent years to foster a new set of guidelines and considerations for roof design, construction, and sustainability.

Located in the heart of San Francisco's Golden Gate Park, the new California Academy of Sciences replaces an outmoded, earthquake-damaged complex of buildings with a remarkable new facility that promotes the Academy's goals to "explore, explain and protect the natural world." The Academy is expected to attract millions of local, national, and international visitors, thereby reconfirming its historic importance as the oldest scientific institution in the American West and setting a bold model for integration of sustainable technology, natural systems, design innovation, and public education.

Under the sculptural form of a 1.01-hectare living roof, the 37,160-square-meter museum houses the Steinhart Aquarium (the oldest such facility in the United States) and Morrison Planetarium as well as 18 million scientific specimens, more than 10,000 live animals, space for education and research, and new exhibits such as a multilevel, glass-enclosed rainforest dome. As part of the design team's commitment to sustainability, the new building reduces the former facility's physical footprint and surrounding pavement by approximately 6,070 square meters, creating space for new gardens that transition to adjacent mature park land.

Since the building opened in 2008, the living roof has proved to be a highlight interpretive attraction that is introducing visitors to a living experiment in native plant restoration in the midst of a major city. In addition to a comprehensive set of technologies relating to building systems—from water recycling in the basement-level aquaria to synchronized ventilation openings in the building curtain walls and roof domes—the living roof captures stormwater, improves air quality by creating and scrubbing oxygen, mitigates microclimatic anomalies, and provides habitat for migratory and local wildlife.

The architect Renzo Piano's initial design concept was to lift the natural landscape on top of the three-story building, creating a dramatic living roof. The roof's contours conform to the major exhibit components and research, collections,

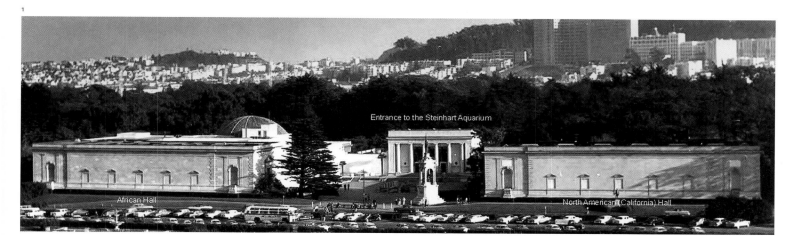

Entrance to the Steinhart Aquarium

African Hall

North American (California) Hall

and administration facilities below, and romantically echo the seven major hills of San Francisco. The two largest domes, with their strategically placed skylights, rise above the planetarium and rainforest exhibit. The landscape architect embraced this approach and collaborated closely with the design team to develop the innovative design and implementation techniques required for such a unique project.

Because the domed portions of the living roof are as steep as 45 degrees in some places, the team developed full-scale models to test the multilayered soil-drainage section and anchoring system that form the foundation to receive the plant materials. A grid of intercept channels created by linear rock-filled baskets (gabions) provides both surface-flow drainage and midslope support for the 7.62-centimeter layer of planting media and the preplanted, biodegradable coir (coconut husk) flats. Plants established in the biodegradable flats off-site, to the landscape architect's specifications, were transported to the site in refrigerated trucks on bakery racks, then hoisted atop the roof and laid by hand onto the planting media sublayer within the gabion channel grid. The coir flats provide temporary support until the plants become well established on the rooftop. Over time, the flats will disintegrate and become part of the soil system.

The resulting vegetated roof includes nearly 500,000 native California plants, all of which require limited or no supplemental irrigation. All plants were selected to be adaptable to the site and attract local butterflies, birds, and insects, some of

them endangered. In addition, the small stature of the selected plants helps to maintain a manicured appearance and express the rolling forms of the roof structure. A 325-square-meter observation deck with interpretive signage provides access to the living roof as well as magnificent views to Golden Gate Park and the de Young Art Museum, completed in 2005. The deck accommodates 200 people and earned innovation LEED credit for using the roof as an exhibit to raise public awareness. Additional native annuals, perennials, and grass species were introduced around the observation deck to realize the tested and recommended palette while increasing the biodiversity of the exhibit.

Sustainability features of the 15.24-centimeter-deep living roof include a reduction of stormwater runoff by at least 90 percent (up to 7.5 million liters of water per year), reduced energy needs for air conditioning, and longer roof life (potentially doubling the life of the roof membrane). Additionally, the extended roof plane forms a broad shade canopy over the building's perimeter circulation and outdoor gathering spaces, and houses 62,000 photovoltaic cells to supply almost 213,000 kilowatt-hours of clean energy per year (about 5 percent of the new Academy's needs), thereby preventing the release of more than 204,115 kilograms of greenhouse gas emissions.

1

Founded in 1853 as a scientific academy, the institution is the oldest of its kind on the American west coast. In 1906, an earthquake destroyed the original building and many of the artifacts and collections. In 1916, the Academy was reopened in Golden Gate Park but suffered earthquake damage again in 1989. This eventually forced the Academy to close again and in 2005 construction began on the new home for the storied institution.

2 (previous spread)

The new Academy is now officially the greenest museum in the world. In 2008, the U.S. Green Building Council issued its formal rating for the new Academy, awarding it the highest possible certification: LEED Platinum. It remains the largest public Platinum-rated building in the world, and—with a total score of 54 points—it also ranks among the world's most sustainable museum buildings. Aside from being a model for green building construction, the unique building design continues to attract 1.6 million visitors annually. (www.calacademy.org, 2009)

3a + b

The two largest hills on top of the roof house the Academy's rainforest and planetarium. The concrete formwork of the domes included circular openings that would serve as motorized skylights and help ventilate hot air from the building. Insulation, reservoir drainage board and support strapping were then layered on top of the concrete before the planting media was added.

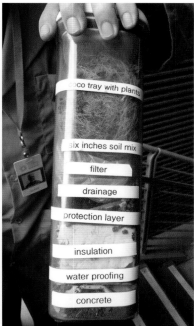

coco tray with plants

six inches soil mix

filter

drainage

protection layer

insulation

water proofing

concrete

4a – 4c

To keep the soil from slipping down the steep hills, SWA devised a structural drainage system using a 7.3-by-7.3-meter grid of rock-filled wire baskets called gabions. In addition to allowing for drainage and providing a soil curb, the gabions are used as footpaths for the maintenance crews that traverse the steep slopes on a regular basis.

To deliver established plants, and ease installation, Rana Creek (restoration ecology and environmental consultants) devised and patented biodegradable planter trays made from coconut husk fiber—a waste product from the coconut industry. The Bio-Tray is held together with natural latex and includes *Mycorrhizal inoculum*, beneficial fungi to

initiate microbial activity and mediate nutrient cycling. Laid on the roof like tiles, the trays degrade within three years, leaving behind a colorful carpet of mature, root-stabilized vegetation.

5

VENTILATION/LIGHT

Circular skylights protrude from the roof mounds. These motorized light fixtures include heat sensors which trigger an opening as temperatures rise above a certain degree.

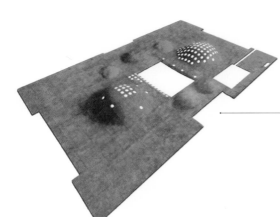

PLANTING

The roof is covered with a half million plants native to the Bay Area. 50,000 43 x 43 cm biodegradable trays housed the young plants and formed the blanket of vegetation covering the roof. As flowers bloom and plants grow, the roof constantly changes with the seasons, while continually providing habitat to a number of bird and insect species.

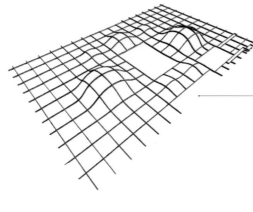

GABION GRID

The 60-degree slopes on the two largest mounds posed a unique and challenging proposal for installation and maintenance on the building's roof. The solution of using a gabion grid, embedded into the insulation layer, created pervious curbing and helped to provide soil purchase, in addition to allowing workers to navigate the terrain.

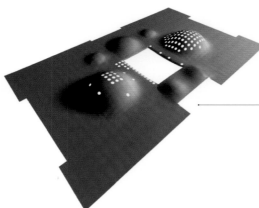

STRUCTURE

Seven mounds make up the structure of the California Academy of Sciences roof. The 1.01-hectare roof is 12 meters off the ground and houses the Morrison Planetarium, Kimball Natural History Museum and Steinhart Aquarium.

A. coconut fiber tray

A 100% biodegradable tray holds the soil and young plant seedlings. The trays are made from the waste products generated by the coconut industry.

B. engineered soil

Six inches of soil (composed of 40% organic matter, 15% sand, and 45% minus scoria) is laid beneath the coconut fiber trays, providing a substrate for plant roots to grow into as they become established.

C. + E. fabric filter

This polypropylene fabric filter helps contain the soil and keep it from washing away, while also acting as a barrier between the planted surface and the building insulation.

D. drainage board

Made of strong recycled materials, the boards help in the regulation and drainage of rain/irrigation water that percolates through the soil and fabric filter.

F. insulation

The insulation works with the vegetation to keep the building interior roughly ten degrees cooler than a standard roof. It also lowers the noise frequency by forty decibels.

G. protection board and waterproof membrane

This thin-material fabric (usually PVC vinyl) separates water and drainage runoff from the insulation layer and away from the structure of the roof.

H. concrete

The structural formwork which makes up the building's mounded roof.

I. stainless steel gabion baskets

Filled with lava rock, the gabions provide structural support and aid in drainage.

J. irrigation system

The system of irrigation is computerized and regulated by an on-site weather station, designed to respond to current conditions. Irrigation water comes from storage reservoirs within the park, rather than relying on the City.

5

The entire roof can be seen as a series of layers. The gabion grid sits atop the structural form, vegetation sits within the grid, and finally ventilation skylights protrude from the top.

6

The three-dimensional rendered section illustrates in greater detail all of the layers which went into the project's construction and how the planting and drainage system was applied to the sloping roof.

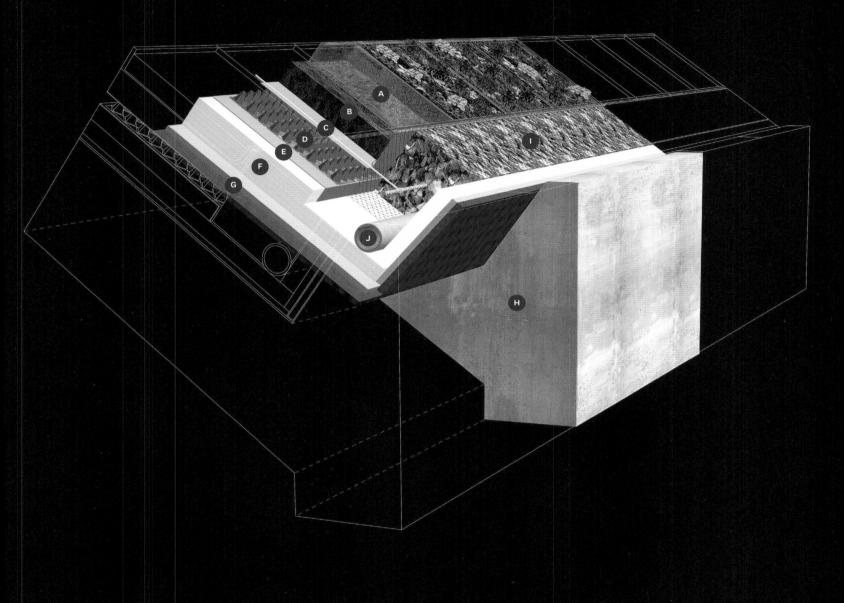

In order to survive past their installation, the rooftop vegetation needed a shallow, strong root structure and the ability to resist high winds and ocean air. Native plants were selected for the Academy's roof because of their proven adaptability to these conditions. Aside from initial watering, the chosen species required minimal care and maintenance once established. In the event irrigation is needed, a weather-controlled system provides water to the roof from reservoirs within the Park (independent from the City's potable water system).

8
The design team tested over 30 native plant species to determine which would survive on the roof. The plants grew in planter boxes for two years without fertilization or irrigation. Nine finalists were selected (both annual plants and perennial wildflowers) for their survivability as well as their ability to attract butterflies, birds, and insects.

9
Perennials included the beach strawberry (*Fragaria chiloensis*), sea thrift (*Armeria maritima*), selfheal (*Prunella vulgaris*), and Pacific stonecrop (*Sedum spathifolium*).

10
Annuals included the California poppy (*Eschscholzia californica*), miniature lupine (*Lupinus bicolor*), goldfields (*Lasthenia californica*), California plantain (*Plantago erecta*), and tidy tips (*Layia platyglossa*).

11

SPECIES DIAGRAM

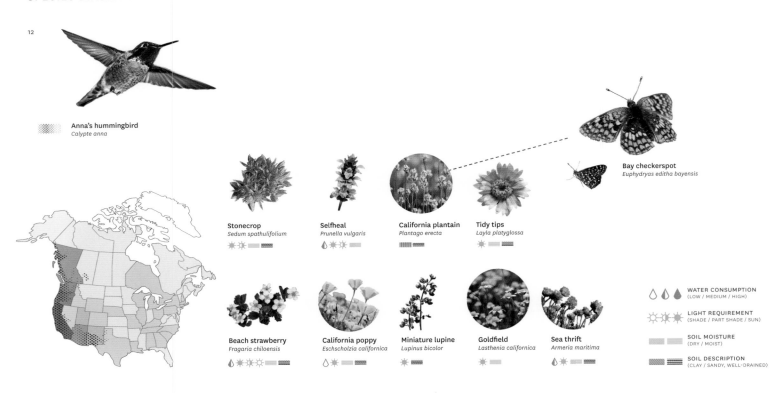

12

Anna's hummingbird
Calypte anna

Bay checkerspot
Euphydryas editha bayensis

Stonecrop
Sedum spathulifolium

Selfheal
Prunella vulgaris

California plantain
Plantago erecta

Tidy tips
Layia platyglossa

Beach strawberry
Fragaria chiloensis

California poppy
Eschscholzia californica

Miniature lupine
Lupinus bicolor

Goldfield
Lasthenia californica

Sea thrift
Armeria maritima

WATER CONSUMPTION
(LOW / MEDIUM / HIGH)

LIGHT REQUIREMENT
(SHADE / PART SHADE / SUN)

SOIL MOISTURE
(DRY / MOIST)

SOIL DESCRIPTION
(CLAY / SANDY, WELL-DRAINED)

11

The Academy's living roof absorbs 5.3 million liters of rainwater each year, thus reducing the amount of stormwater runoff by 93 percent. In the event of heavy rain, water not held in the planting media or the reservoir board immediately below, is directed to a ground water recharge chamber below the building loading dock. In addition, the plants return moisture and oxygen to the air through evapotranspiration. The combined processes help to keep the climate of the building and roof cool for both people and animals.

12

The plants on this roof create habitat for a diversity of pollinating creatures like Anna's hummingbirds (*Calypte anna*), numerous bumblebees and many species of butterflies. Development over the past century has decreased the habitat of the bay checkerspot butterfly. Once seen throughout the San Francisco, San José, and Oakland areas, today their small populations are limited to regions of San Mateo and Santa Clara. The green-roof vegetation provides nectar for the Bay Checkerspot and could help to reestablish its population in the Bay Area.

14

13a – 13c

The technology that went into the design of the green roof has now become part of educational outreach programs at the Academy. Students, teachers, and visitors are invited to learn about how the system works and to understand the materials that went into creating the unique landscape.

14

In addition to the living roof, the landscape architect designed the new entries and the side gardens created by the new building's more compact footprint. These ground-level areas provide flexible outdoor rooms for cafes, receptions, exhibits, sculpture, and casual outdoor use. Weather-based, high-efficiency irrigation technology helps to reduce water usage in these areas. Planting design ensures that a minimum of 30 percent of impervious (non-roof) surfaces will be shaded.

NINGBO ECO-CORRIDOR

Tranquil Waters

Located in the heart of the Yangtze River Delta on China's coastline, Ningbo is one of China's oldest cities, with a current population of about 5 million inhabitants. Ningbo, meaning "tranquil waters," overlooks the Hangzhou Bay and rests within a matrix of industrial lands, water canals, and a delta landscape of tributary streams and wetlands. In 2002, the government enacted a set of development objectives to increase the core urbanized area while still allowing for the continued maturity of their foreign trade port and the viability of Ningbo as a major metropolitan area of economic importance. A parallel agenda was set to index the water resources of the city—canals, wetlands, fishing ponds, rivers, streams, and estuaries—and evaluate their combined ecological impact on the rapidly expanding urban center.

To approach the complicated task of evaluation, a 100-hectare area within the heart of Ningbo's East Town comprised of fish ponds, agricultural lands, and industrial areas was identified and master-planned. The proposed plan revitalizes and regenerates the environments to create a green lung for the city, providing recreation, education, and cultural facilities. Programmed uses such as hiking, biking, and running combine with water-based activities such as interpretive overlooks, boating, and fishing to support the goals of creating an environment where recreation and ecology are inextricably linked.

A hydrological flow pattern based on water flow within the Hangzhou Bay Delta was introduced as the primary organizing system in the project and was conceived as a slow-moving, meandering water body that references the historic lowland floodplain. The design creates habitat for flora and fauna through an integrated constructed open-space system of active and passive recreational uses set within a hydrological framework of wetlands, open water and operable gates.

Acting as an ecological corridor, the project performs as a living filter, actively improving the condition of the city's water resources on a daily basis. The current canal water quality is classified as Level V by Chinese water-quality classification—restricted to industrial and agricultural uses and not fit for human recreation. To expedite the water-filtration process beyond what can be achieved by simply planting passive water plants, the consultant team studied how natural filtration systems work and developed a highly orchestrated ecological water filtration system. Water quality is achieved through a series of biofilm filtration systems that use microorganisms to treat polluted water. Patented by BioMatrix of Scotland, the biofilm technology employs islands of vegetation structured onto floating circular frames that are anchored out in the water. Biofilm microorganisms and selected plant species break down or absorb pollutants from the canal water. The project improves the condition of the water to Level III or better—able to support habitat ecology and suitable for recreation. Wetlands, riparian plantings, bioswales, and waterbodies that provide filtration, aeration, and retention, work together in setting a new precedent for water-quality infrastructure in China.

SCOPE AREA WITHIN EXISTING CONTEXT

MASTERPLAN

2

3

1. Water Jet
2. Expanded Water Body
3. Wind Mills on Mound
4. Outdoor Teaching Space
5. Nature Study
6. Underground Garbage Facility
7. School
8. BBQ Area
9. Land Art Pedestrian Bridge
10. Bio-Retention Basin
11. Bio-Ponds
12. Wellness Gardens
13. Sand Volleyball Court
14. Children's Playground
15. Bio-Dry Creek
16. Main Pedestrian Loop with Bike Lane
17. High-rise Residential Building
18. Pedestrian Bridge over Main Creek
19. Pump House Facility
20. Outdoor Swimming Pool
21. Sculpture Garden
22. Campus
23. Water-Cleansing System
24. Pedestrian Bridge and Overlook
25. Boat Dock
26. Observation Tower
27. Children's Learning Center
28. Basketball Court
29. Skateboard Park
30. Volleyball Court
31. Parking Lot
32. Community Village
33. Waterfront Platform
34. Rock-Climbing Area
35. Neighborhood Center
36. Nature Study
37. Offstream Wetland
38. Community Garden
39. Boardwalk
40. Water-Edge Promenade
41. Primary Wetland

0   175   250   500   750   1000m

1

The city of Ningbo covers an area of 9,365 square kilometers with a population of around 5 million. Water is a major element for the city with its proximity to the Hangzhou Bay and to the intersection of the Yuyao and Fenghua Rivers. A network of canals reinforces this theme, as water is integrated into the fabric of the city. The canals are used for transportation and irrigation, but the system also collects runoff from industry and agriculture, which has rendered much of the water unsafe for human interaction or recreation.

2

Aerial view showing the site boundary. The design addresses the integration of urban development and established agriculture and industry.

3

The master plan for the site provides sustainable habitats that educate the public on ecological processes while creating constructed open-space systems for recreation and adaptive reuse. Wildlife ecosystems, stormwater filtration and active or passive human habitation occur at different moments along the corridor as it transitions between adjacent land uses.

4

4
The aerial perspective shows how these
systems interact and integrate. Buildings
emerge from the meandering green corridor
and give a sense of scale.

SITE ANALYSIS

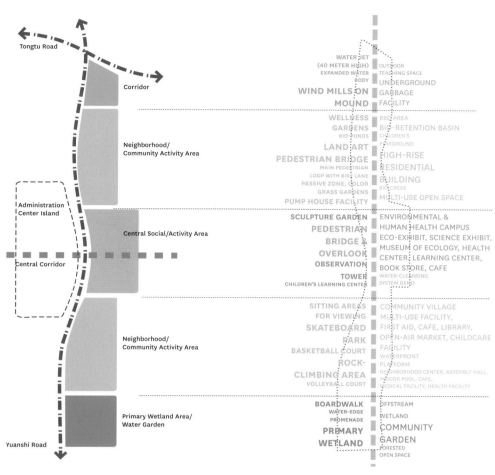

5

Tongtu Road

Corridor

Neighborhood/
Community Activity Area

Administration
Center Island

Central Social/Activity Area

Central Corridor

Neighborhood/
Community Activity Area

Primary Wetland Area/
Water Garden

Yuanshi Road

WATER JET
(40 METER HIGH)
EXPANDED WATER
BODY
WIND MILLS ON
MOUND

OUTDOOR
TEACHING SPACE
UNDERGROUND
GARBAGE
FACILITY

WELLNESS
GARDENS
BIO-PONDS
LAND ART
PEDESTRIAN BRIDGE
MAIN PEDESTRIAN
LOOP WITH BIKE LANE
PASSIVE ZONE, COLOR
GRASS GARDENS
PUMP HOUSE FACILITY

BBQ AREA
BIO-RETENTION BASIN
CHILDREN'S
PLAYGROUND
HIGH-RISE
RESIDENTIAL
BUILDING
BIO CREEK
MULTI-USE OPEN SPACE

SCULPTURE GARDEN
PEDESTRIAN
BRIDGE &
OVERLOOK
OBSERVATION
TOWER
CHILDREN'S LEARNING CENTER

ENVIRONMENTAL &
HUMAN HEALTH CAMPUS
ECO-EXHIBIT, SCIENCE EXHIBIT,
MUSEUM OF ECOLOGY, HEALTH
CENTER, LEARNING CENTER,
BOOK STORE, CAFE
WATER-CLEANSING
SYSTEM DEMO

SITTING AREAS
FOR VIEWING
SKATEBOARD
PARK
BASKETBALL COURT
ROCK-
CLIMBING AREA
VOLLEYBALL COURT

COMMUNITY VILLAGE
MULTI-USE FACILITY,
FIRST AID, CAFE, LIBRARY,
OPEN-AIR MARKET, CHILDCARE
FACILITY
WATERFRONT
PLATFORM
NEIGHBORHOOD CENTER, ASSEMBLY HALL,
INDOOR POOL, CAFE,
MEDICAL FACILITY, HEALTH FACILITY

BOARDWALK
WATER-EDGE
PROMENADE
PRIMARY
WETLAND

OFFSTREAM
WETLAND
COMMUNITY
GARDEN
FORESTED
OPEN SPACE

6

7

5
Diagrammatic site analysis of the 3.3-kilo-meter eco-corridor allowed for definition of zones of activity and programmatic use. The intent was to have the design connect with the adjacent urban fabric, creating seamless integration, and reflecting a symbiotic relationship between city and environment.

6
Rendering of how the site is used and oper-ates. Aquatic filtration systems are at work, helping to produce clean water for wildlife habitat creation, while people can use the new infrastructure of pathways, bridges and pools along the canals for active and passive recreation.

7
Rendering of the wind turbines which would be employed on site as part of a strategy for sustainable energy production.

8

9

10

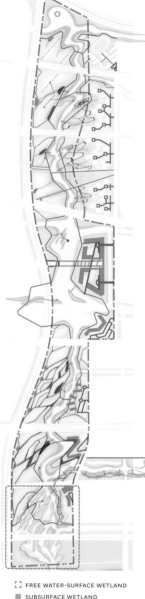

WETLAND STRATEGY

11

- ▬ SEASONAL WETLAND
- ▬ PERENNIAL WETLAND
- ▬ SUBMERGED DEEP AND FLOATING AQUATICS

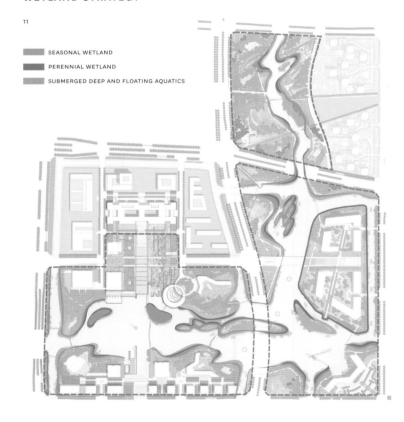

- ── 0 M / 5 M/ 10 M CONTOUR
- ── 1 M INTERVAL CONTOUR
- --- 1.27 M CONTOUR
- 3.59 SPOT ELEVATION
- +3.7 FFE ELEVATION
- 1 CONTOUR LINE ELEVATION

- ⊡ FREE WATER-SURFACE WETLAND
- ▪ SUBSURFACE WETLAND
- ▪ RAIN GARDEN
- ■ BIO-RETENTION BASIN
- ⬚ INFILTRATION BIOSWALES
- ⬚ VEGETATION BIOSWALES
- ▪ RIPARIAN BUFFER STRIPS
- ⬚ AERATION
- ▪ GREEN BUILDINGS
- ■ POROUS & PERMEABLE PAVING

8

The site was devoid of topographic variation. To create a landscape reminiscent of the surrounding mountain ranges, fill dirt from construction was used to construct dramatic landforms. These changes in topography provide a more dynamic spatial experience, create more challenging terrain for exercise, and allows for ecological diversity and the establishment of habitat niches.

9

The ecological scheme divided the site into different categories including wetlands, riparian zones, bioswales, water filtration, green building, and energy production. Stormwater is filtered in bioswales and retention ponds before being released into the canal system, at a dispersed rate, to prevent scouring of the canal banks.

Riparian plantings and wetlands work with mechanical aeration devices to improve water quality and create habitats for wildlife. Green materials and LEED practice was used for all new buildings on site, and renewable energy was introduced through wind turbines and photovoltaic cells.

10

Images of the wildlife, which is supported by riparian and wetland habitats created within the project design.

11

The existing vertical banks of the waterways are replaced with soft-sloping vegetated banks composed of a diverse assemblage of riparian plant communities. These communities will provide a green buffer and containment sink, to retain and remove contaminants from runoff. Additionally, the planted edge creates a critical zone for wildlife habitat.

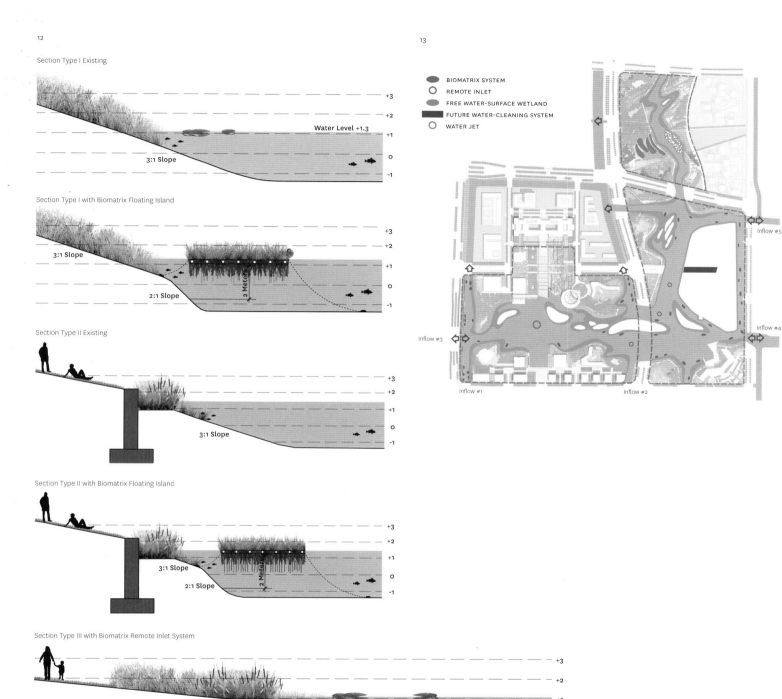

12

Section Type I Existing

+3
+2
Water Level +1.3
+1
3:1 Slope
O
-1

Section Type I with Biomatrix Floating Island

3:1 Slope
+3
+2
+1
2:1 Slope
.2 Meters
O
-1

Section Type II Existing

+3
+2
+1
3:1 Slope
O
-1

Section Type II with Biomatrix Floating Island

+3
+2
+1
3:1 Slope
.2 Meters
O
2:1 Slope
-1

Section Type III with Biomatrix Remote Inlet System

+3
+2
+1
O
3:1 Slope
-1

13

BIOMATRIX SYSTEM
REMOTE INLET
FREE WATER-SURFACE WETLAND
FUTURE WATER-CLEANING SYSTEM
WATER JET

Inflow #5
Inflow #3
Inflow #4
Inflow #1
Inflow #2

12

Floating ecological systems, known as Biomatrix units, treat water through aeration and the movement of water over plant roots. The Biomatrix system combines developments in ecological engineering with biofilm technology for effective wastewater treatment. The sections illustrate how the Biomatrix filtration system is anchored, and how plant roots are able to penetrate the floatation structure. The system circulates water though a biofilter on the floating island, providing an aerobic environment suitable for biological nitrogen removal. Selected vegetation and the use of biofilms function to provide a living habitat for continual re-inoculation of the canal with beneficial bacteria. Biofilms hold micro-organisms like bacteria, fungi, and algae that ingest and filter contaminates from the water. Plant roots also absorb additional pollutants from the water, which are then stored in the plant biomass. (www.biomatrixwater.com)

13

Diagram of the in-canal treatment system which regulates biological oxygen demand (BOD). BOD is the measure of oxygen required by bacteria to break down organic compounds under aerobic conditions. The system involves a stair-stepping series of free water-surface wetlands that are designed to treat canal water through a cascade and filtration effect, while creating aesthetic appeal to the landscape.

14a

Bird Perch and Observation Deck

14b

Land Art Park

14a + b
A site cross section through the eco-corridor illustrates the changes in topography and programmatic use. The highlighted portion shows in detail the observation deck and bird perch, which serves not only as land art but also as wildlife habitat.

15a 15b 15c

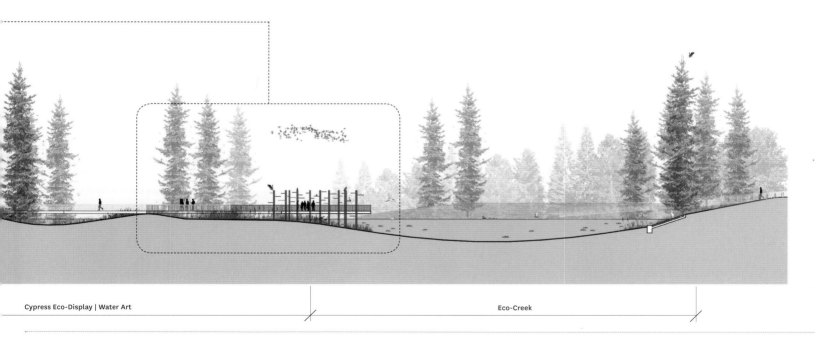

Cypress Eco-Display | Water Art

Eco-Creek

15a – 15c
Bird perches provided inspiration for
the land art.

TACOS ARIZAS

OPEN

TACOS · BURRITOS ·

ASADA   ASADA
LENGUA   CABEZA
PASTOR   LENGUA
CABEZA   PASTOR
BUCHE   CHORIZO
CHORIZO   POLLO   CHORIZO
POLLO   CARNITAS   POLLO
CARNITAS   BUCHE   CARNITAS
TRIPITAS   TRIPITAS   TRIPITAS

CHORIZO
CARNITAS   CARNITAS
TRIPITAS   TRIPITAS

EMERGENCY

4EU9382

SO

AGG REG ATE

Landscape infrastructure is often seen as piecemeal objects. When consolidated, the collective whole has the ability to remediate and sometimes even reverse negative impact.

Hundreds of taco trucks line LA streets, alleyways, parking lots, and parks in search of hungry stomachs. Operating exclusively within the public right-of-way, taco trucks (and their more gourmet offspring) have solidified their position as one of Los Angeles's most popular alternatives to sit-down dining. Tacos Arizas can be found on the corner of Sunset and Logan in Los Angeles every night, seven days a week.

LEWIS AVENUE CORRIDOR

Catalytic Landscape

From the amazing desert landscape of Red Rock Canyon to the cultural spectacles of the Strip, Las Vegas is an amalgam of extreme experiences symbolizing the past, the present, and the future through its constantly evolving urban fabric. In the early 1800s, areas of the Las Vegas Valley contained artesian wells and supported meadows (vegas in Spanish), hence the name Las Vegas. Over time, the city has replaced some of those meadows with an urban mat of development and bills itself as the entertainment capital of the world. Today, the city seems to have become a living cartoon of itself, where exaggeration and contradiction is commonplace. Las Vegas hosted an estimated 36 million visitors and 19,000 conventions in 2009 alone. The resident population of 558,383 in 2008 was greatly outnumbered by this transient population. An annual rainfall of 10.1 centimeters and daytime temperatures of 40 degrees Celsius in the summer challenge a sustainable lifestyle in the desert.

For a city intent on being all things to all people, its very essence seems all but lost in the latest entertainment or gambling venue. Upon closer examination, however, pockets of real everyday life can be found in the older residential communities, parks, and downtown area, and in various annual events.

Through the collaboration of the City of Las Vegas Office of Cultural Affairs and the Las Vegas Arts Commission, what was once a single-use parking lot and alley is now a highly functional, linear urban park. Connecting a new Regional Justice Center and a new U.S. Federal Courthouse, the project offers a continuous canopy of shade and active programming for three city blocks. The corridor has provided strong interconnectivity for the downtown and has helped unify and revive the office and residential core. Acting as a hub, Lewis Street Corridor has become a catalyst for private office, retail, and residential development. Soon after the project's completion, the city experienced a wave of urban housing developers wanting to build unsolicited mid- and high-rise market-rate housing along both sides of the corridor. As the corridor continued to draw development interest, the open space itself has started to symbolize the beginning of an old Las Vegas renaissance intent on carving out its identity based on a pedestrian sensibility rather than a simulacrum of exported icons.

In its unimproved condition, Lewis Street was overscaled, comprised of narrow sidewalks with no shade, and unsafe during the evening hours. The street did not function as a collector street or a major service corridor. It was clear early

1   2   3

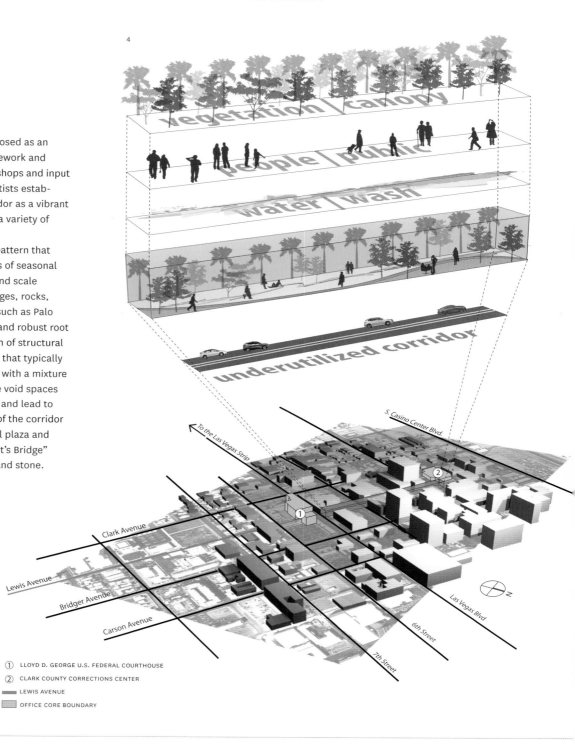

on that this single-use corridor should be repurposed as an aggregate of a larger pedestrian circulation framework and open-space system. A series of community workshops and input from the Las Vegas Arts Commission and local artists established the vision for the future Lewis Street Corridor as a vibrant public gathering space that could be utilized for a variety of events, programs, and functions.

The design logic is derived from the natural pattern that desert washes create in the landscape after years of seasonal rainfall. These washes are regional in character and scale yet contain common elements such as eroded edges, rocks, cracked earth, waterfalls, and native vegetation such as Palo Verde and Mesquite trees. To encourage healthy and robust root growth, trees were planted in a continuous trough of structural soil that would maintain the same compaction as that typically found under sidewalks (95 percent) but specified with a mixture of clay, nutrient-rich soil, and aggregate to create void spaces in the substrate to encourage the spread of roots and lead to healthy and mature canopies. The spatial layout of the corridor is comprised of four main areas: a multifunctional plaza and arroyo, a tree-lined pedestrian walkway, the "Poet's Bridge" and a waterfall surrounded by native vegetation and stone.

① LLOYD D. GEORGE U.S. FEDERAL COURTHOUSE
② CLARK COUNTY CORRECTIONS CENTER
▬ LEWIS AVENUE
▫ OFFICE CORE BOUNDARY

1
With lights that are visible from space, nighttime on the Las Vegas Strip provides a platform for questionable spectacle. Twenty percent of the entire state of Nevada's electricity goes into lighting just the casinos that line the Strip. The 5.6 giga-watts of electricity used by the casinos is equal to the output of five large coal power plants.

2
Just west of Las Vegas lies Red Rock Canyon showcasing the scenic desert landscapes of the region. Prehistoric plate tectonics produced the sublime rock formations of limestone and red sandstone for which the area is known. The dynamic topography lends itself to a diversity of desert environments, from wooded canyons to seasonal washes and to exposed rock faces.

3
Lewis Avenue runs perpendicular to Las Vegas Boulevard, north of the Strip. The image shows existing street conditions, which served primarily as a parking lot for the area's office core. Continuous asphalt and concrete paving was uninviting and offered no protection from the often harsh and hot environment.

4
Rather than viewing the site as a negative, it was seen as an opportunity to transform an underutilized street into a lush community corridor. Anchored by the newly renovated U.S. Federal Courthouse and the Clark County Corrections Center, design for Lewis Avenue was broken into a series of programmatic elements (water, people, and vegetation). The water element would reference the seasonal washes of the regional desert landscape. Public activities would provide a social element. And finally, vegetation would transform the site, creating contrast and canopy.

5

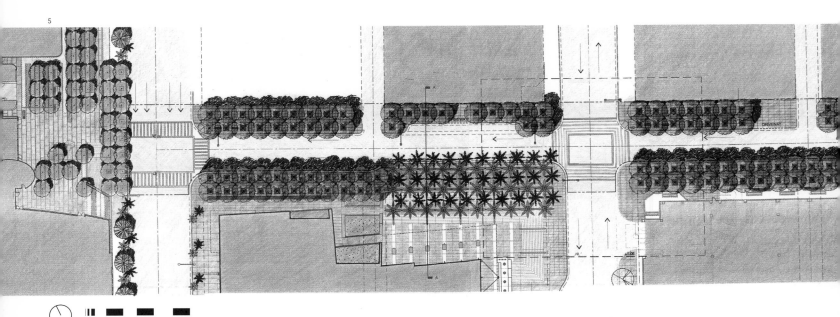

6

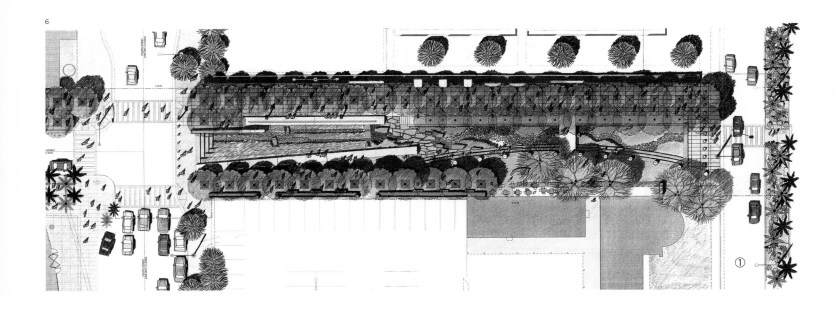

5

At 400 meters in length the project spans
four city blocks of Lewis Avenue. The planting scheme seen in the master plan drawing
provides linear continuity and establishes
site identity. The overall design is rooted
in the character and materiality of the new
pedestrian corridor at the east end of the
project boundary.

6

The detail from the illustrative plan highlights the 3,400-square-meter pedestrian
corridor, which sets up a leisurely seven
to ten minute walk through the area's
business district. The design drawing
accentuates the different ground conditions,
complexity of plantings, and changes in
programmatic use.

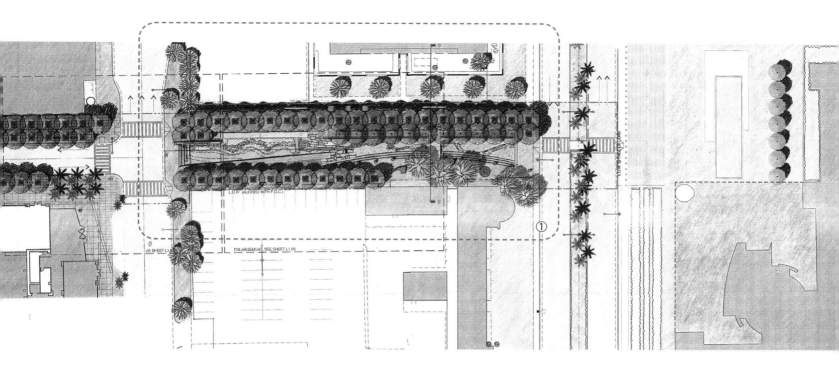

7

7
Community outreach and workshops were
an integral part of the project; perspective
sketches served as an early means of providing a sense of place and a vision of the site's
transformation. The image looks towards the
new U.S. Federal Courthouse building and
shows how the site could be inhabited and
used by local residents and visitors.

9a

9b

10

8 (opposite)
The aerial image, looking east, shows integration of the designed landscape into the fabric of the city. Lewis Avenue Corridor becomes a diversion for the people of the area as the street is completely redefined.

New vertical elements break up the space between ground plane and building roof, while the horizontal infrastructure begins to link both pedestrian routes and the street to the larger context.

9a + b
The designed streetscape that lines Lewis Avenue provides visual and linear connections to Las Vegas Boulevard and Freemont Street. The sidewalks were widened to 6 meters, and then paved with porous materials to aid in the retention of stormwater runoff.

Rows of ash trees (*Fraxinus pennsylvanica*) provide shade from the heat and sunlight. These trees were chosen for their delicate leafy structure, drought tolerance, and their adaptability to a range of soil conditions.

10
At the intersection of Fourth Street, Lewis Avenue terminates in the pedestrian corridor. The streetscape typology continues through the site, while pathways, vegetation, and water create a meandering and lush environment. In dramatic fashion, the infrastructure of buildings is visually replaced with a canopy of leaves and an understory of vegetation.

11

12

13a

13b

11
Water is introduced to the site on a plinth that sits 3 meters above street level and cascades down a stone face into a linear collection basin. The falling water momentarily silences the sounds of everyday city life, and the rock façade establishes a materiality which is continued through the site. Water is recirculated through a closed-cycle system.

12
From the collection basin, water flows in a loose meandering fashion through the corridor. While linear in nature, its curvature and uneven pattern contrasts the geometry seen in the planting design. Plants and materials chosen were meant to allude to the region's natural desert landscape.

13a + b
Water moves in linear basins, through laid stone walkways and over pebble embankments. The entire system of water was lowered 60 centimeters below street level, allowing for steps and seating along its course.

14 (opposite)
The flow of water is slow, allowing pools to form. This image depicts the inviting reflective surface of the water and the quiet ambiance produced as the sun sets.

15a – 15d

As evening falls, the mood changes. Lighting was added in the design to showcase the different landscape elements even after the sun has gone down. The stimulating effects encourage use and exploration of the site well past business hours.

16 (opposite)

Different visual planes were established through variations in plantings and changes in hardscape. The ground is sunken, differentiating it from walkways, while the vertical growth of Mexican grass trees (*Dasylirion longissima*) forms a kind of low wall that grows up to the elevation of the seat walls. The canopy of Palo Verde trees (*Cercidium microphyllum*) provides yet another visual and spatial plane, helping to bring the scale of the surrounding buildings down to the level of the pedestrian. The Palo Verde tree is native to the southwestern United States and northern Mexico. As a drought-deciduous species, it will drop its leaves and smaller branches in severe dry conditions to prevent water loss through transpiration. The tree survives by photosynthesizing through its bark. Yellow flowers bloom in late spring. The Palo Verde tree is an important habitat species for the desert, providing shelter for birds and rodents and food for other animals.

17

Additional imagery gives a sense of the site's spatial character, while calling attention to the introduction of color to the Lewis Avenue Corridor. Seasonality can be read as the plants bloom and grow, offering different environments throughout the year. Date palms (*Phoenix dactylifera*), Palo Verde and mesquite trees (*Cercidium microphyllum* and *Prosopis pubescens*) create the canopy, while the red-flowered false yucca (*Hesperaloe parviflora*, shown in bloom) and Mexican grass tree (*Dasylirium longissima*) provide texture and color to the understory.

18

Large stone pieces were laid to create unique walkways, which cross over the water system. This image shows a portion of the corridor where water is currently not present. However during periods of high rain this area can absorb water and runoff, much like the seasonal arroyos and washes found within the Nevada landscape.

19a

19b

19c

19d

19a – 19d
These images illustrate how the public interacts with the project. Shade is a welcomed amenity for local residents and workers. The ambiance and passive spaces invite people to sit and relax, or cool theirfeet in the water. Events and shows bring people to the site for social gathering, while the promenading trees create a venue for vendors or artists to display their work.

20
The Mexican grass tree belongs to the agave family, a native to the deserts of the south-western United States and Mexico. Its long straight leaves can grow up to 1.5 meters in length, providing distinctive vertical mass-ing. The species is drought-tolerant and thrives in full sun. In early summer a large spike with a whitish green flower emerges from the plant and blooms.

21a

21b

22

After everything else has taken its toll and gone
loneliness is living in someone else's song.
—John Emmons

I think she is strange, America.
—Andy Hall

Who hasn't seen the moon's reflection in the surface of the water
and remembered looking into eyes just about everything.

Because self-indulgence
is the highest achievement
of Western Civilization.
Because "star-crossed"
sounds better
than "stardust". —Gregory Crosby

21a + b
The red-flowered false yucca is a native to
the deserts of central Texas. Chosen for its
tolerance to drought and high heat, this species is readily adaptable to many different
soil types. A favorite of hummingbirds, the
pink flowers bloom in late spring through
early summer with shoots growing up to 1.5
meters in height.

22
The Las Vegas Arts Commission was actively
involved with the Lewis Avenue project and
sponsored the first public art initiative for
the site. Etched prose and poetry from Las
Vegas artists can be found along one of the
bridges spanning the water.

GUBEI PEDESTRIAN PROMENADE

Pedestrian Streets

Historically, streets are the places where people from all parts of society converge. The culture of a place can be revealed through the ways people use the streets to meet their daily needs. The city street is also the means to measure the sentiments of citizens, their worldview, civic pride, and attitude about public life in general. One could argue that a growing city's economic and social well-being could be gauged from the streets through the amount of pedestrian movement, the concentration of retail activities, and the voices of street vendors pushing their wares through the city's alleyways and corridors. In Jane Jacobs' *Death and Life of Great American Cities* (1961), the author connects the presence of pedestrian activity to a city's prosperity: "Lowly, and unpurposeful and random as they may appear, sidewalk contacts are the small change from which a city's wealth of public life may grow."[1] The pedestrian, it turns out, defines the authenticity of the city.

1 Jane Jacobs, *Death and Life of Great American Cities*, New York: Vintage, 1961, p. 72.

2 Michelle Wallar, "How to Create a Pedestrian Mall." *Culture Change*. http://www.culturechange.org/issue14/pedestrianmall.html. (accessed June 12, 2010).

3 Jane Jacobs, *Death and Life of Great American Cities*, op. cit., pp. 220–221.

If pedestrian activity increases, then so may certain aspects of mixed-use development. Increased density questions the role of the vehicle within these public corridors heavily used by pedestrians. By closing a road and redirecting traffic flow onto other road networks, the vacated street becomes the new medium in which to evolve the programmatic use of the entire right-of-way of the street, that is, the building-to-building dimension becomes the occupiable space and opens up new opportunities for programming urban surfaces for pedestrians, commercial activity, residential uses, events, and other civic-minded programs. "Pedestrians use 20 times less space than an automobile, and are able to communicate and interact with one another as they travel."[2] Nowhere is the potential of this new pedestrian occupation more visible than in the transformation of streets in China, where some of its oldest pedestrian streets form a strong cultural link between the country's storied past and its current aspirations. At 845 meters long, Qianmen Street, for example, has recently experienced its fifth restoration within

the changing urban fabric of historic Beijing. The history of Qianmen Street stretches back to the Yuan Dynasty (1206–1368), when its latticework of alleys gave rise to a major commercial district. Lantern fairs, theaters, teahouses, cultural events, and festivals all took place within this street. With vehicular traffic diverted to adjoining streets, Qianmen Street witnessed the demise of historic structures making room for new buildings, a restored rail-car line, international establishments, and an increased pedestrian presence related to a renewed vigor of making what was old new again. In contrast, Shanghai maintains a relatively new pedestrian street named Nanjing Road. Unlike the historic preservation of Qianmen Street in Beijing, Nanjing Road has evolved over time and remains the most famous shopping and entertainment-oriented street in Shanghai. The street's iconic supersized billboards internally lit with neon lights have been on the cover of many books and magazines, symbolizing the modernization of China and its important role in the global economy. Averaging 35 meters in width and 700 meters in length, this pedestrian-only corridor is flanked by two linear parks and exemplifies the fast-forward orientation of the city's burgeoning appetite for international recognition and identity.

The emergent typologies of pedestrian streets in China present an interesting case study. Where Qianmen Street looked to the past, Nanjing Road looked to the future, yet another case may symbolize the present. A new typology of pedestrian streets based on residential densities has emerged in Shanghai. The Gubei Pedestrian Promenade seeks to add yet another layer of complexity to the pedestrian street typology. The Changning District (of which Gubei is part) maintains a population density of 183 persons per hectare, similar to Koreatown in Los Angeles at 162 persons per hectare. Yet as a separate master-planned area, Gubei consists of 5,800 dwelling units in 54 thirty-story towers and spreads over a nine-block area of 6.4 hectares, creating a spike of population equivalent to 937 persons per hectare (Manhattan has 400 persons per hectare). This kind of density has defined a new kind of pedestrian street.

In 1961, Jane Jacobs posited that "people gathered in concentrations of city size and density can be considered a positive good, in the faith that they are desirable because they are the source of immense vitality, and because they do represent, in small geographic compass, a great exuberant richness of differences and possibilities, many of these differences unique and unpredictable and all the more valuable because they are."[3] The new paradigm here is the introduction of population density first, quickly followed by cultural development and programming. Jacobs goes on to argue that "density should be enjoyed

as an asset and their [people's] presence celebrated: by raising their concentrations where it is needful for flourishing city life, and beyond that by aiming for a visibly lively public street life and for accommodating and encouraging, economically and visually, as much variety as possible."

Objectively, the Gubei Pedestrian Promenade seeks to achieve three primary goals: First, the project orientation is public and thus has tremendous potential to benefit the greater community. Second, the scale of the project has a significant impact on the overall city ecology via a planted urban forest that mitigates heat-island effect. Third, the linear nature of the open space and its ability to connect and extend movement beyond the site's given envelope can nurture positive transformation along adjacent streets.

The Gubei Pedestrian Promenade is comprised of three blocks of open-space plan of plazas, gardens, and parks supported by community retail, commercial, and arts programs. Vehicle circulation is limited to two streets that divide the project into three main zones: retail, community, restaurants. Each part strives for a unique identity through the design and layout of tree species, materiality, form, and color. The project has become a catalyst for heightened pedestrian activity of all kinds. An amphitheater, water features, and shaded gardens support this activity through flexible design and planning considerations, for example, ginkgo (*Ginkgo biloba*) and Japanese

zelkova (*Zelkova serrata*) are arranged in compact formal groves to encourage seating/dining, while adjacent areas remain open for emergency vehicles and public gatherings. Three architectural follies designed by SWA provide leasable space within the promenade and infuse an urban character typically found in older pedestrian streets around the world.

Much has been written about Shanghai, its kaleidoscopic history and status as China's "window to the world." Among great cities, modern Shanghai is unique in its approach to arts and culture, the shifting nature of its citizens (permanent and transient), and the speed with which values become obsolete. In a city that strives to stay ahead of everything, Shanghai's complex history continues to reassert itself, offering captivating imagery from art forms, architecture, and fashion from a bygone era. It is understandable that for a city that experiences transformation overnight, the need to preserve its identity through the assertion of its past becomes even more pronounced. Fortunately, for landscape architects faced with this dilemma the wealth of historic references offers infinite inspiration.

1
Gubei Pedestrian Promenade prior to design and construction.

2a – 2d
Historic images of daily life in traditional Shikumen housing.

DIAGRAMMATIC CONTEXT MAP

3

4

DENSITY DIAGRAM

	LOS ANGELES	PUXI OF SHANGHAI	SAN FRANCISCO	MANHATTAN
AREA	1,214.9 km²	288 km²	121 km²	87.5 km²
DENSITY	3,168 persons/km²	22,950 persons/km²	6,688.4 persons/km²	27,490.9 persons/km²
POPULATION	3,849,378	6,609,610	808,976	1,634,795
OPEN SPACE	17.24 km²	139.00 km² (Shanghai City)	23.94 km²	10.95 km²
PERCENT	1.4%	2.19% (Shanghai City)	19.8%	12.5%
OPEN SPACE PER PERSON	4.48m²	7.36m² (Shanghai City)	29.59m²	6.70m²

5

3

Gubei Pedestrian Promenade covers an area of 4.6 hectares, spanning four city blocks, stretching approximately 800 meters in length, and between 40 and 80 meters wide. The map highlights the project area and adjacent pedestrian streets (shown in green). Surrounding streets shown in purple are larger arterial roads.

4

Diagram showing a comparison of population density relative to open space between major U.S. cities and Shanghai. (Shanghai is comprised of Pudong, districts east of Huangpu River, and Puxi, districts west of Huangpu River.)

5

Residential blocks are connected via a dense streetscape planting of shade trees, shrubs, and ground covers.

6

A bird's eye view of the Gubei Pedestrian Promenade captures a sense of the site's density, and the integration of landscape with infrastructure. The photo also gives a visual understanding of the amount of open space and tree canopy the project provides. The site design is broken down into three segments (the west, central, and east blocks). Each of these blocks is defined by intersecting neighborhood streets and through different program and designed elements. The west block is associated with dining, while the central block is focused on community, and the east block is associated with retail. The entire promenade is flanked on either side by 20–30-story residential towers with shops, restaurants, and retail on the ground floor. The design language for the site reflects a hybrid integration of western axiality, symmetry, and conceptual clarity, while capturing the eastern sensibility of intimate scale, views, and the enjoyment of the garden as part of daily life.

7a + b

Views of Gubei Pedestrian Promenade showing aspects of design and scale.

8

Open-Space Park

Project West Entry

Outdoor-Dining Island

Pedestrian Connection to Neighborhood

Glass Tile Fountain

Pedestrian Crossing
Continuous Street Tree Planting

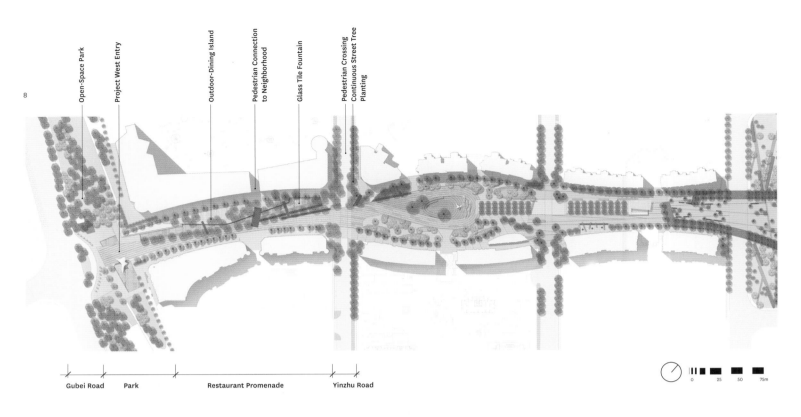

| Gubei Road | Park | Restaurant Promenade | Yinzhu Road |

0   25   50   75m

9

10

11

8
Master plan for Gubei Pedestrian Promenade, highlighting the west block. The site was broken into three segments or "blocks," each with different programmatic activities. The west block is associated primarily with outdoor dining plazas connected by a sculptural water feature.

9
Red maples (*Acer rubrum*) are used along the street for continuity and formality. Their large leaves provide shade and a bright red color in the fall. Chinese fringe flower (*Loropetalum chinense var. rubrum*) and cordyline (*Cordyline spp.*) create a subtle carpet of texture at the ground level. The plant selection was to vary in height, texture, and seasonal interest.

10
The sculptural water feature is comprised of green glass tiles and black stone strips shaped and terraced to capture the nuances of falling water. Contextually, the feature provides spatial division for the west block —redirecting the main pedestrian flow to the south while carving out large wooden terraces to the north for outdoor dining, relaxing, and music performances.

11
Large wooden terraces and seatwalls are situated along fountain edges for viewing of the water cascades, while bridges criss-cross the linear fountain to provide access, views, and moments of respite.

BRIDGE SEATING

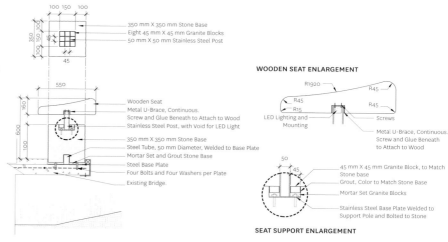

100 150 100

350 mm X 350 mm Stone Base
Eight 45 mm X 45 mm Granite Blocks
50 mm X 50 mm Stainless Steel Post

45

WOODEN SEAT ENLARGEMENT

13

550

Wooden Seat
Metal U-Brace, Continuous.
Screw and Glue Beneath to Attach to Wood
Stainless Steel Post, with Void for LED Light
350 mm X 350 mm Stone Base
Steel Tube, 50 mm Diameter, Welded to Base Plate
Mortar Set and Grout Stone Base
Steel Base Plate
Four Bolts and Four Washers per Plate
Existing Bridge.

R1920
R45
R45
R45
R15
LED Lighting and
Mounting
Screws
Metal U-Brace, Continuous.
Screw and Glue Beneath
to Attach to Wood

50
45
45 mm X 45 mm Granite Block, to Match
Stone base
Grout, Color to Match Stone Base
Mortar Set Granite Blocks
Stainless Steel Base Plate Welded to
Support Pole and Bolted to Stone

SEAT SUPPORT ENLARGEMENT

12a

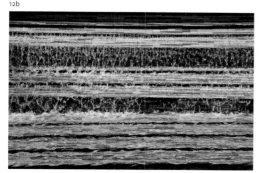

12b

14a   14b

WEST FOUNTAIN GLASS TILE SCHEME

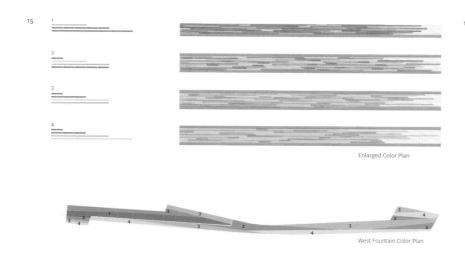

15

1

2

3

4

Enlarged Color Plan

West Fountain Color Plan

16

12a + b
Cascading water creates ambiant noise and is visually engaging in the daytime and at night.

13
Construction detail of the stone bollard railing.

14a + b
The stone bollard railing and a wooden seat-wall both contribute to pedestrian safety.

15
Color studies of glass tiling layout showing the proportion and distribution of four color variations from light green to deep green.

16
Aerial view of a pedestrian bridge crossing. The adjacent paving materials consist of wood, stainless steel edging, glass tiles, and granite pavers from local quarries.

MASTER PLAN: CENTRAL BLOCK

18

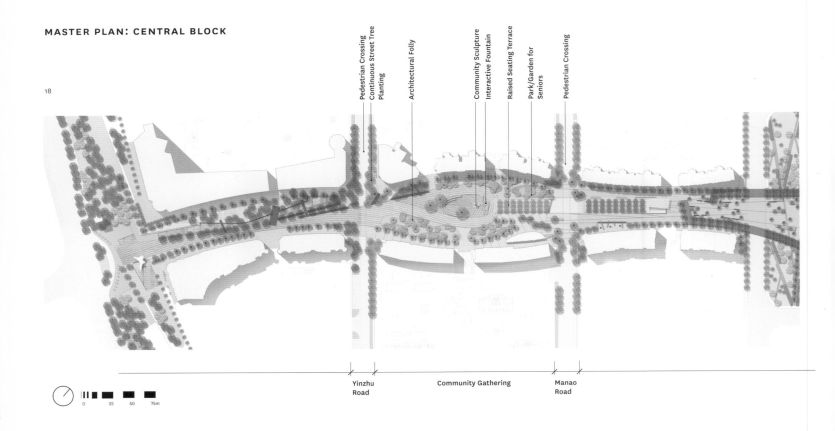

Pedestrian Crossing
Continuous Street Tree Planting
Architectural Folly
Community Sculpture
Interactive Fountain
Raised Seating Terrace
Park/Garden for Seniors
Pedestrian Crossing

0   25   50   75m

Yinzhu Road

Community Gathering

Manao Road

19

20

21

17 (Previous spread)
A group of women strolling through the promenade after a visit to the local market. Open space, restaurants, retail shops, and commercial lobbies engage outdoor programs, colors, and geometries, offering a new kind of public space for the area—one that was inspired by community participation and encourages cultural interaction and identity.

18
The master plan for the central block is focused primarily on community programs and is anchored by a large plaza for special events, gatherings, social activities, and holiday celebrations.

19
Dense planting frames the central plaza to provide scale and separation of activities.

20
Surrounding the central plaza are small cherry gardens for small group gatherings. Curved benches offer a variety of seating experiences, while the porous paving maximizes walkable surfaces and allows for stormwater infiltration.

21
Pedestrian bridges cross over vegetated swales designed to filter stormwater and create shelters for urban wildlife.

22a

22b

22c

22d

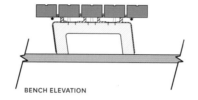

BENCH ELEVATION

23

POLYCARBONATE BENCH

FIBER GLASS BLOCK LAYOUT

The First Row: Color A (2 small modules and 2 large modules)
The Second Row: Color B (1 small modules and 3 large modules)
The Third Row: Color B (1 small module and 2 large modules)
The Fourth Row: Color B
The Fifth Row: Pattern Type A

Small-Module Fiber Glass Block (180 X 600 X 100 mm typ.)

Small-Module Fiber Glass Block (180 X 1200 X 100 mm typ.)

Void Fiber Glass Block
Fiber Glass Block

BENCH ELEVATION

Fiber Glass Block

180 mm X 100 mm Void Fiber Glass Block for LED Lighting

180 mm X 100 mm Fiber Glass Block with Grove

12 mm Stainless Steel Frame, typ.

6 mm Stainless Steel Plate, typ.

Stainless Steel Bench Leg

450

85°

ENLARGED PLAN—END CONDITION A

180 mm X 100 mm Fiber Glass Block

Stainless Steel Frame Below

ENLARGED PLAN—END CONDITION B

180 mm X 100 mm Fiber Glass Block at Edge Condition

Stainless Steel Frame Below

BENCH SECTION

SCREW CONNECTIONS

260 260
80 90
80 180 90 150 140

450
50
290

LED Lighting Device
Screw to Connect Void Block
LED Tube
Bracket on Steel Plate
Connector Bolt

STAINLESS STEEL FRAME

Steel Bench Leg Below
Stainless Steel Frame Below
180 mm X 100 mm Fiber Glass Block at Edge Condition

Steel Dowel
Continuous Footing

22a – 22d
Custom benches, made of translucent polycarbonate, were designed specifically for the central block. The benches are 1 meter wide and embedded with LED lighting to create an intense red glow.

23
Construction details of the custom polycarbonate bench.

24

25

26a

27a

26b

27b

27c

UNIT PAVING DETAIL

300

85° Paver layout orientation

150

AXONOMETRIC VIEW OF UNIT

Adjacent paved or planted area per plans

Filler Planting

Amended Soil

Walls of Precast Concrete Masonry

Sand Base

Compacted Sub-Base

150

100 75

SECTION

24
Aerial view of the central block architectural folly. The large metal-paneled structure creates a focal point within the plaza. The structure will serve as a small tapas bar and an art gallery.

25
Image of the folly from the ground level. Its unique shape and colored-metal panel roof provides a striking sculptural center-piece for the site.

26a + b
Details of granite paving units used through-out the promenade. Three shades of warm-toned granite pavers and episodic black granite segments were used to transition the paving "fabric" from light cream to reddish brown to heighten the sense of depth and movement as one traverses from the west block to the central plaza.

27a – 27c
Porous paving allows for stormwater infiltration and a walkable green surface area. Custom precast concrete units were inspired by traditional clay roof tiles used throughout China.

28a

28b

28c

28d

28e

28a – 28e
Images of the site in use. A young girl skates through the circular water fountain, playing in the interactive jets. A toddler cycles through the water feature. Throughout the site, there is outdoor seating and plazas with shade trees, offering spaces for people to gather and relax. Concert venues are erected on a seasonal basis to take advantage of the plaza's size and orientation. Retail shops and restaurants take up much of the first-floor development with apartments located in the upper stories.

MASTER PLAN: EAST BLOCK

29

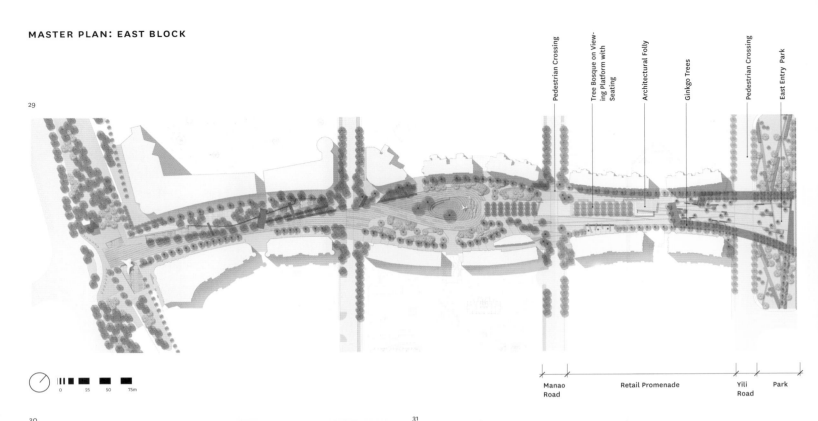

Pedestrian Crossing

Tree Bosque on Viewing Platform with Seating

Architectural Folly

Ginkgo Trees

Pedestrian Crossing

East Entry Park

0 25 50 75m

Manao Road | Retail Promenade | Yili Road | Park

30

31

32a

32b

32c

29
The east block of the master plan is primarily associated with retail and other commercial programming. An elevated tree bosque extends into the central block, providing seating and connectivity between the two blocks.

30
The east block includes an arrangement of wooden benches, surrounded by sweet olive trees (*Osmanthus fragrans*), while a zelkova (*Zelkova serrata*) bosque frames a raised seating area that extends halfway into the central block, creating an urban "living room" underneath a shaded canopy.

31
Aerial view of the wooden benches in context of stone paving patterns.

32a – 32c
Pedestrian activities within the east block.

33

34

WOODEN BENCH

DETAIL SECTION

35

LONGITUDINAL SECTION

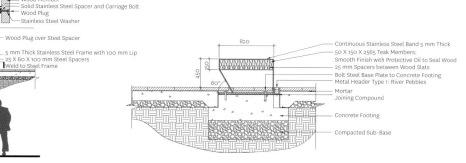

25
Wood Member
Solid Stainless Steel Spacer and Carriage Bolt
Wood Plug
Stainless Steel Washer

Wood Plug over Steel Spacer

5 mm Thick Stainless Steel Frame with 100 mm Lip
25 X 60 X 100 mm Steel Spacers
Weld to Steel Frame

Continuous Stainless Steel Band 5 mm Thick
50 X 150 X 2565 Teak Members:
Smooth Finish with Protective Oil to Seal Wood
25 mm Spacers between Wood Slats
Bolt Steel Base Plate to Concrete Footing
Metal Header Type 1: River Pebbles
Mortar
Joining Compound
Concrete Footing
Compacted Sub-Base

ELEVATION

36a

36b

33
A linear arrangement of wooden benches gives identity to the block.

34
A promenade of ginkgo trees line retail store fronts.

35
Construction detail of the wooden bench.

36a + b
Final views from within the east block depicting sweet olives (*Osmanthus fragrans*) surrounded by double rows of ginkgo trees. The east block functions primarily as a multipurpose open space: tai chi in the early mornings, favorite lunch spots for office workers, and weekend children destinations for children on roller skates, tricycles, and skateboards.

MILTON STREET PARK

Ecological Embankment

The urban infrastructure of cities, although designed for high efficiency, is often limited to monofunctional use. This is appropriate for freeways and railways, where safety, access, and ease of maintenance rely on a single function. Other infrastructures however, such as stormwater channels, are questionable as single-use corridors. The opportunity to embed overlapping functions within these channels presents a significant design strategy for cities today. Los Angeles, for example, has kilometers of underutilized waterway infrastructure waiting to be discovered and repurposed for the benefit of natural resources and the sustainability of the city.

The Ballona Creek watershed is the third-largest urban watershed in the Los Angeles metropolitan area, encompassing 337 square kilometers, including all or part of Los Angeles, Beverly Hills, Culver City, Inglewood, Santa Monica, and West Hollywood. Centuries ago, Ballona Creek, the watershed's primary conduit, was used by Native Americans for transportation and fishing. Later, settlers used the creek for irrigation and transformed the banks into lands for agriculture and ranching. By the 1920s, rapid development of the city created an impervious surface area so significant that the creek became a seasonal flooding nuisance. In response to this dilemma, the once meandering stream, running through the Ballona Creek watershed, was converted to a 14.5-kilometer flood-control channel stretching from the Santa Monica Mountains to the Pacific Ocean. In 1935, for safety and efficiency of moving stormwater, the creek was straightened and the embankment paved by the U.S. Army Corps of Engineers. A few years later, rocks quarried from Catalina Island were used to line the bottom of the creek. These rocks were eventually paved over with concrete, solidifying Ballona Creek as the largest all-concrete storm drain within the watershed. Today Ballona Creek passes through an urban area of 3 million people and drains directly into the Santa Monica Bay. While channelization has facilitated flood management, it has simultaneously modified natural hydrologic functions, decreased plant and wildlife diversity, and degraded much of the surface and ground water quality within the area. Socially, parts of the creek have become invisible; perception of these areas as unsafe has classified much of the waterway as lacking in civic identity.

Today the concrete embankments of Ballona Creek serve two purposes: ongoing stormwater management and recreation with an active bike path. One side of the creek has been maintained as a Class 1 bike path, dedicated exclusively to bicyclists and pedestrians, connecting the "Strand" (beach bike path) in Marina Del Rey to Culver City and into Los Angeles. 14.5 kilometers in length, the bike trail runs parallel to the creek and was one of the first in the region to be used daily by cyclists, runners, strollers, and skaters for both pleasure and commuting. Increased usage of the trail and community-backed initiatives to restore the creek to some semblance of its former ecological profile (following success with the Ballona wetlands) prompted the Mountains Recreation and Conservation Authority (MRCA) to identify a parcel of land along the creek that could deliver on the creek's potential as both a natural resource and a recreation corridor. The MRCA intended to establish a precedent for a new urban park that could address a diverse user group, mitigate stormwater runoff, improve water quality, create habitat, increase open space, and provide access points for passive and active recreation. An undeveloped linear parcel of land along Ballona Creek, near the bottom of the watershed, was identified and proposed as a park. The project, known as Milton Street Park, became a joint effort between the MRCA, community stakeholders, and SWA to embark on the incremental transformation of the creek, beginning at this pilot site. Through a series of public meetings and presentations, the project developed a program-based identity whose aim was to enhance the bike trail with a public park, reinforce native plantings, create a bird-watching/creek platform, introduce seating areas, facilitate stormwater management, and create educational opportunities via interpretive ecological habitats.

Throughout the design process, it became clear that what the park really needed was a robust, multifunctional identity rooted in the reestablishment of native ecologies and open to diverse users. With this framework, the approach to the landscape was to weave together active and passive recreation programs with structured ecological systems that would take on the immediate sub-watershed and encourage a viable ecology that could be observed and understood by all park users. Trees are envisioned as a "drift" that would flow through the site, punctuated by a flexible "waterfront" open space at its geographic center. This open space provides the community with a place to picnic, to observe the creek, to hold outdoor classroom sessions, and to host events and gatherings. Multiple paths allow easy access between the recreational fields to the

1a

north and Ballona Creek to the south. Slopes and embankments along the park are planted with native species, promoting sustainability and habitat creation. The planting plan establishes continuity throughout the park while offering an opportunity to educate visitors about the varied ecological communities of the region. Plants chosen belong to the coastal sage shrub ecosystem, which includes coastal prairies, riparian vegetation, and chaparral/oak woodlands.

By revealing the site's invisible ecologies, the park and its infrastructural systems (water, circulation, and plants) might nurture a new sensibility in urban park design for the area. By instilling ecological meaning and program into a small park next to this channelized waterway, the intention is to help people envision what the entire corridor could become.

1b

2

3

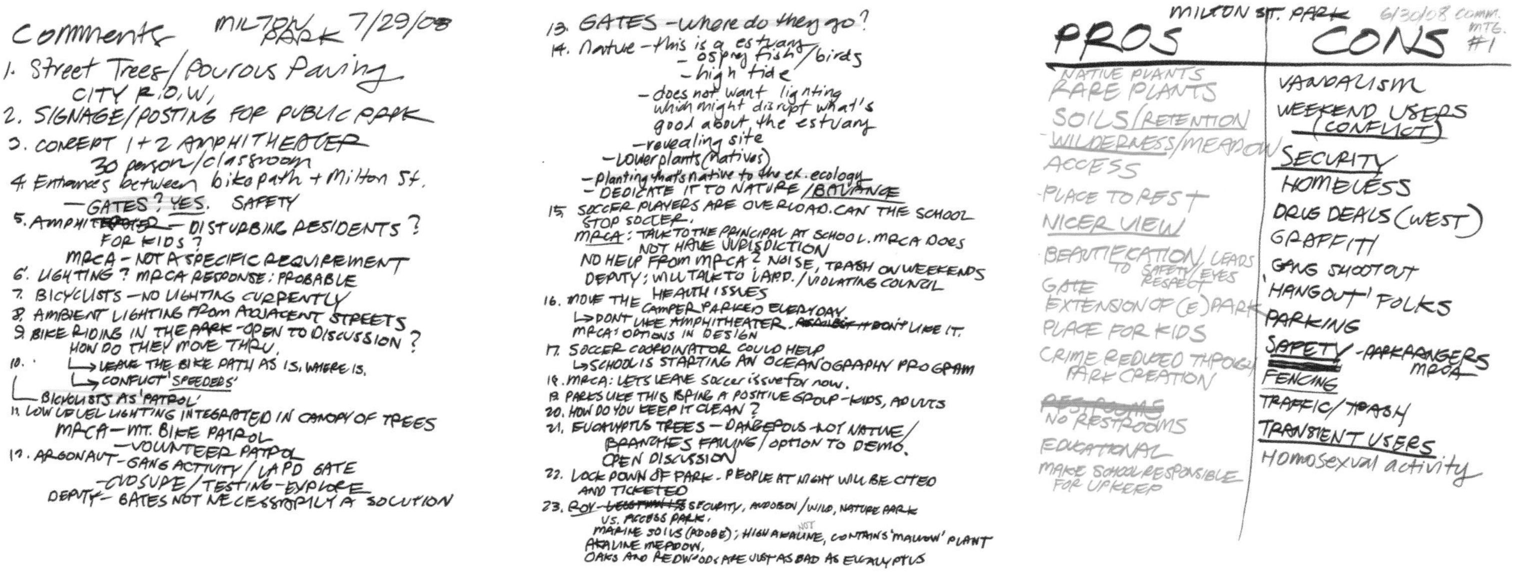

Comments MILTON PARK 7/29/08
1. Street Trees/Pourous Paving
CITY R.O.W.
2. SIGNAGE/POSTING FOR PUBLIC PARK
3. CONCEPT 1+2 AMPHITHEATER
30 person/classroom
4. Entrances between bike path + Milton St.
—GATES? YES. SAFETY
5. AMPHITHEATER — DISTURBING RESIDENTS?
FOR KIDS?
MRCA – NOT A SPECIFIC REQUIREMENT
6. LIGHTING? MRCA RESPONSE: PROBABLE
7. BICYCLISTS — NO LIGHTING CURRENTLY
8. AMBIENT LIGHTING FROM ADJACENT STREETS
9. BIKE RIDING IN THE PARK – OPEN TO DISCUSSION?
HOW DO THEY MOVE THRU.
10. → LEAVE THE BIKE PATH AS IS, WHERE IS.
→ CONFLICT 'SPEEDERS'
BICYCLISTS AS 'PATROL'
11. LOW LEVEL LIGHTING INTEGRATED IN CANOPY OF TREES
MRCA — MT. BIKE PATROL
—VOLUNTEER PATROL
12. ARGONAUT – GANG ACTIVITY / LAPD GATE
–CLOSURE / TESTING – EXPLORE
DEPUTY – GATES NOT NECESSARILY A SOLUTION

13. GATES – where do they go?
14. Nature – this is a estuary
– osprey fish/birds
– high tide
– does not want lighting which might disrupt what's good about the estuary
– revealing site
– Lower plants (natives)
– planting that's native to the ex. ecology
– DEDICATE IT TO NATURE / BALANCE
15. SOCCER PLAYERS ARE OVERLOAD. CAN THE SCHOOL STOP SOCCER.
MRCA: TALK TO THE PRINCIPAL AT SCHOOL. MRCA DOES NOT HAVE JURISDICTION
NO HELP FROM MRCA? NOISE, TRASH ON WEEKENDS
DEPUTY; WILL TALK TO LAPD. / VIOLATING COUNCIL
HEALTH ISSUES
16. MOVE THE CAMPER PARKED EVERYDAY
→ DONT LIKE AMPHITHEATER. ~~[illegible]~~ DON'T LIKE IT.
MRCA: OPTIONS IN DESIGN
17. SOCCER COORDINATOR COULD HELP
→ SCHOOL IS STARTING AN OCEANOGRAPHY PROGRAM
18. MRCA: LETS LEAVE soccer issue for now.
19. PARKS LIKE THIS BRING A POSITIVE GROUP – KIDS, ADULTS
20. HOW DO YOU KEEP IT CLEAN?
21. EUCALYPTUS TREES — DANGEROUS NOT NATIVE / BRANCHES FALLING / OPTION TO DEMO.
OPEN DISCUSSION
22. LOCK DOWN OF PARK – PEOPLE AT NIGHT WILL BE CITED AND TICKETED
23. ROY – ~~[illegible]~~ SECURITY, AUDOBON / WILD, NATURE PARK VS. ACCESS PARK.
MARINE SOILS (ADOBE); HIGH ALKALINE, CONTAINS 'MALLOW' PLANT (NOT)
ALKALINE MEADOW,
OAKS AND REDWOODS ARE JUST AS BAD AS EUCALYPTUS

MILTON ST. PARK 6/30/08 COMM. MTG. #1

PROS	CONS
NATIVE PLANTS	VANDALISM
RARE PLANTS	WEEKEND USERS (CONFLICT)
SOILS / RETENTION	SECURITY
WILDERNESS / MEADOW	HOMELESS
ACCESS	DRUG DEALS (WEST)
PLACE TO REST	GRAFFITI
NICER VIEW	GANG SHOOTOUT
BEAUTIFICATION / LEADS TO SAFETY / EYES RESPECT	'HANGOUT' FOLKS
GATE	PARKING
EXTENSION OF (E) PARK	SAFETY – PARK RANGERS MRCA
PLACE FOR KIDS	FENCING
CRIME REDUCED THROUGH PARK CREATION	TRAFFIC / TRASH
~~RESTROOMS~~ NO RESTROOMS	TRANSIENT USERS
EDUCATIONAL	Homosexual activity
MAKE SCHOOL RESPONSIBLE FOR UPKEEP	

1a + b
Milton Street Park is a proposed 4,856-square-meter linear urban park alongside the Ballona Creek bike path. The site images show the undeveloped parcel that stretches over 305 meters in length and is linked on both ends by previously developed portions of the bike trail.

2
Community involvement was a central part of the design process. The landscape architects, in conjunction with the Mountains Recreation and Conservation Authority, conducted numerous community meetings including a public charrette to ensure design consensus. Through this collaboration, the proposed park will include native plantings, bird-watching platforms, bike trail enhancement, stormwater collection, and a strategy for habitat creation and protective fencing.

3
Notes taken at the community meeting held in July 2008. Interaction between residents and designers allowed for compromise and the creation of a public park that would serve the needs of the people.

WATERSHED MAP

REGIONAL CONTEXT MAP

4

5

WATERWAYS
BIKE PATH
BALLONA WATERSHED
HISTORIC WETLANDS BEING PRESERVED

BIKE PATH
CITY LIMITS

MILTON
STREET PARK

BALLONA
WETLANDS

AREA
PARKS

1. WOODBINE PARK
2. MEDIA PARK
3. BALDWIN HILLS REC CENTER
4. RANCHO CIENEGA SPORTS CENTER
5. CULVER CITY PARK
6. KENNETH HAHN STATE PARK
7. KENNETH HAHN STATE REC AREA
8. NORMAN O. HOUSTON PARK
9. LADERA PARK
10. BLANCO PARK

11. EL MARINO PARK
12. CULVER SLAUSON PARK
13. FOX HILLS PARK
14. LEAVEY FIELD
15. WESTCHESTER REC CENTER
16. GLEN ALLA PARK
17. ADMIRALITY PARK
18. BURTON CHASE PARK
19. DEL REY LAGOON PARK

MASTER PLAN

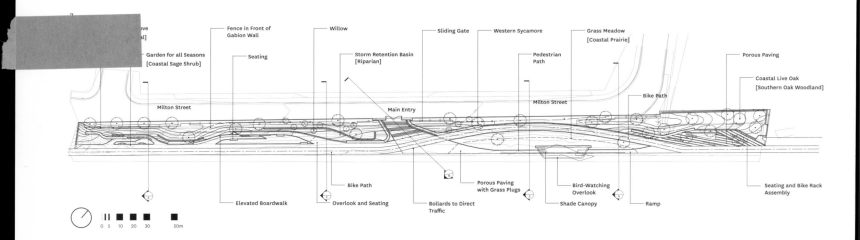

0 5 10 20 30   50m

4

Map of the Ballona watershed, which covers much of the greater Los Angeles area, stretching from the Santa Monica Mountains to the Pacific Ocean. Ballona Creek runs through the watershed, discharging into the Santa Monica Bay. Running parallel to the creek is the Ballona Creek bike path, which begins in Marina Del Rey and continues into Culver City. Portions of the bike path pass through the existing Ballona wetlands. This delicate habitat supports estuarine and brackish marshes along with coastal sage shrub communities.

5

The regional map situates Milton Street within the larger city fabric and shows its proximity to other community parks/recreational opportunities. Creating connection into the regional bike path network became part of the larger project scope.

6

Diagram illustrating the local hydrology of the Milton Street project area. Two sub-watersheds surround Milton Street by the Del Rey Middle School. Sub-watershed A covers 9.9 hectares. Storm drains for this watershed capture and divert approximately 1,230 cubic meters of water into Ballona Creek. Sub-watershed B covers 8.7 hectares and diverts approximately 1,150 cubic meters of water. An upstream dam separates fresh water from the Santa Monica Mountains and local city runoff from the brackish water from Santa Monica Bay.

MILTON STREET SUB-WATERSHED MAP

6

	SUB-WATERSHED A	SUB-WATERSHED B
AREA	9.9 Hectares	8.7 Hectares
VOLUME	1233.48 m³	1147.13 m³
IMPERVIOUS SURFACES	7.3 Hectares	6.5 Hectares
PERVIOUS SURFACES	2.6 Hectares	2.2 Hectares

—— BIKE PATH
—— HYDROLOGY
—— STORM DRAIN
▨ MILTON STREET PARK
▪ MILTON STREET SUB-WATERSHEDS [A-B]

8

7

The master plan for the project incorporates the established program and designed elements (outlined in the community meeting) and also includes seating areas, outdoor picnic areas, a grass meadow, overlooks, and an elevated boardwalk. Visitors and residents to the park will experience a number of different native Southern California ecosystems and will be able to connect into the larger regional bike network. The concept of "nature drift" is expressed in a flow of trees that moves along the length of the site. Medium-sized shade trees highlight this experience, punctuated by open green space. Multiple pathways allow easy access between the recreational fields to the north and Ballona Creek to the south.

8

Perspective section of the park design as it extends out from the street. Numerous pathways provide opportunities for various types of recreation, while vegetation offers shade as well as habitat for local wildlife. A fence extends the length of the park for protection, and gabion walls allow for separation and topographic change.

PLANTING DIAGRAM

9

RIPARIAN
COASTAL PRAIRIE
CHAPARRAL | OAK WOODLAND
COASTAL SAGE SHRUB

| COASTAL SAGE SHRUB | RIPARIAN | COASTAL PRAIRIE | CHAPARRAL | SOUTHERN OAK WOODLAND |

The coastal sage shrub plant community is characterized by low-growing aromatic and drought-deciduous shrubs, adapted to the semi-arid Mediterranean climate of the coastal lowlands.

Riparian plant communities are found along the shores of fresh water rivers and lakes. Cottonwoods and willows typically dominate the landscape closest to the water while sycamores and oaks thrive on the outer floodplain.

California's coastal prairies are the most species-rich grassland types in North America. Characteristic species include Douglas iris, seaside daisy, Blue-eyed grass, and California oat grass.

Chaparral plant communities consist of densely growing evergreen scrub oaks and other drought-resistant shrubs. Species often grow so densely that the landscape is almost impenetrable to animals or humans. Native species to the California chaparral include the toyon, manzanita and scrub oak.

Oak Woodland is widespread at lower elevation in coastal California, interior valleys of the Coast Ranges, and in a ring around the California Central Valley Grasslands. The Oak Woodlands of Southern California are dominated by oaks and understory grasses, herbs, and shrubs.

STORMWATER DIAGRAM

10

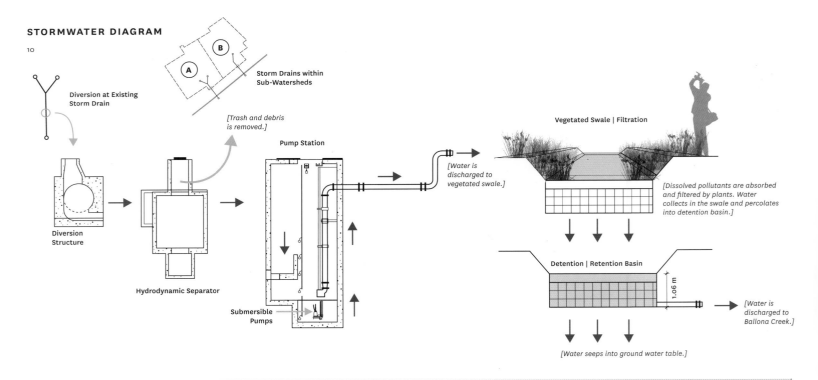

Diversion at Existing Storm Drain

Storm Drains within Sub-Watersheds

[Trash and debris is removed.]

Pump Station

[Water is discharged to vegetated swale.]

Vegetated Swale | Filtration

[Dissolved pollutants are absorbed and filtered by plants. Water collects in the swale and percolates into detention basin.]

Diversion Structure

Hydrodynamic Separator

Submersible Pumps

Detention | Retention Basin

1.06 m

[Water is discharged to Ballona Creek.]

[Water seeps into ground water table.]

9

The Milton Street Park plant palette is inspired and derived from local native plant communities. Coastal sage shrub, coastal prairie, riparian, chaparral, and oak woodland ecosystems have historically formed a patchwork of overlapping ecotones throughout the Los Angeles Basin. The plants selected all belong to the coastal sage shrub community, but also branch out and thrive in the other communities. This planting plan establishes continuity with the adjacent restored Ballona wetlands to educate visitors about the various dynamic plant communities of the region.

10

The diagram illustrates the stormwater treatment process for urban runoff used at Milton Street Park. The strategy includes a series of best management practices, which will improve the quality of runoff diverted through the site prior to discharge into Ballona Creek. First, water is directed at the existing storm drains into a diversion structure. Water then moves into a hydrodynamic separator unit that effectively removes trash and debris from the runoff. Water is then pumped via an underground system to designed bioswales with vegetated buffers. Here plants absorb dissolved pollutants and water is filtered as it settles. A detention/retention basin sits below the swales and collects water as it percolates through. Clean water slowly seeps into the water table and is also released into Ballona Creek.

A second perspective section offers a view of the bird-watching overlook and shade canopy. The design provides for both active recreation (along the creek) and passive enjoyment (within the shaded, more intimate portions of the park). Aside from the

network of pathways, open space in the park provides places to picnic, hold outdoor classrooms, or host community events.

Rendering of the canal overlook and the various ecologies established on either side of the bike path. The creek fosters marsh and estuary wildlife, while the planting scheme along the bank supports native insects, birds, and animals, and offers a mosaic of the larger California landscape.

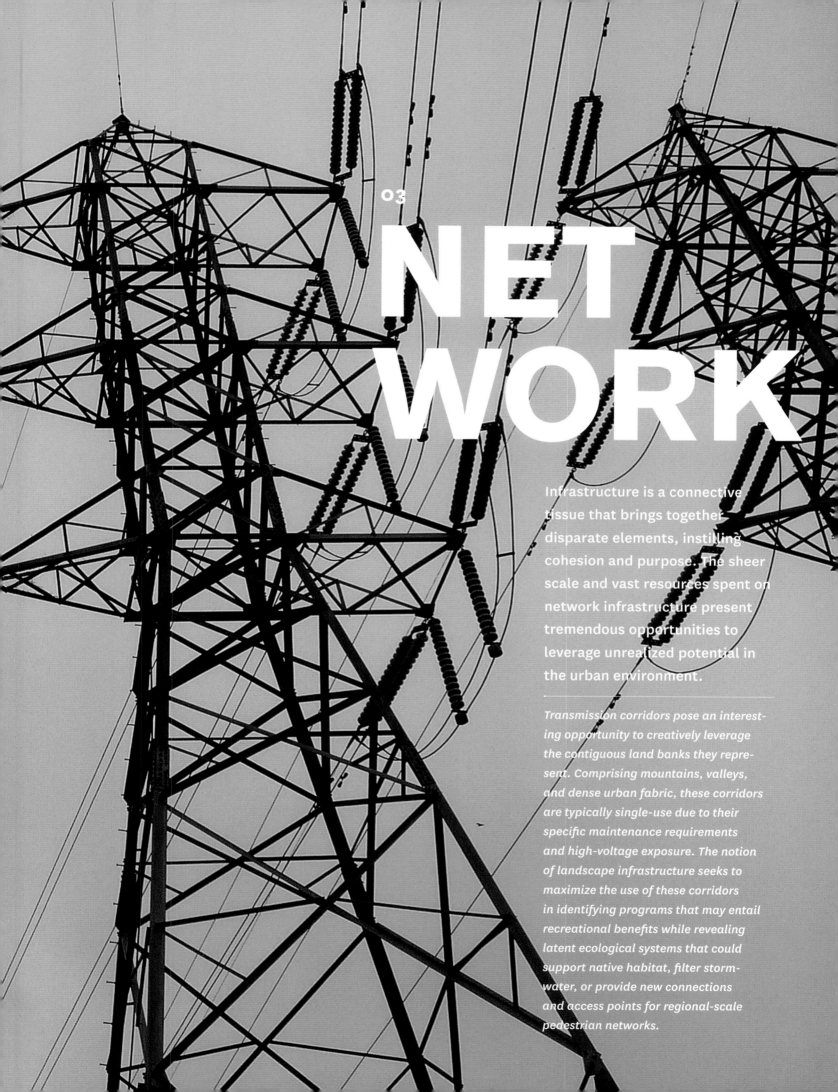

NET
WORK

Infrastructure is a connective tissue that brings together disparate elements, instilling cohesion and purpose. The sheer scale and vast resources spent on network infrastructure present tremendous opportunities to leverage unrealized potential in the urban environment.

Transmission corridors pose an interesting opportunity to creatively leverage the contiguous land banks they represent. Comprising mountains, valleys, and dense urban fabric, these corridors are typically single-use due to their specific maintenance requirements and high-voltage exposure. The notion of landscape infrastructure seeks to maximize the use of these corridors in identifying programs that may entail recreational benefits while revealing latent ecological systems that could support native habitat, filter stormwater, or provide new connections and access points for regional-scale pedestrian networks.

SHUNDE NEW CITY

Ecological Derivatives

The 36-square-kilometer competition master plan for Shunde New City brings together environmental infrastructure and layered transportation to create a new, multinodal urban fabric. The city of Shunde sits within the Pearl River Delta. Design for the New City will weave together 72 square kilometers of the delta into a network of island villages. The delta is the second-largest bird migration and estuary habitat in Southeast Asia. It is the seasonal home to thousands of bird species, including swans and cranes that travel from as far as Russia and Australia to stay in the warmer climate of Southern China. Situated within this fertile delta, Shunde is bisected by waterways and has a history of fish farming, agriculture, and flower cultivation. In recent years, the city has also become a manufacturing center, known for the production of many household appliances and electronics.

The design for Shunde New City took inspiration from land patterns found within the delta. This concept was translated into a framework for individual islands, comprised of multi-use villages adjoined by a series of greenbelts, water corridors, trails, and wetlands. Regional connectivity was achieved through intercity rail, in addition to a local monorail system, water taxis, and freeway connections. This network of transit provides a strategy for integrating housing, commercial, and high-tech research development into a more harmonious connection with the natural environment. Interconnected transportation expands the local industries and offers opportunities to reduce traffic, while promoting a vibrant, dense, and efficient place to live.

A strategy for land utilization maximizes the social and economic value of Shunde New City, while expanding its ecological potential. The master plan divides the city into districts that include a civic and cultural center, financial center, office campus, academic campus, and resort. Within these districts, individual islands are developed with residential, industrial, commercial, educational, and cultural uses. Narrow streets and smaller city blocks promote a human-centered, walkable environment. These 200-by-200 meter city blocks contrast with much of the proposed development in China, which tends to anticipate heavy traffic and expedient development, often calling for city blocks twice that size. Aside from providing a more intimate environment, the smaller block sizes also allow for greater architectural variation and for the preservation of the local cultural identity. Buildings have no setbacks from the street, creating comfortable, tree-lined spaces that add to the site's human-oriented design.

Proposed waterways facilitate transportation and provide flood-storage capacity for the city. This system also collects wastewater for treatment in four sewage plants, based on natural cleansing systems. Urban corridors and greenbelts line or criss-cross the network of rivers and canals. These designed greenbelts incorporate wetlands and bioswales, forming a system for urban runoff filtration. Forested edges along the greenbelts establish wildlife sanctuaries and generate habitat for migratory bird populations. This urban forest edge also offers the potential for carbon sequestration. A comprehensive trail network parallels the greenbelts, encouraging recreational use and educational interpretation.

1a

1b

1c

1a – 1c
The landscape provided inspiration for the
design of the new city. Its setting, in the
Pearl River Delta, is characterized by agricultural use as well as a network of canals
and waterways.

2a

2b　　　　　　　　　　2c

2d

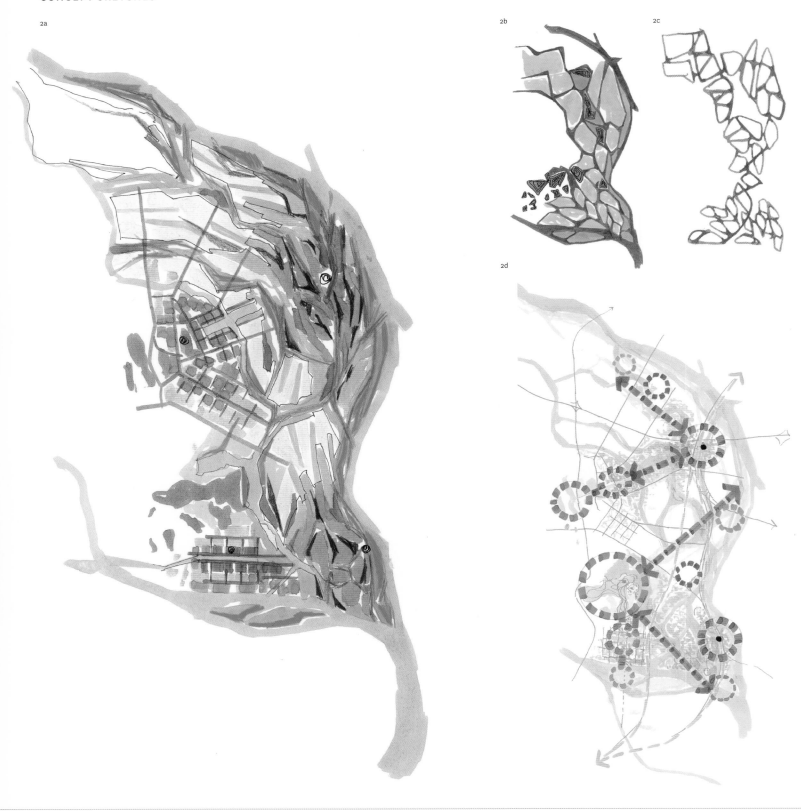

2a – 2d
Early conceptual sketches offer a diagrammatic look at an integrated urban and natural
pattern depicting four urban and transportation centers. Inspired by the movement of
water within the Pearl River Delta, landform
islands, waterways, and forests weave
together both human-made and natural systems into a comprehensive green network.

3 (opposite)
Three-dimensional perspective of the waterways and proposed infrastructure that
connect Shunde New City into a web of
transportation and urban life. The canal
system moves through the city, providing
recreational corridors for residents.
Bridges and tree-lined promenades invite
interaction with the waterways and facilitate
movement through the different islands.

4

5

URBAN FOREST
WETLAND

```
||  ■■   ■     ■     ⊘
0  200  600  1400   3000m
```

4
The site master plan shows in detail the
network of waterways and interconnecting
greenbelts, along with proposed development (which includes civic, financial,
residential, resort, and educational uses).

5
The diagram of the proposed greenbelt
highlights the urban forest and wetlands
which make up the interconnecting greenbelt system. Wetlands and bioswales are
implemented for water filtration and also
help redefine the water edge. The urban
forest creates contiguous linear habitat
for wildlife and migratory birds.

HYDROLOGICAL SYSTEMS DIAGRAM CIRCULATION DIAGRAM TRANSIT DIAGRAM

6

EXISTING
PROPOSED
● GATE

7

WATER TAXI
TRAIL NETWORK

8

- - - - - REGIONAL RAIL   LIGHT RAIL
——— MONORAIL   ○ TRANSIT CENTER
——— SUBWAY

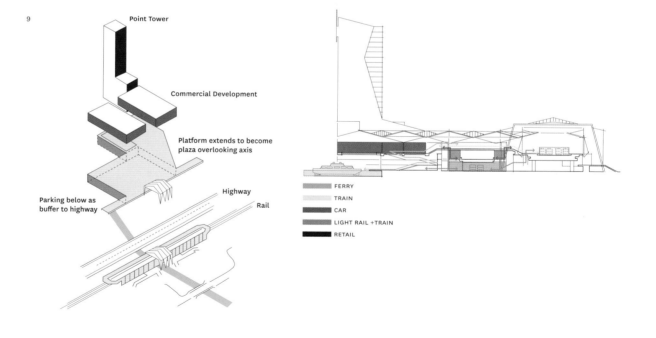

9

Point Tower

Commercial Development

Platform extends to become
plaza overlooking axis

Parking below as
buffer to highway

Highway

Rail

FERRY
TRAIN
CAR
LIGHT RAIL +TRAIN
RETAIL

6

The water system diagram illustrates how proposed canals and rivers link directly to the existing levee pump and gate system. Waterways define the various areas of Shunde New City, but also become a way of traveling between islands and offer another means of recreation.

7

The diagram of water taxi routes and trail networks shows one layer of transportation within the site. Shunde is designed as a walkable series of neighborhood island villages with water taxi stops located at roughly 500-meter intervals.

8

The final circulation diagram shows a map of other means of transportation which run through the city. A monorail loop linking village centers and bicycle trails following the rivers, canals, and boulevard corridors, provides local connections. The main rail lines, along with the subway offer regional connections.

9

A diagrammatic section shows how the vertical layering of transportation and land use come together at the multimodal stations. Regional rail, local rail, water taxi, bus, freeway and pedestrian trail systems link in the context of greenbelt gardens and building structures.

KATY TRAIL

Trails from Rails

Every year, kilometers of abandoned railway lines throughout the United States are transformed into vibrant recreational corridors supporting millions of users and communities. As a networked infrastructure, this transformation has responded to an urban populace hungry for access to open space. A nonprofit organization based in Washington, D.C., named aptly Rails-to-Trails has made its mission to create a nationwide network of trails from former rail lines. The program aims to help enhance America's environment, transportation, economy, neighborhoods, and people. Established in 1986, Rails-to-Trails has helped to oversee the conversion of more than 30,577 kilometers of rail-trails throughout the United States and another 14,484 kilometers are waiting to be built. The organization received additional support in 1991 with the passage of the Intermodal Surface Transportation Efficiency Act, which provides federal grant funding for many of the Rails-to-Trails projects. Katy Trail, in Dallas, Texas, is a recent Rails-to-Trails project, located in the densest portion of the city connecting more than 300,000 residents, who live or work within 1.6 kilometers of the path, to the 50 hectares of urban park land.

Katy Trail, formerly known as the Missouri-Kansas-Texas (MKT) Railroad, operated as the main link for residents of Dallas to the east coast for more than 100 years. On June 6, 1870, the MKT Railroad Company won a construction race, earning the right to build across the Red River and into Texas. In 1871, the Missouri line was continued south and connected to the Kansas line in Parsons. And in 1872, the rail line spanned the Red River and linked with the Houston and Texas Central lines, completing the MKT route. In the 1980s, after a century of operation, the rail closed and was abandoned. The portion of the railway running through Dallas represents a remarkable resource for the residents of the area for recreation and unification of the city's urban parks. In 1997, community members and city leaders came together to form Friends of the Katy Trail, a nonprofit organization aiming to preserve the greenbelt running along the MKT tracks. In addition to its preservation, the rail line was transformed into a linear urban park through the densest parts of Dallas, featuring a 5.6-kilometer pedestrian and bicycle path weaving through 12 hectares of nature. Friends of the Katy Trail spearheaded efforts to advocate and raise funds for its master planning and development. Upon completion of Phase 1 of the Trail Master Plan, the trail will be composed of a 3.6-meter bicycle and skate path and a parallel 2.4-meter soft-surface jogging path made of recycled tires. Six major access points are identified and include kiosk structures and drinking fountains. The trail extends from Airline Road to the American Airlines Center and links the Mockingbird DART station to the west end of downtown Dallas; plazas and entrances help to link the trail to the additional 38 hectares of city park land.

Katy Trail serves as a transportation and recreational corridor for jogging, biking, walking, and nature interpretation, bringing together 20 neighborhoods and connecting people to the central business district, the Dallas Theater Center, Southern Methodist University, and the Trinity Trails network. The master plan for the trail encouraged the use of native plant species that would help to reestablish tallgrass prairie to the area. Agriculture and urban development have contributed to a 99 percent loss of this prairie ecosystem. Friends of the Katy Trail and Audubon Texas worked to eradicate invasive Bermuda grass. They then planted the trail with native grasses and wildflowers. More than 100 decorative light poles were installed along the trail to provide visibility after the sun goes down and in the early morning. Friends of the Katy Trail estimate that approximately 2,000 people a day use the trail now. The North Central Texas Council of Governments estimates that upon completion nearly 1.6 million people will use it every year.

1

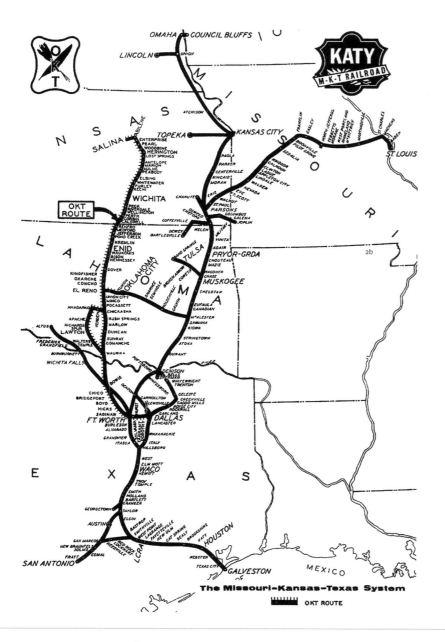

2a

2b

3

1

Map of the Missouri-Kansas-Texas Railroad: the railway was the first to enter Texas from the north. It began operation in 1887, and was the primary means of transportation for residents of Dallas to the east coast.

2a + b

Painted signs and the old rail cars from the MKT line serve as pieces of the site's history. The railroad through Dallas closed in the 1980s and quickly became a neglected infrastructure. Like many of the historic railroads throughout America, the abandoned Katy line presented an opportunity for a Rails-to-Trails initiative, transforming the site into a linear public park.

3

The city of Dallas is home to a population of more than 3 million, and of this number approximately 300,000 live within 1.6 kilometers of the Katy Trail. The railroad location and the concentration of local residents promoted the formation of "Friends of the Katy Trail," a nonprofit organization that helped raise funds for the project.

4

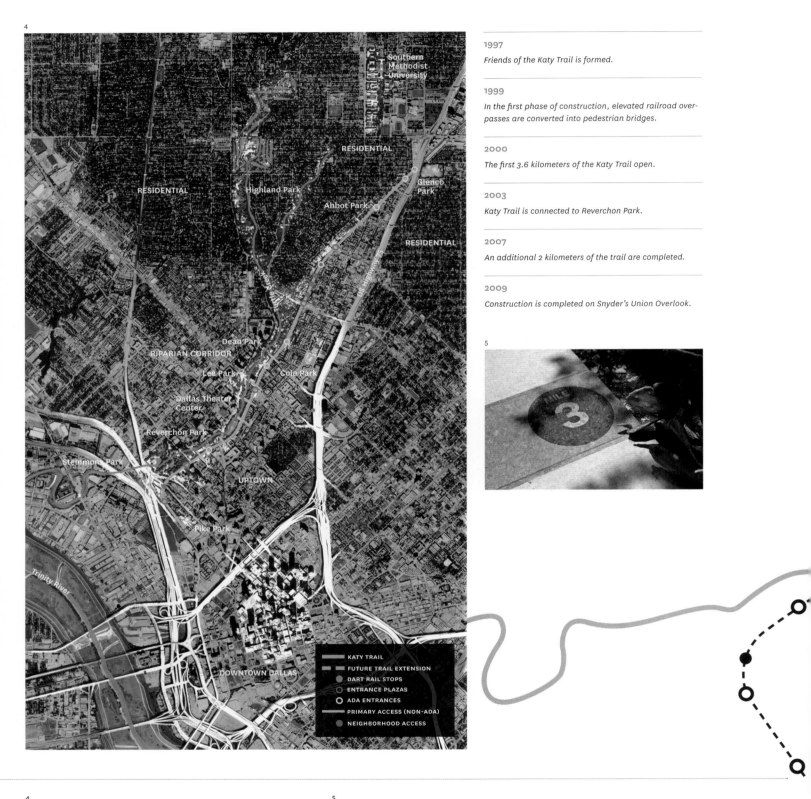

KATY TRAIL
FUTURE TRAIL EXTENSION
DART RAIL STOPS
ENTRANCE PLAZAS
ADA ENTRANCES
PRIMARY ACCESS (NON-ADA)
NEIGHBORHOOD ACCESS

1997
Friends of the Katy Trail is formed.

1999
In the first phase of construction, elevated railroad overpasses are converted into pedestrian bridges.

2000
The first 3.6 kilometers of the Katy Trail open.

2003
Katy Trail is connected to Reverchon Park.

2007
An additional 2 kilometers of the trail are completed.

2009
Construction is completed on Snyder's Union Overlook.

5

4
Map of the regional context surrounding Katy Trail. Located just north of downtown the trail connects Pike Park to Glenco Park, following the Turtle Creek greenbelt, and linking into 50 hectares of urban park land. The 7.2-kilometer trail includes four major accessible (ADA-compliant) entrances, three major connections, ten additional ADA entrances, and seven stair entrances. The master plan for the project was based on four primary goals: to create a safe and easily accessible trail system, to celebrate the history and natural environment of the area, to promote community involvement and stewardship, and to establish a beautiful urban city park.

5
The mile markers on the Katy Trail are imbedded into the concrete path and show the distance from the end in the direction users are traveling.

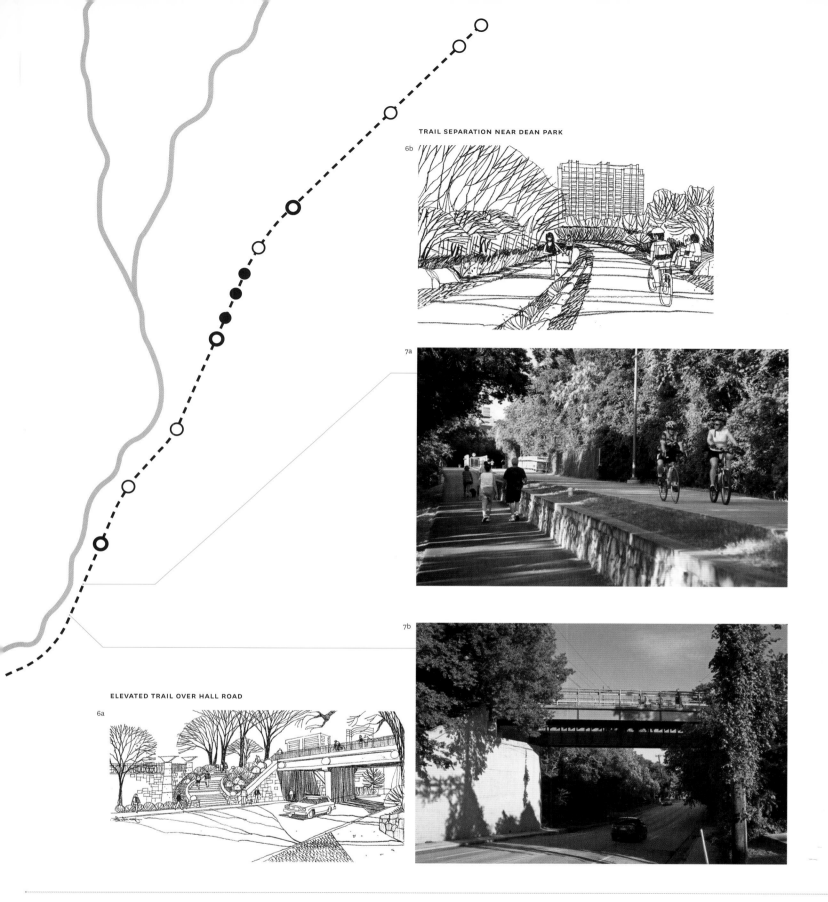

TRAIL SEPARATION NEAR DEAN PARK

6b

7a

7b

ELEVATED TRAIL OVER HALL ROAD

6a

6 a + b

Early conceptual sketch illustrating accessibility and how the trail navigates through
the city. This vision was translated into a
built reality as the elevated railroad overpasses were converted into pedestrian trail
bridges in 1999 as part of the first phase of
construction. A second sketch highlights
the proposal for two separate but parallel
trail systems.

7 a + b

As the actual site image shows, a 3.6-meter
concrete path serves the faster bikers, skaters, and inline skaters, while the 2.4-meter
path—made of ground, recycled rubber
tires—serves the walkers and joggers.

SNYDER'S UNION OVERLOOK

8

ENTRY STAIRS TO KATY TRAIL

9

NEAR THE AMERICAN AIRLINES BUILDING

10

8
The trail extends from the American Airlines Center just north of downtown through urban park land, and the riparian landscape of Turtle Creek, into neighborhoods and communities, and ends near Southern Methodist University. A number of overlooks and plazas are incorporated into the trail as places to rest or gather. In 2009, Snyder's Union Overlook was completed. The wooded awning provides shade for visitors and gives the plaza a unique character.

9
There are seven stair entrances to Katy Trail from the surrounding neighborhoods. These provide access, while also serving as an additional recreational element for more strenuous workouts.

10
Joggers near the beginning of the trail (by the American Airlines Building). The linear infrastructure connects people, as users find their way along pathways that wind through the woods in the middle of the densest part of Dallas.

11

12

13

11

Plantings along the trail were meant to reference the historic native landscape. Tallgrass prairie species such as sideoats grama (*Bouteloua curtipendula*), little bluestem (*Schizachyrium scoparium*), Indian grass (*Sorghastrum nutans*), switchgrass (*Panicum virgatum*), and big bluestem (*Andropogon geradii*) are planted along trail edges to help reestablish a grassland habitat. Trees along the trail are all native hardy trees, and were planted to replace any dying or diseased trees. Those species planted are classified as "urban forest trees" and include species of oak (*Quercus sp.*), redbuds (*Cercis canadensis*), and chinaquapins (*Castanea purnila*).

12

As a former railroad, the trail maintains its function as a transportation corridor, moving people through the city and the landscape. The network of powerlines and utilities were built along the railroad as part of the city's urban infrastructure and have now become part of the Katy Trail.

13

Designed signs direct the movement of people and mark the Katy Trail.

KNOX STREET INTERSECTION

14

PLAZA ENTRANCE TO REVERCHON PARK

15

14
The trail passes through different neighborhoods and communities. Since the initial 3.6 kilometers were completed in 2000, there has been an upsurge in property values and real estate sales. The image shows the intersection of Katy Trail with Knox Street,

as people rest along benches and walkers/joggers pass by designed vertical light fixtures. As a safety measure, 145 lights were added; they glow from 5 a.m. to sunrise and again from sunset until 11 p.m.

15
A large trellis marks the entrance plaza to Reverchon Park. Native crossvine (*Bignonia capreolata*) grows up the structure, providing both shade and visual interest along the trail.

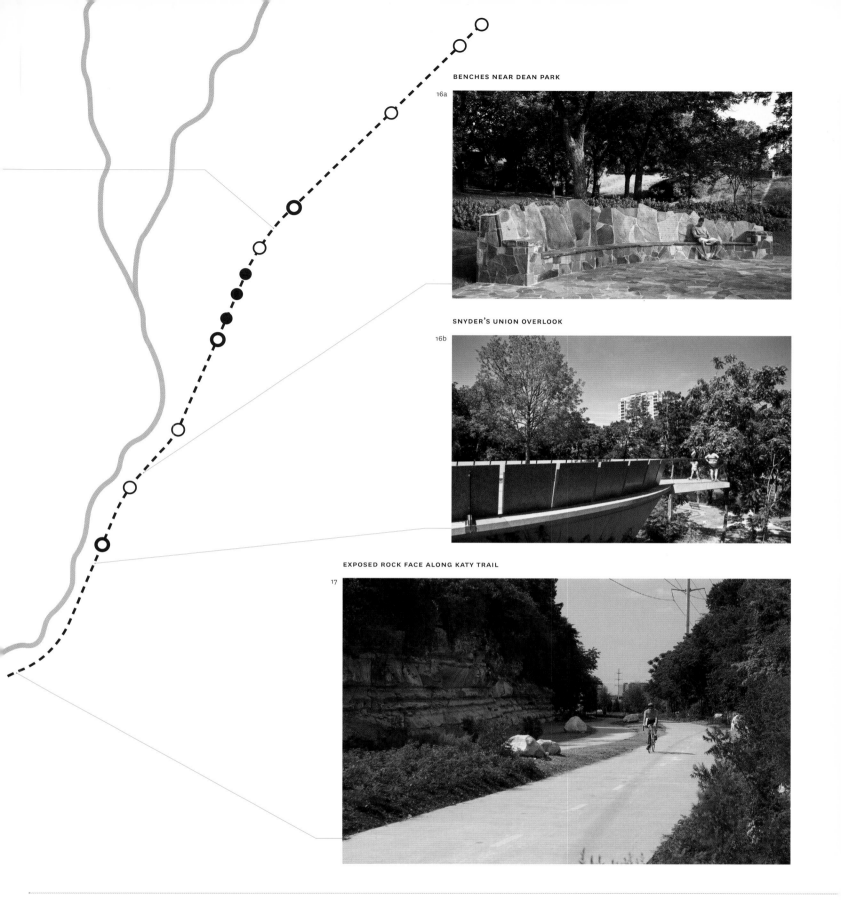

BENCHES NEAR DEAN PARK

16a

SNYDER'S UNION OVERLOOK

16b

EXPOSED ROCK FACE ALONG KATY TRAIL

17

16a + b
Different constructed elements along the trail add complexity and variation to the site. The curved stone bench references the rock outcroppings that can be found along the trail and throughout the region, and the overlook at Snyder's Union provides a view of Robert E. Lee Park.

17
A biker along the Katy Trail. As an urban park, the trail promotes daily exercise and recreation for residents of Dallas (a city with an obesity rate approaching 50 percent). For eleven straight years the Katy Trail has sponsored a 5-kilometer run/walk, which helps to raise money for maintenance and construction, and also promotes a healthy lifestyle. Aside from increasing physical activity for the city residents, the trail infrastructure also helps the environment by reducing vehicle emissions if people use the pathway for their commute or travel.

BEIZHI RIVER WATERFRONT

Infrastructure of Pleasure

The city of Fuyang in Zhejian Province, like much of China, is experiencing a familiar pattern of prevalent development—transitioning from an agricultural and industrial society to that of a service-oriented city. With rapid expansion into water-based infrastructure, recreation, and increasing density in the residential sector, infrastructure becomes a mechanism for defining purpose and program, while establishing a set of relationships between city and landscape. Fuyang is located within the Yangtze River Delta, bisected by the Beizhi River and also influenced by the Fuchun River. The river corridors fluctuate based on tides and seasonal flooding, ultimately affecting accessibility. This case study focuses on a proposal for the transformation of the Beizhi River into a networked ecology based on water recreation and sports programming. The Beizhi River runs through Fuyang, with the city's downtown to the north and Dongzhou Island to the south. Ancient sediment deposits from the larger Fuchun River formed an island, land mass that caused a diversion in water flow that became the Beizhi River. Fifty years ago, in response to seasonal flooding, the river was dammed, and since then has served as an irrigation reservoir for Dongzhou Island. In contrast to the Fuchun River, which serves as a major transportation artery for the region, the two dams along the Beizhi River impede water flow and limit its use, both recreationally and commercially. Recent development demands aimed at maximizing open space and waterfront land use in the face of increased population density call for a rethinking of the role of the Beizhi River.

The growth of Fuyang into a metropolis has led to a series of city initiatives to index available open space for the potential to maximize program and accessibility, including a government-sponsored competition for the reestablishment of the Beizhi River as a viable hydrological and ecological corridor. The 17-kilometer waterfront serves as a framework for the redefinition of Fuyang, providing a new identity for the region, oriented toward a balanced lifestyle of work, recreation, and leisure. The concept of "Acu-pleasure" takes the attitude that the removal of two dams within the Beizhi River presents an opportunity to create a layered ecological and recreational landscape for Fuyang. Strategic interventions [acupuncture] seek to remove the impediments and identify new linkages, enhance human experience [pleasure] while strengthening the ecological viability of the region. The design approach to restoring the river includes the protection and creation of densely vegetated parks along the embankments, and the filtration of stormwater within the immediate watershed. Removal of the dams helps to restore former water fluctuations and to reintroduce a historical set of riverbank conditions, based on fluvial morphology. Improved hydrologic flow reestablishes the Beizhi River as a habitat and ecological network that could extend and connect development throughout Fuyang and Dongzhou Island and into the larger regional context of the Fuchun River.

The linear waterfront stretches 17 kilometers and is focused on open-space planning and development. Design for the corridor is driven by strategies that include reconnecting the north-south forest corridors from the mountains to the riverfront, establishing wetland habitats along the riparian edge to increase species richness and cleanse stormwater runoff, retaining the existing agricultural landscape to ensure economic viability to farmers, and encouraging an array of sports and recreational programs throughout the year. Landscape linkages defined by trails, boardwalks, linear parks, and seasonal riparian corridors provide interconnectivity and become an ecological framework for improving water quality while nurturing habitat and wetland vegetation. Programming ideas for the corridor incorporate a variety of water-based recreation such as sailing, dragon-boat racing, waterskiing, canoeing, and kayaking, mixed with land-based recreation such as biking, hiking, running, kite flying, and picnicking. As a network of infrastructure these various systems of ecology, history, recreation, and economy serve as the basic framework of city and growth, as well as an infrastructure of pleasure revealed through public enjoyment and well-being.

1a

1b

2

1a + b

The project site is located along the Beizhi River in Dongzhou, a growing area of the city of Fuyang. Design for the 17-kilometer waterfront open space aims to reconnect forest corridors from the mountains to the riverfront, establish wetland habitats to increase species richness, cleanse stormwater runoff, and provide an array of sports and recreation programs to reinforce the city's vision as a destination for activity and wellness.

2

The city of Fuyang has a history of paper-making dating back to the Song Dynasty (960–1279). Archeological excavation in Fuyang revealed the earliest ancient paper-making workshop ever discovered in China. Today the paper industry remains an important part of the area's history and contributes significantly to its economic development.

CONTEXT DIAGRAM

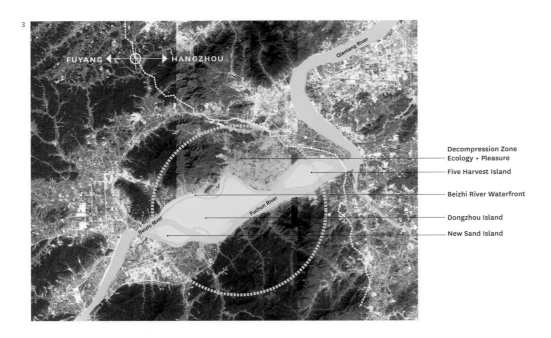

Decompression Zone
Ecology + Pleasure

Five Harvest Island

Beizhi River Waterfront

Dongzhou Island

New Sand Island

SITE AILMENTS

Local Connector
Hard Edge

Isolated
Landform

Disturbed
Ecosystem

Industrial Development
Toxic Runoff

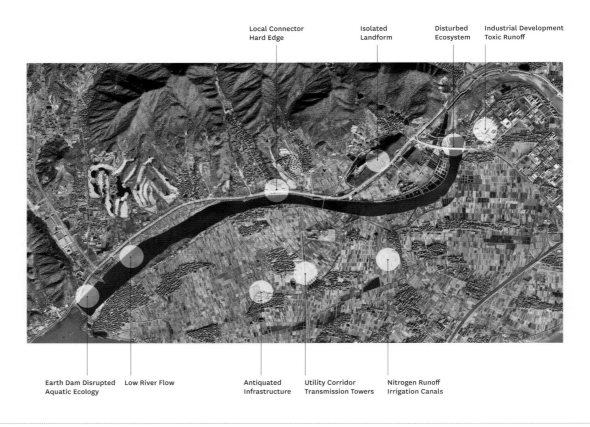

Earth Dam Disrupted
Aquatic Ecology

Low River Flow

Antiquated
Infrastructure

Utility Corridor
Transmission Towers

Nitrogen Runoff
Irrigation Canals

3

The map provides a regional orientation of the project site. The Qiantang River splits to form the Fuchun and Beizhi Rivers. The city of Fuyang lies at this juncture, southwest of Hangzhou. Islands are formed where the rivers have diverged and are incorporated into the design for the Beizhi River Waterfront. Mountainous terrain surrounds the site, enveloping what can be seen as a "decompression zone" surrounding the waterfront. This area becomes a tranquil valley, surrounded by mountains and combining ecological preservation with recreation and pleasure.

4

The overarching design concept for the riverfront is based on the idea of "Acu-Pleasure." This begins with the removal of dams within the Beizhi River, allowing the river to flow freely. The idea of acupuncture is realized as physical interventions that rectify the site ailments and redirect the area towards a restored and balanced equilibrium.

5

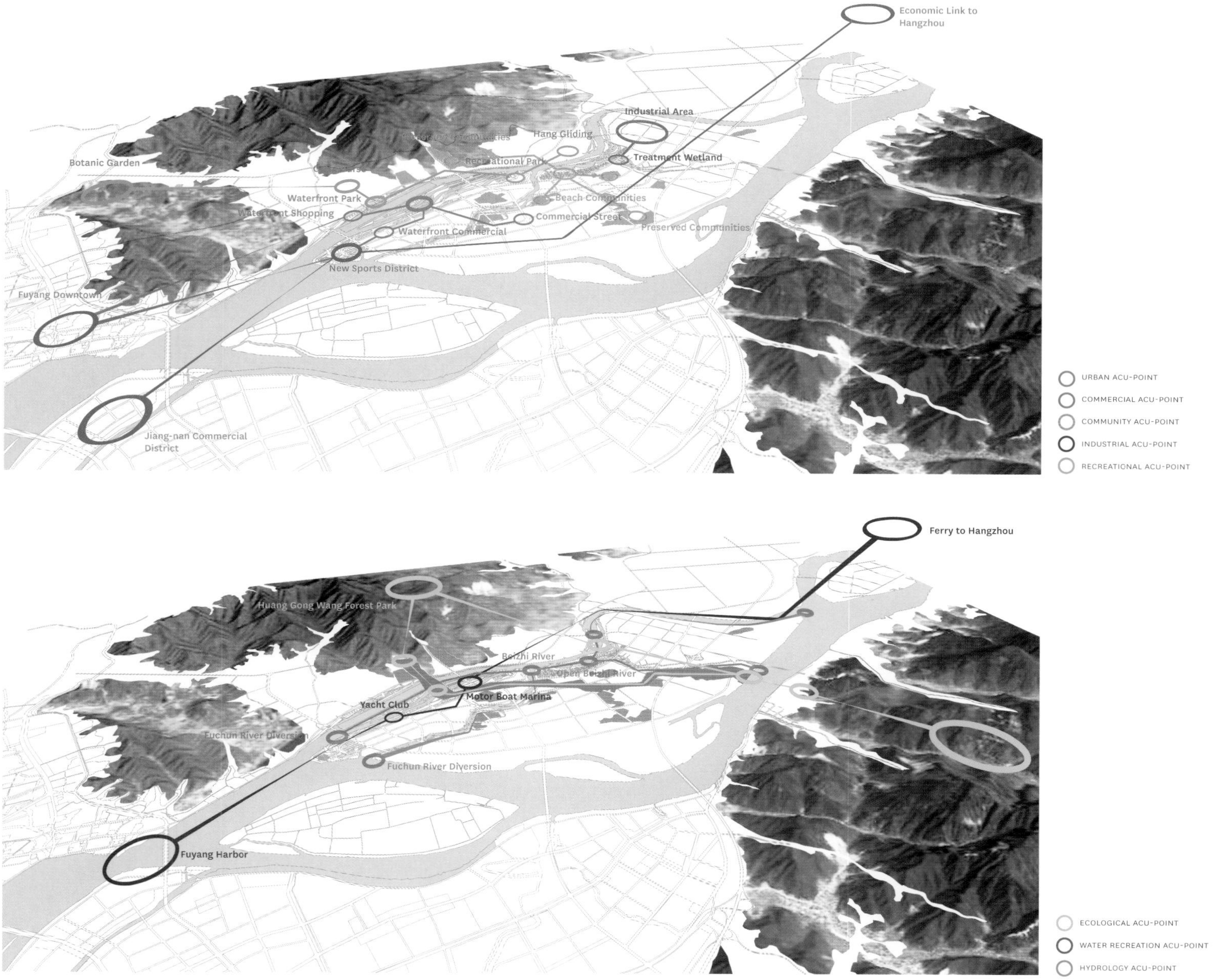

URBAN ACU-POINT

COMMERCIAL ACU-POINT

COMMUNITY ACU-POINT

INDUSTRIAL ACU-POINT

RECREATIONAL ACU-POINT

ECOLOGICAL ACU-POINT

WATER RECREATION ACU-POINT

HYDROLOGY ACU-POINT

5
Concept diagrams define the different
"acupuncture points" that become part of a
landscape system which includes ecology,
hydrology, culture, and commerce. These
systems are given identity through different
types of programming, and function together through a network of paths, corridors,
and destinations.

6

7

6

The landscape master plan for the 17-kilo-meter-long site is focused on a variety of recreational uses and accessibility, while maintaining ecological function and an appropriate scale. By removing the dams, the hydrology of the larger Fuchun River system becomes part of the Beizhi River system, creating higher-velocity water flow and increased wildlife.

7

Bird's eye perspective of the development of Dongzhou Island and its connection to the Beizhi River Waterfront.

DIAGRAM OF PEDESTRIAN CIRCULATION

8

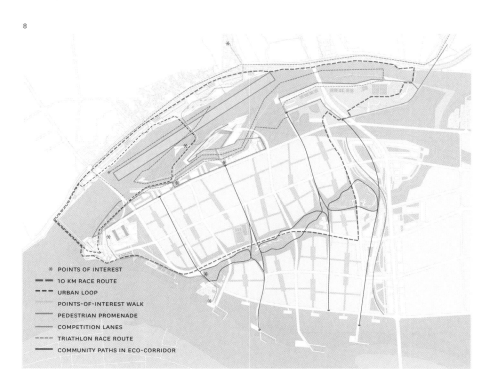

* POINTS OF INTEREST
— — 10 KM RACE ROUTE
- - - URBAN LOOP
POINTS-OF-INTEREST WALK
PEDESTRIAN PROMENADE
COMPETITION LANES
- - - TRIATHLON RACE ROUTE
COMMUNITY PATHS IN ECO-CORRIDOR

DIAGRAM OF HYDROLOGY AND ECOLOGY

9

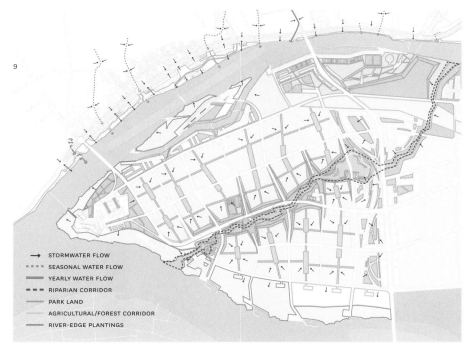

→ STORMWATER FLOW
· · · · SEASONAL WATER FLOW
YEARLY WATER FLOW
- - - RIPARIAN CORRIDOR
PARK LAND
AGRICULTURAL/FOREST CORRIDOR
RIVER-EDGE PLANTINGS

0 100   300   500   700   900m

8
Circulation through the site is primarily multimodal (accommodating bikers, inline skaters, joggers, and pedestrians). Trails are set aside for pedestrians and joggers, while others are meant to serve those on wheels.

9
The ecological component of the design is integrated into the development strategy. Through a combination of habitat zones and connected green corridors the entire riverfront is incorporated into the larger landscape region. An understanding of hydrology was an essential part of the project, as water flow continues to affect site topography,

soil structure, and erosion. Without the presence of dams, the river moves unobstructed, providing an opportunity for water activities such as speed boating, sailing, and kayaking. A small diversion just south of the river brings water eastward into Dongzhou Island and creates an amenity for smaller boats. Water quality is achieved

through structured, man-made ecological systems that support recreation and interpretive education.

PROGRAMMATIC ZONES

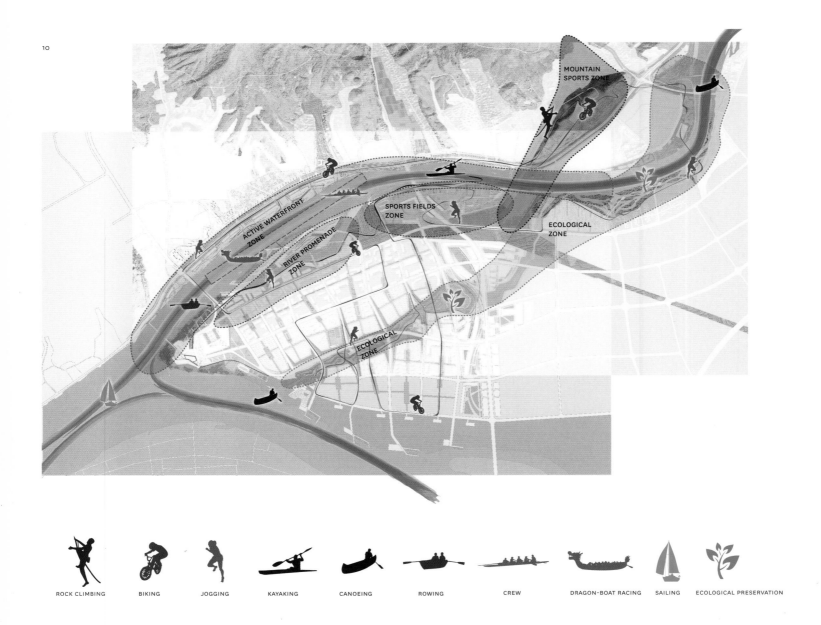

ROCK CLIMBING   BIKING   JOGGING   KAYAKING   CANOEING   ROWING   CREW   DRAGON-BOAT RACING   SAILING   ECOLOGICAL PRESERVATION

10
Diagram highlighting use. Recreational
activities are established throughout the
site, as Fuyang has been named the "City of
Sports." The variety of programs provides
opportunities for bike and boat races as well
as marathons and triathlons. Passive recreation is incorporated into the design as well,
creating a multifunctional corridor.

11a

11b

11c

11d

11e

11a – 11e

Various activities can be accommodated throughout the site, while the transformation of the river and surrounding landscape is accentuated. Along with everyday use, the multimodal paths provide venues for specific races and athletic competitions. The river accommodates a variety of different types of watercraft due to its depth, which allows for both recreational events and leisure.

12a

12b

12c

12d

12e

12a – 12e

These renderings show the site as a series of systems and interconnected corridors. Pathways follow the river embankment, with portions of the circulation network breaking off to form seating structures and docks. The main road artery along the waterfront is also redesigned. Street trees and vegetation provide visual appeal while serving to reduce stormwater and the urban heat-island effect. With sidewalks and pathways, the street too becomes multimodal.

13

13
Additional bird's eye perspective of the
entire site including the riverfront as well
as Dongzhou Island.

IN CRE MENT

The incremental nature of infrastructural projects bears directly on a city's ability to sustain growth through a measured period of time.

Shanghai's transportation network has matured to include a state-of-the-art magnetic rail system and freeways capable of sustaining a robust metro-politan population of over 19 million people. Incremental changes to the urban fabric of China's storied city on the Huang Pu River is necessary for the maturation and growth of its core identity. Perhaps the recently installed blue LED lights underneath the Yan'An elevated freeway is an attempt to convey a sense of what Shanghai is now and a prelude of things to come in the future.

CENTRAL OPEN SPACE IN MAC

Density Transfer

As part of the Republic of Korea's vast urban-planning strategy for decentralization, an international competition for the Multifunctional Administrative City (MAC) was established. With the phased relocation of twelve governmental ministries, six government agencies, and other state-run organizations currently located in Seoul, MAC will serve as the new administrative center for South Korea. Situated outside of Seoul, the proposed city will help to alleviate density, and balance growth and development in the nation's capital. The competition brief called for an innovative master-plan strategy that would establish MAC as a model city of sustainable growth for future generations with a large open space functioning as the foundation of the urban landscape. The 72-square-kilometer site presents an opportunity to embrace the existing watershed ecologies, topography, and transportation infrastructure, to create a dynamic design approach. A modular grid system was employed to integrate park and urban infrastructure as a framework for flexible, programmatic open space and development, which would adapt to current and future populations. Program and infrastructure became the catalyst for determining the future shape, function, and form of the new city.

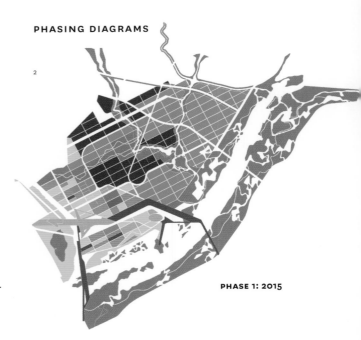

PHASING DIAGRAMS

2

PHASE 1: 2015

1

SEOUL METROPOLIS
23.4 million
GROWTH RATE 1.38%

Inchoen

MULTIFUNCTIONAL
ADMINISTRATIVE CITY
0.5 million

Daejun

Daegu

Ulsan

Kwangju

Pusan

SOUTH KOREA
47.3 million
GROWTH RATE 0.55%

The "Park City" design for MAC was based on two basic ideas: production and consumption. A phased strategy was developed that would evolve through the interaction of these two forces. Master planning for the site would begin with a densification of the civic core, allowing for reclamation of much of the land that had originally been planned for development. The grid layout was applied to this open space as a pattern for changeable programmatic park land. Additional strategies for the master plan included the introduction of a civic circuit—a continuous loop of plazas and bridges, providing public space and allowing the majority of the river banks to remain as natural habitats. The plan also outlined programmatic centers that would create integration between the urban and the natural realm.

Phasing for Park City was broken into three sequences. In the first phase, a cultural complex and urban promenade would be built to become the first active programs that would link city to park. In addition, a wetland park and ecological corridor would be established as part of the beginning of a sustainable and hydrologic strategy for the city. This phase was designed to accommodate the predicted 2015 population of 150,000. At only 30 percent of the city's projected population capacity, much of the open space would not require activation and would remain in production, as either rice fields or nurseries. Phase Two would accommodate the predicted population growth of

3

4

URBAN ACTIVITY
ACTIVE
CULTURE
PASSIVE
AGRICULTURE
NURSERY
ENERGY
ECOLOGY

PHASE 2: 2020

PHASE 3: 2030

the city to 2020. Park land would grow toward the east side of the site, which would ultimately influence the direction of future development. Finally, in Phase Three, the park would be in its final state with the city's population at its target maximum of 500,000. Most of the production park land, natural land within the categories of nurseries, energy, agriculture, and ecology, would have been replaced by a consumption park program, land that will be developed for urban activity, active programming, passive programming, and cultural activities, while planted forests would have become fully mature and integrated into the surrounding natural environment. While this is the final phase, no conceptual boundary is established for the site; thus the park can expand beyond the city and begin to coalesce new urban development with the existing park system.

A series of specifically designed elements provide an armature for the flexible, changing park program. A 40-meter-wide urban promenade links the different centers within the site. The promenade is limited to pedestrians, but includes stops for the local shuttle-bus system. At the city's entry point, buildings are clustered and adjoined by a grand plaza, which serves as a "stage" for a multitude of public events. Smaller, 5-meter-wide pedestrian routes follow the grid system through the city, becoming less rigid and more organic as they meander outside of the civic core. Both jogging and bicycle circuits are incorporated into the circulation. At varying lengths, these trails take advantage of topography changes and are able to accommodate different levels of recreational use. A series of wetland parks are incorporated to help cleanse stormwater, provide flood control, and nurture wildlife. This system of wetlands along with established riparian corridors act as ecological connectors, linking the urban park system to the surrounding mountains and rivers.

1

Multifunctional Administrative City, occupying approximately 72 square kilometers, lies south of Seoul and within the Chungcheongnam-do Province of Korea. With an expected population growth of half a million within the next few years, MAC became an ideal location for implementing a strategy of park and urban infrastructure that is flexible and adaptable.

2

The design was broken into phases that would allow for the park to adapt to changes in population. In Phase One, much of the land remains under production; at these early stages, program elements such as circulation, entry and access points, cultural venues and open spaces are added that will trigger future development within the park.

3

In Phase Two the population is expected to grow to 200,000 and thus more park program will take over production lands. By converting lands within each grid unit, urban development is progressively introduced to the surroundings. Along the waterfront, mid-density housing is added, while planted forested sites begin to mature.

4

The final phase of the project occurs in 2030, when the expected population growth will reach the city's maximum capacity. At this stage, much of the production land has been converted to park land, and forested sites have fully matured. In addition, tree hospitals and sustainable energy sources are introduced, creating a well-balanced city that integrates the land's resources with urban development.

DESIGN STRATEGY

5

URBAN GRID SYSTEM

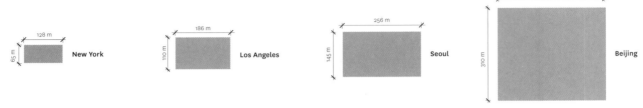

New York 128 m × 65 m

Los Angeles 186 m × 110 m

Seoul 256 m × 145 m

Beijing 350 m × 310 m

PARK GRID SYSTEM

AGRICULTURAL GRID SYSTEM

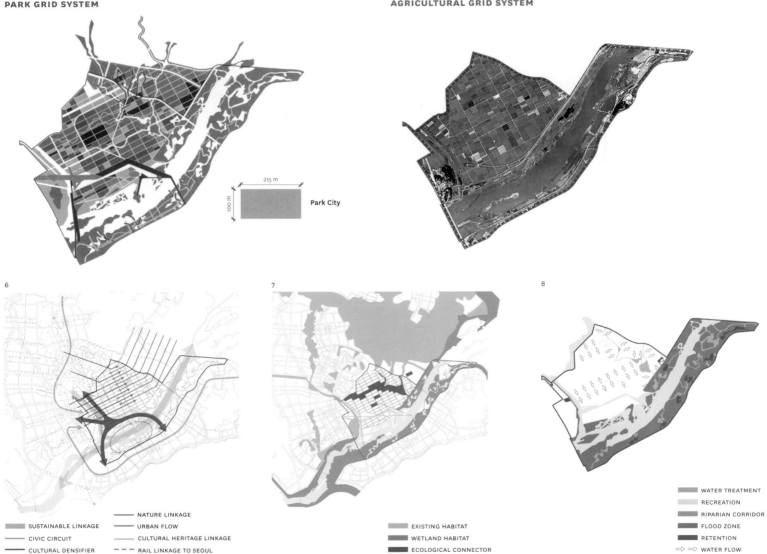

Park City 215 m × 100 m

SUSTAINABLE LINKAGE
CIVIC CIRCUIT
CULTURAL DENSIFIER
NATURE LINKAGE
URBAN FLOW
CULTURAL HERITAGE LINKAGE
RAIL LINKAGE TO SEOUL

EXISTING HABITAT
WETLAND HABITAT
ECOLOGICAL CONNECTOR

WATER TREATMENT
RECREATION
RIPARIAN CORRIDOR
FLOOD ZONE
RETENTION
WATER FLOW

5
The modular grid system derived from city blocks becomes a means of parceling the site and creating a pattern for growth and expansion that fits into a scale appropriate to the area. The existing agricultural grid further provides a framework for the proposed urban park system.

6
Connections within the site and programmed spaces help to link the project with the regional context.

7
Ecological connections are made through a riparian corridor that links Wonsubong, the tip of Hwangak mountain, and Jeonwol mountain to the Gum River through the eastern edge of the park, while a second corridor ties the urban park system to the surrounding mountains. Added wetland parks, along with water treatment ponds and nine retention pools, help provide flood control, create habitat, and provide a visual amenity for the city.

8
The most important hydrological issue in Park City is flood control. Nine water retention pools are proposed along the Gum River, following the given areas and locations. The pools will have multiple functions including stormwater treatment ponds, bird sanctuaries, wildlife habitat, and wetland parks.

CONCEPTUAL LANDSCAPE MASTER PLAN

9

10

11

12

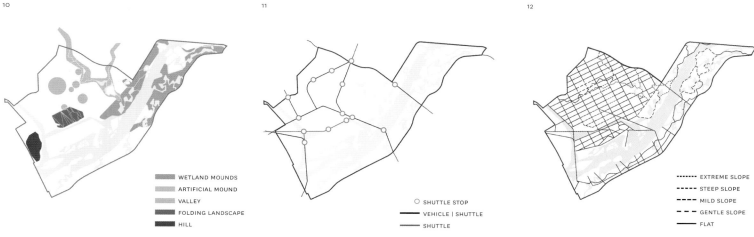

WETLAND MOUNDS
ARTIFICIAL MOUND
VALLEY
FOLDING LANDSCAPE
HILL

○ SHUTTLE STOP
— VEHICLE | SHUTTLE
— SHUTTLE

········· EXTREME SLOPE
------- STEEP SLOPE
-- -- MILD SLOPE
-- - GENTLE SLOPE
— FLAT

9

The master plan for the MAC competition establishes a series of programmatic centers surrounded by a fluctuating park system. The cultural center includes a performing arts complex, a history and folk museum, and an amphitheater. A sports center includes soccer stadiums, a basketball arena, and tennis facilities. The administrative and civic center establishes the remaining initial program. Open space used for production or consumption surrounds these developed nodes, while a network of circulation and ecological corridors provides connection through the site.

10

In addition to the existing natural topography, artificial topography is created on the site in the form of circular mounds (in the center of the city) and a folding landscape that integrates buildings into the park space.

11

Walkability is promoted throughout the site. Thus vehicular traffic is restricted, and residents are encouraged to take the shuttle bus. The shuttle bus is the only means of access to certain areas of Park City, apart from walking.

12

The main pedestrian circulation routes follow the grid structure while within the city. As routes head out of town, they loosen and become more organic, taking advantage of topography changes. A jogging and bicycle circuit includes 1–20-kilometer-trail loops that accommodate varied users and levels of recreation.

13

GRID UNIT PHASING

15a

EXAMPLE 1

| FZ | Phase 1: Flood Zone | → | WL | Phase 2: Wetland | → | PA | Phase 3: Picnic Area |

EXAMPLE 2

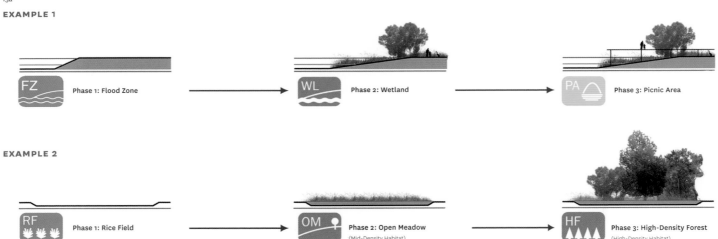

| RF | Phase 1: Rice Field | → | OM | Phase 2: Open Meadow (Mid-Density Habitat) | → | HF | Phase 3: High-Density Forest (High-Density Habitat) |

13

The rendered image illustrates how the landscape folds to incorporate both city and park into an almost continuous stretch of programmatic open space. The pedestrian urban promenade can be seen in front, providing recreation and connection.

14

Imagery of the juxtaposition of land uses within the open park spaces. Land still used for production abuts with land that has been converted to consumption.

15a + b

The illustrations show how phasing may occur within a given grid unit. In addition to programmatic changes, habitat diversity and density increases, soil composition is altered, and land is reused.

14

15b

EXAMPLE 3

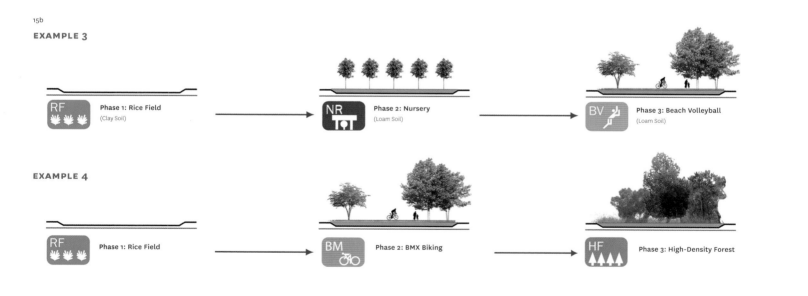

RF — **Phase 1: Rice Field** (Clay Soil) → NR — **Phase 2: Nursery** (Loam Soil) → BV — **Phase 3: Beach Volleyball** (Loam Soil)

EXAMPLE 4

RF — **Phase 1: Rice Field** → BM — **Phase 2: BMX Biking** → HF — **Phase 3: High-Density Forest**

16 (next spread)

The program evolution diagram is overlaid on a rendering of what the site could look like in 2030. Park City originates from the existing agricultural conditions of the lands and transforms into a diverse accumulation of programmatic spaces. The majority of the agricultural land is dedicated to nurseries, energy, crops, and ecology. This land can adapt with development and urban activity into places of active and passive recreation and cultural venues.

JEFFREY OPEN SPACE TRAIL

Urban Trail Blazing

America's National Trails System totals more than 96,560 kilometers in all 50 states (longer than the interstate highway system) and is comprised of various types designated as scenic, historic, recreational, multifunctional, and rails-to-trails conversions. Enacted in 1968, the National Trails System Act authorized the creation of a national trail system to promote a deeper appreciation for natural open-space systems and their latent ability to connect people with the natural, historic, and cultural heritage of the American landscape. As a basic component of recreation, the simple trail was envisioned as an essential part of everyday life. In Orange County in Southern California, the 20,200-hectare Irvine Ranch Wildlands and Parks preserved open space integrates a 35.4-kilometer trail connecting the Weir Canyon Wilderness Area to the Pacific Ocean. Aptly named the Mountains-to-Sea Trail (MST), the trail allows joggers, bikers, and walkers an unparalleled experience of the area's biological and geological features.

The MST contains important natural habitats and unusual geological formations that support hundreds of species of plants and animals including eagles, badgers, mountain lions, tecate cypress trees (*Cupressus forbesii*), and many rare types of birds, reptiles, amphibians, and plants. However, near the center of this open-space preserve, between the foothills and the coast, lies a relatively flat area comprised of a complex web of freeways, bridges, tunnels, and a burgeoning new residential population of mixed-density housing supported by commercial developments. Given its status as a National Recreation Trail, providing access to the MST was important, but equally important was addressing the growing community's desire for open space that could spatially accommodate increased residential densities by providing multipurpose recreation fields and space for picnicking and relaxation.

The response to these desires came by way of the Jeffrey Open Space Trail—Segment 2, a 1.6-kilometer multipurpose trail and recreation corridor linked to the contiguous MST, which leads through a local park in the foothills north of the city of Irvine, and the many residential neighborhoods to the south. The entire trail consists of four segments with an overall length of 4.4 kilometers: Segment 2 was the first to be realized. The land that formed the basis for the design and implementation of the Jeffrey Open Space Trail could be characterized as relatively flat, laden with roadways, and punctuated by a mobile-home park, a temporary storage facility, and a former packaging facility. The corridor itself was widened to 100 meters in some sections to fully accommodate the intended recreational and cultural programs developed during the initial outreach effort. Programs such as kite flying, butterfly gardens, seating areas, interpretive signage, art, and active and passive recreation were the desired uses of the 28.3-hectare park that were ultimately implemented.

Since 2004, nearly 10,000 new homes were realized within a few kilometers of the newly constructed Jeffrey Open Space Trail. Because of its scale, the trail acts as a distribution of recreational and natural systems set within an urban fabric of dense residential development. The linear park corridor consists of a multifunctional bicycle and pedestrian trail that passes through informal landscapes sculpted and informed by foothill topography and a planted regime of native trees, shrubs, and grasses to restore the historic ecologies of the area. The trail itself maintains a 3.3-meter-wide paved surface for bicyclists and inline skaters and a parallel 1.5-meter-wide decomposed granite path for joggers, runners, and walkers. The approach to the planting design is structured around the alignment of the trail and considers spatial and visual experience, habitat creation, water-harvesting strategies, and an integrated system of vegetated swales to filter and recharge the aquifer. This approach is supported by topographical landforms to filter and channel stormwater, open meadows, and seasonal arroyos. It is integrated with interpretive panels to commemorate significant events in the region's cultural and natural history—the role of Native Americans of the region, the establishment of the Spanish ranchos, the evolution of the agricultural heritage of Irvine Ranch, and the development of the city itself.

1

2

3

1

The map shows the 35.4-kilometer Mountains-to-Sea Trail located within the 20,200-hectare Irvine Ranch Wildlands and Parks. These lands have been identified by The Nature Conservancy as one of the top 50 priority conservation landscapes in California for their extraordinary concentration of unique plant and animal species.

2

This commemorative mosaic tile was integrated into a stone bench. While the first orange trees were planted in California in 1804, they were not exported in any significant quantity until the early 1900s with the establishment of packing houses such as Irvine Valencia Growers packing house in Orange County 1926. The earliest California orange crops consisted of Navel oranges and Valencia oranges which ripened in the summer in Orange County.

3

A community programming workshop for the proposed Jeffrey Open Space Trail was held in 2003. Residents participated in a series of workshops focused on identifying the key elements and landscape character of the trail. A consensus plan eventually identified a combined bicycle and running trail set within a "woodsy" landscape fabric of undulating hills and valleys.

DIAGRAMMATIC LANDSCAPE PLAN

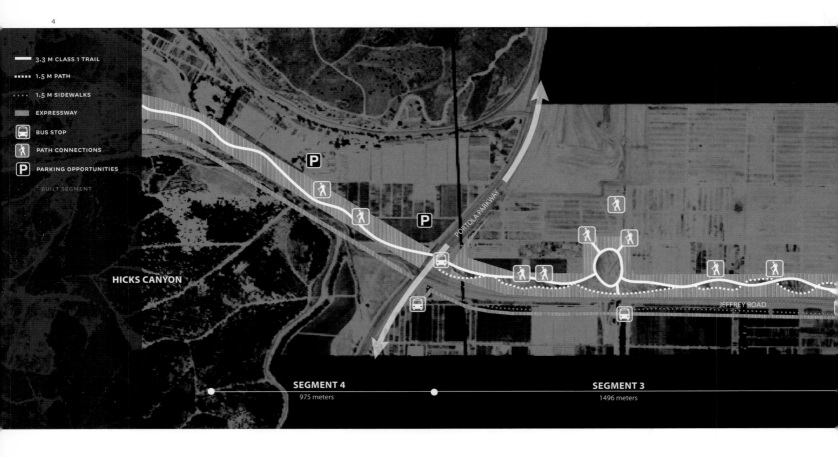

4

- ▬ 3.3 M CLASS 1 TRAIL
- ▪▪▪▪ 1.5 M PATH
- ⋯⋯ 1.5 M SIDEWALKS
- ▨ EXPRESSWAY
- 🚌 BUS STOP
- 🚶 PATH CONNECTIONS
- 🅿 PARKING OPPORTUNITIES
- BUILT SEGMENT

HICKS CANYON

PORTOLA PARKWAY

JEFFREY ROAD

SEGMENT 4
975 meters

SEGMENT 3
1496 meters

LANDSCAPE DIAGRAMS

5a

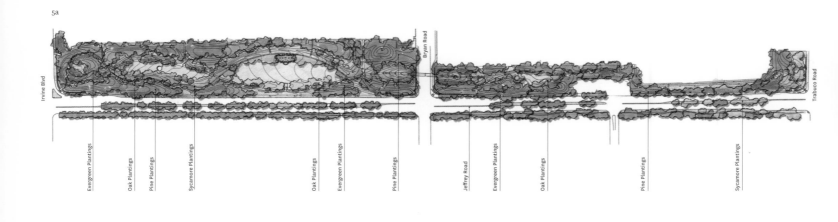

Irvine Blvd

Evergreen Plantings
Oak Plantings
Pine Plantings
Sycamore Plantings
Oak Plantings
Evergreen Plantings
Pine Plantings
Bryan Road
Jeffrey Road
Evergreen Plantings
Oak Plantings
Pine Plantings
Sycamore Plantings
Trabuco Road

4
Overall master plan of the Jeffrey Open
Space Trail. The trail is comprised of four
segments totaling 4.4 kilometers in length.
The plan consists of 3.3-meter-wide class
1 trails (which prohibit mountain bikes
and motorized vehicles), 1.5-meter-wide
bicycle and pedestrian paths, and 1.5-meter-
wide sidewalks.

5a + b
Schematic landscape diagrams of the
Jeffrey Open Space Trail. A planting diagram
illustrates the "woodsy" character of the
park design, while the ground plane diagram
illustrates trail layout, understory planting,
undulating landforms, and drainage.

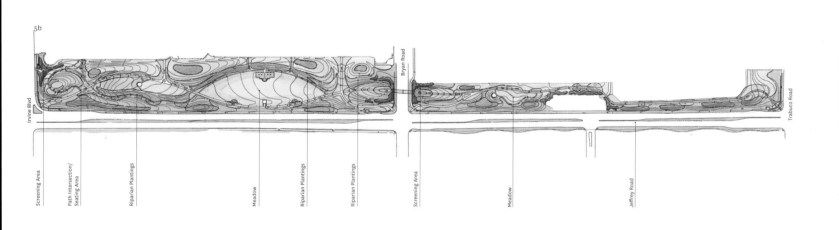

5b

Irvine Blvd

Bryan Road

Trabuco Road

Screening Area

Path Intersection/
Seating Area

Riparian Plantings

Meadow

Riparian Plantings

Riparian Plantings

Screening Area

Meadow

Jeffrey Road

SECTION DETAIL

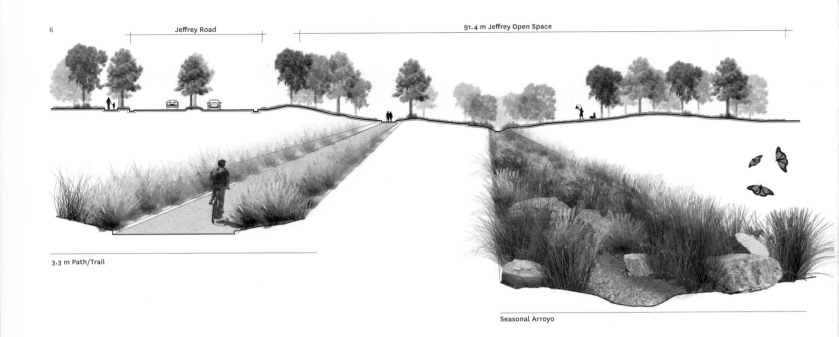

6

Jeffrey Road

91.4 m Jeffrey Open Space

3.3 m Path/Trail

Seasonal Arroyo

7

6
Section cut through Segment 2 of Jeffrey Open Space Trail. Recreational pathways and the seasonal arroyos are shown in detail as two conditions along the trail.

7
Bicyclists enjoy a sunny afternoon on the trail. According to the National Association of Homebuilders, the most desired amenity of prospective buyers is walking and jogging trails. The group surveyed people nationwide and found that trails were preferred 57 percent of the time (parks came in at 54 percent), and it was predicted to increase. Trails were also the highest preference in every ethnic group.

8
The context of native grasses, relic structures, existing trees, neighborhood fabric
and the Cleveland National Forest beyond
provide a compelling framework for the
newly integrated Jeffrey Open Space Trail.

9
Native and semi-native grasses prevail,
giving definition and character to the
trail itself.

10
Dense vegetation of fescue (*Festuca sp.*),
California gray rush (*Juncus patens*), Aleppo
pine (*Pinus halepensis*), and California
sycamore (*Platanus racemosa*) encourages
habitat creation as well as a memorable experience for runners, walkers, and residents
looking for an escape.

Seasonal arroyos are structured in parallel with the trail to direct and filter localized stormwater runoff. Native grasses, rocks, gravel, and white alder trees (*Alnus rhombifolia*) offer an interpretive identity to the arroyo and its latent ecological functions.

The arroyo disappears into a wooded section of the trail's open-space system. Visitors to the park can venture off the designated trail and explore more naturalized areas.

13a + b
Historic wooden columns preserved and integrated into the park design. Remnant wooden posts are all that remains of the historic packing house once occupied by the Irvine Valencia Growers of Orange County. Both the posts and the layout of the building's original footprint have been pre-served as a cultural landmark and part of the trail experience. The main purpose of the packing house was to protect the fruit from injury and decay during its journey from the citrus groves to the consumer.

14
The trail uses a previously underutilized tunnel for contiguous pedestrian and bicycle circulation. Other grade separators occur throughout the park, providing key points of access between residential developments.

15a

15b

16a

16b

16c

15a + b
A variety of sedges were planted within the arroyo where the seasonal rainfall enhances their range. Sedges are particularly adaptable to wet, poorly drained soils, but can also be found in upland riparian habitats and at mountain elevations.

16a – 16c
Native California grasses were planted along the trail, referencing the coastal sage scrub and grassland habitats that are protected on the Irvine Ranch. These species are drought-tolerant and many attract a variety of wildlife who feed on the flowers and seeds.

17a – 17c
Concrete etchings and mosaic tiles educate visitors about the historical and cultural heritage of the Irvine Ranch.

17a

17b

17c

MASTER PLAN FOR THE NORTH LAKE REGION OF CHONGMING ISLAND

Cultured Ecology/Ecological Culture

The master plan for the North Lake Region of Chongming Island, a site along the north branch of the Yangtze River, in Shanghai, provides for the redevelopment of 34.5 square kilometers in the northern portion of the world's largest alluvial island at 1,042 square kilometers. The plan addresses global issues of sustainable development, carbon sequestration, and wetland restoration, while providing for the educational and recreational needs of the residents of Shanghai. It offers several innovations in dealing with ecological and economic sustainability. The project is located at the mouth of the Yangtze River Delta, where substantial habitat degradation, wetland destruction, and water pollution have reached a point of critical concern and threaten the delta's overall ecosystem. The North Lake Region is zoned by the City of Shanghai for eco-tourism, ecologically sensitive agriculture, and a strategic open-space reserve. The planning approach incorporated this zoning with innovative strategies for landscape restoration that met or exceeded the current income of existing agricultural practices while manifesting carbon-offsetting programs and catalyzing research-and-development partnerships. Throughout the planning process, questions of how to blend urbanity with nature resulted in the idea that a cultured ecology could yield an ecological culture for Chongming Island. Reclaiming the ecological integrity of the North Lake Region is dependent on a clear understanding of the landscape systems of the site.

In collaboration with the Shanghai Urban Planning Administration, the landscape architects (SWA) identified the regional context, hydrology, sedimentation, historic land creation, vegetation, and agricultural uses. These studies assisted in understanding the predevelopment conditions of the largely engineered site. Currently the island has only 6,000 hectares of wetlands, in comparison to 47,000 hectares of farmland. Wetlands are second only to tropical rain forests as the most endangered habitats in the world—an argument for restoring farmland on the island to wetlands. In order to initiate this process, levees would need to be removed, which could severely affect farmer's traditional methods. As a potential solution, research was conducted into the feasibility of using afforestation and carbon-offsetting programs to economically compensate farmers for the replacement of traditional rice fields. The goals for the planning and design of the North Lake Region were as much tied to the implementation strategy as they were to the physical layout of the plan. Five prevailing goals assisted SWA in addressing the City of Shanghai's program:

1. Create a landscape structure that restores ecological function while adequately providing economic alternatives to farmers.
2. Achieve the City of Shanghai's program of having a nature-based refuge for the benefit of citizens and tourists.
3. Connect the land to existing and proposed regional systems throughout Chongming Island.
4. Create an open-space program of environmental restoration that will eliminate the impact of the historical large-scale levees.
5. Develop an open-space system that will also support ongoing international research regarding wetland creation and community-scale environmental interpretation.

SWA further identified important implementation strategies that would help promote initiatives within the master plan. The initial strategy, "Redefining Public-Private Partnerships," responds to the ownership of lands within the project. A land transfer of individual ownerships will allow high and dry land to be exchanged for low wetlands to achieve the appropriate development as well as proliferate the creation of wetlands throughout the site by the Shanghai Planning Bureau. The second strategy, "Partnerships for Growing Ecological Lands," is focused on the benefits of planting and maintaining forests for economic sustainability, beyond intrinsic environmental and social benefits. The afforestation program is based on the economic model of a carbon-offsetting program in which the government would pay

farmers or individuals for their forested land that they can then use as carbon credit. As an economic crop, forests in similar regions have yielded $120-per-hectare/year for planting and $45-per-hectare/year for health maintenance. Extending this to the upland areas, a conservative estimate for afforestation is approximately $50,000/year for the area dedicated to forest in the master plan. The third strategy, "Evolving Crops," sets in motion a partnership between the research community and agricultural landowners, as a way to provide economic income equal to grain production. In this strategy farmed land is rented to researchers for transformation into coastal wetlands and for the study of estuary habitat and coastal sedimentary processes. The fourth strategy capitalizes on the abundance of sediment in the Yangtze River and the innovation of population-based programming by the City of Shanghai. This program introduces site densification through the accretion of sediment and the creation of high land. The City of Shanghai Planning Bureau has identified a land-use ratio of one person for every 0.65 hectares. The strategy called "Adding Land—Adding Program" is based on the understanding that population-based programming is related to the total area of high land. It creates high land through sedimentation catches, providing area on which the farmer can generate income. These programs would reduce the distance traveled by vehicle and the associated carbon emissions.

The "New Terrain for the North Lake Region" is governed by a strategy for passive management of sedimentation to improve water quality while capitalizing on the potential to create land. It is a plan that provides for the restoration initiatives needed to improve a degraded ecosystem while setting in motion a set of implementation strategies that address the economic issues surrounding large-scale landscape improvements. The project focused on gathering critical environmental data, understanding current and historic socio-economic conditions, and providing planning concepts that solve problems of ecological and economic sustainability. This framework offers a vision for developers, city officials, designers, and planners to create open space and address environmental issues.

1

The design concept for Chongming Island refers to a dynamic strategy that expands on the existing highly engineered system of levees and canals, which allows agriculture to exist on land initially unfit for cultivation in the north reach of the Yangtze River and North Lake District. This strategy simultaneously introduces new landscape processes through environmentally sensitive, ecological, and agricultural experimentation. The site's projected features include sustainable aquaculture, wind farms, treatment wetlands, organic agriculture, local nurseries, farm and lake resorts, a health spa, a performance center, and a youth camp.

SEDIMENT CHRONOLOGY OF YANGTZE RIVER DELTA

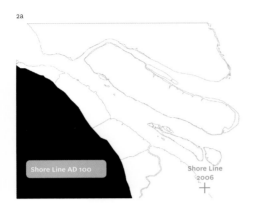

2a

Shore Line AD 100

Shore Line 2006

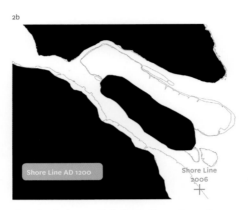

2b

Shore Line AD 1200

Shore Line 2006

Chongming Island appeared in the Yangtze River mouth some 800 years ago and divided the river into the North Branch and South Branch. At this time the North Branch was the main discharge channel.

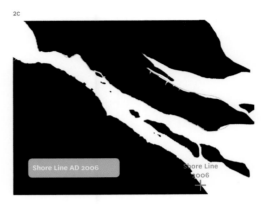

2c

Shore Line AD 2006

Shore Line 2006

The South Branch bifurcated into the North Channel by Changxing Island, which emerged from the South Branch. Jiuduan Shoal appeared after the 1954 flood.

HYDROLOGY OF YANGTZE RIVER DELTA

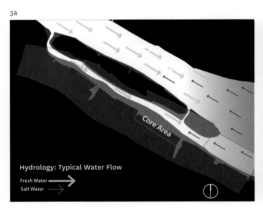

3a

Core Area

Hydrology: Typical Water Flow

Fresh Water
Salt Water

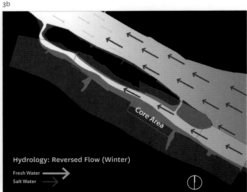

3b

Core Area

Hydrology: Reversed Flow (Winter)

Fresh Water
Salt Water

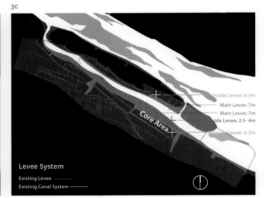

3c

Core Area

Inside Levee: 4-5m
Main Levee: 7m
Main Levee: 7m
Side Levee: 2.5- 4m
Inside Levee: 4-5m

Levee System

Existing Levee
Existing Canal System

2a – 2d

The diagrams show the changing geo-morphology of the Yangtze River Delta. Deposition and erosion of sediments over time have created what is now one of the largest alluvial deposits in Asia.

3a – 3c

The hydrology of the Yangtze River Delta experiences two distinct periods of current flow. The primary period occurs from February through October where the dominant flow originates from the river. The result is a lower salinity rate due to the influx of fresh water. In the months from November through January, the reverse occurs where the dominant flow comes from the East China Sea, increasing the salinity rate. It is during these months that the North Lake is replenished, resulting in visibly bluer water. The overall system is controlled by the ubiquitous levee structures which typically stand at an elevation of 7 meters.

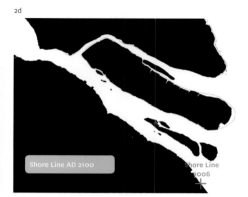

Shore Line AD 2100

Shore Line 2006

Currently the North Branch is shrinking and Chongming Island is gradually linking with the north bank of the Yangtze River. Finally Chongming Island will be connected to Jangshu Province. The east side of Chongming Island is predicted to increase. Several huge shoals will create a vast land area in the future

4

SEDIMENT TRANSPORT
Statistics in Yangtze River

Total Sediment Transport: Annual in Yangtze River
486 million tons

Total Sediment Deposit at Branches in Vicinity of the River Mouth
155

Total Sediments Transported to the Hangzhou Bay
238

Total Sediment Transported to the Ocean
92

Sea Bed Elevation: 1900

Sea Bed Elevation: 2000   + 8 meters

Haihe River

Yellow River

Yangtze River

ANNUAL SEDIMENT LOADS

Haihe River: Sediments from the Sea Cause a Small River Mouth
182 million tons

Yellow River: Fan-Shaped Delta
1000

Yangtze River: Bifurcation of Channels with Delta Islands
486

HIGH TIDE +6.00

LOW TIDE +2.80

4

As development upstream continues, research illustrates that the sedimentation process will accelerate and ultimately cap off the north reach of the river. The design approach would take advantage of the 486 million metric tons of soil and sediment that travel down the river and provide a new landscape for the people of the Shanghai area. The project would expand habitat and increase biodiversity which would improve the function and appreciation of this unique site. At a global scale, the project addresses water-quality degradation and habitat segmentation that are the results of human-induced erosive processes.

5

With a set of strategies for sediment accretion, new habitat can emerge or be cultivated as a means of economic and environmental growth. The diagrammatic section illustrates the formation of an estuary ecosystem and the variety of species such as streambank bulrush (*Scirpus triqueter*), common reed (*Phragmites Australis*), and bunge (*Suaeda glauca*) that make this landscape home.

6

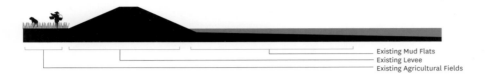

Existing Mud Flats
Existing Levee
Existing Agricultural Fields

Human Cultivation Modules
Sediment Accretion

Accelerated Sediment Accretion

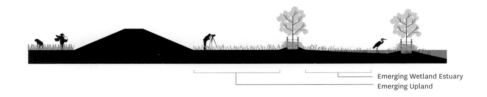

Emerging Wetland Estuary
Emerging Upland

Cultured Ecology/
Ecological Culture

6

Changes to the local levee system are an initial step in altering the site's terrain and function. Depending on location, levees will be removed or new ones constructed, while in other areas sediment will be allowed to accrete, producing new land and promoting new use. Flood-control infrastructure will be maintained but modified in places to create new landscapes.

HABITAT CULTIVATION

7a

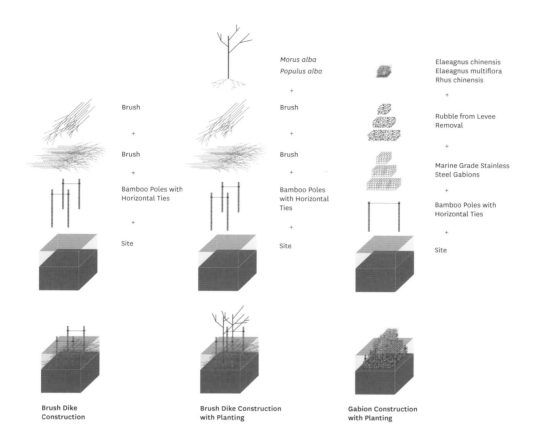

Morus alba
Populus alba

+

Brush

+

Brush

+

Bamboo Poles with Horizontal Ties

+

Site

Brush

+

Brush

+

Bamboo Poles with Horizontal Ties

+

Site

Elaeagnus chinensis
Elaeagnus multiflora
Rhus chinensis

+

Rubble from Levee Removal

+

Marine Grade Stainless Steel Gabions

+

Bamboo Poles with Horizontal Ties

+

Site

Brush Dike Construction

Brush Dike Construction with Planting

Gabion Construction with Planting

MODULE DIMENSION AND DENSITY

7b

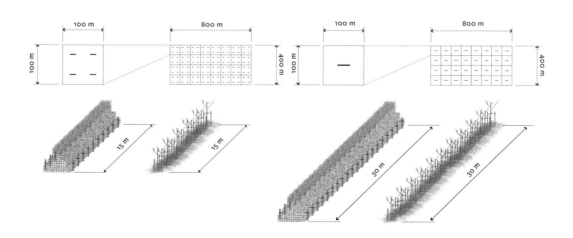

7a + b
The diagrams illustrate methods of habitat cultivation. Structural materials are used to provide support for herbaceous plants and shrubs to take root within newly created coastal wetlands, estuaries, and upland forests.

BIODIVERSITY COMPARISON

8

Column 1 (top)

Herbaceous plants
Imperata cylindrica
Scirpus mariqueter
Scripus triqueter
Phragmites australis
Aeleropus littoralis
Suaeda glauca

Fish + Benthos
Bullacta exarata
Angulia japonica
Coilia ectenes
Coilia mystus
Moerella iridescens
Metaplax longipes
Mugil cephalus
Sinonovacula constricta
Trichiurus haumela

Birds
Calidris alpina
Charadrius alexandrinus
Calidris tenuirostris
Calidris acuminata
Calidris ferruginea

Mammals
Mustala sibirica
Erinaceus europaeus

People
Research Scientists

Column 2 (top)

Herbaceous plants
Imperata cylindrica
Scirpus mariqueter
Scripus triqueter
Phragmites australis
Aeleropus littoralis
Suaeda glauca

Shrubs
Tamarix ramosissima
Eleaegnus multiflora
Eleaegnus umbellata
Rhus chinensis

Fish + Benthos
Bullacta exarata
Angulia japonica
Coilia ectenes
Coilia mystus
Moerella iridescens
Metaplax longipes
Mugil cephalus
Sinonovacula constricta
Trichiurus haumela

Birds
Calidris alpina
Charadrius alexandrinus
Calidris tenuirostris
Calidris acuminata
Calidris ferruginea

Mammals
Mustala sibirica
Erinaceus europaeus

People
Research Scientists

Column 3 (top)

Herbaceous plants
Imperata cylindrica
Scirpus mariqueter
Scripus triqueter
Phragmites australis
Aeleropus littoralis
Suaeda glauca

Shrubs
Tamarix ramosissima
Eleaegnus multiflora
Eleaegnus umbellata
Rhus chinensis

Fish + Benthos
Bullacta exarata
Angulia japonica
Coilia ectenes
Coilia mystus
Moerella iridescens
Metaplax longipes
Mugil cephalus
Sinonovacula constricta
Trichiurus haumela

Amphibians
Cuora trifiscata

Birds
Calidris alpina
Charadrius alexandrinus
Calidris tenuirostris
Calidris acuminata
Calidris ferruginea
Grus monacha
Platalea minor
Podiceps nigricollis
Podiceps ruficollis
Pelicanus philippensis
Ardea cinera
Ciconia ciconia
Ciconia nigra
Hydrophasianus chirurgus

Mammals
Mustala sibirica
Erinaceus europaeus

People
Research Scientists

Column 4 (top)

Herbaceous plants
Imperata cylindrica
Scirpus mariqueter
Scripus triqueter
Phragmites australis
Aeleropus littoralis
Suaeda glauca

Shrubs
Tamarix ramosissima
Eleaegnus multiflora
Eleaegnus umbellata
Rhus chinensis

Fish + Benthos
Bullacta exarata
Angulia japonica
Coilia ectenes
Coilia mystus
Moerella iridescens
Metaplax longipes
Mugil cephalus
Sinonovacula constricta
Trichiurus haumela

Birds
Calidris alpina
Charadrius alexan-drinus
Calidris tenuirostris
Calidris acuminata
Calidris ferruginea
Grus monacha
Platalea minor
Podiceps nigricollis
Podiceps ruficollis
Pelicanus philippensis
Ardea cinera
Ciconia ciconia
Ciconia nigra
Hydrophasianus chirurgus

Mammals
Mustala sibirica
Erinaceus europaeus

People
Research Scientists
Eco Tourists

Coastal Wetlands

Rice

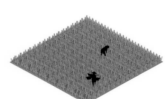

Rice — Column 1

Herbaceous plants
Oryza sativa

Fish + Benthos
Bullacta exarata

Birds
Ardea cinerea

Mammals
Mustala sibirica
Neomys fodiens

People
Farmers

Rice — Column 2

Herbaceous plants
Oryza sativa

Fish + Benthos
Bullacta exarata

Birds
Ardea cinerea

Mammals
Mustala sibirica
Neomys fodiens

People
Farmers

Rice — Column 3

Herbaceous plants
Oryza sativa

Fish + Benthos
Bullacta exarata

Birds
Ardea cinerea

Mammals
Mustala sibirica
Neomys fodiens

People
Farmers

Rice — Column 4

Herbaceous plants
Oryza sativa

Fish + Benthos
Bullacta exarata
Birds
Ardea cinerea

Mammals
Mustala sibirica
Neomys fodiens

People
Farmers

8

As a result of the proposed land transformations, some of the current agricultural lands would ultimately be replaced. In order to compensate farmers for the land lost, an afforestation program was proposed along with a strategy for economic income generated through the cultivation of coastal wetlands. The estuary habitat that surrounds the North Lake Region of Chongming Island supports a tremendous amount of wildlife and biomass. The diagrams illustrate the increase in ecological diversity over time as wetlands develop. Through a rental partnership with the Shanghai Urban Planning Administration these coastal wetlands can be just as economically viable for farmers as crop cultivation.

172

INCREMENT

PROFIT COMPARISON

Developer leases land to Farmer

Developer
[landowner]

Farmer
[lessee]

Developer
[landowner]

Researcher
[lessee]

Shanghai Urban Planning
[program facilitator]

Corporations
[investors]

Developer leases land to Researcher

Researcher pays Developer rent with money from the carbon tradeable offsets program

Researcher participates in Shanghai Urban Planning Administration's carbon tradeable offsets program

Shanghai Urban Planning Administration pays Researcher from a fund created by the sale of carbon tradeable offsets

Shanghai Urban Planning Administration finds Corporations that will invest in carbon tradeable offsets

Farmer pays Developer rent with profits from farming

9
The afforestation proposal is based on the sequestration of carbon, and would provide an additional means of economically balancing the loss in agricultural production. Carbon tradeable offsets could be accrued by the farmers, which would help reduce emissions and create a model for open space in the Yangtze River Delta.

10
This section illustrates the habitat diversity found in fresh water wetlands and upland forests. Cultivated trees within the forest sequester carbon, while wetlands filter and treat waterways and stormwater runoff. Some notable wetland species are common reed (*Phragmites australi*), mud sedge (*Carex limosa*), and ladysthumb (*Polygonum persicaria*).

1 Dongping Forest
2 Typical Habitat Overpass
3 Qianewi Eco-Village
4 Jiangsu Province
5 Shuttle Bus Route
6 North Lake New Town
7 East Wetlands, Interpretive Zone and Research + Development Area

a Nursery
b Sustainable Aquaculture
c Organic Agriculture
d Farm Resort
e Living Machine
f Treatment Wetlands
g North Forest Buffer

h Lake Resort
i Health Spa
j Performance Center
k Youth Camp
l Wind Farm
m Salt Marsh

11

The landscape's central focus was connectivity. The new habitats and ecosystems created within the site would become corridors to the adjacent Dongping Forest to the west, the new forests proposed in the center of Chongming Island, and to the estuarine landscapes to the east. The master plan highlights different areas of program and development and how systems connect to the larger regional landscape.

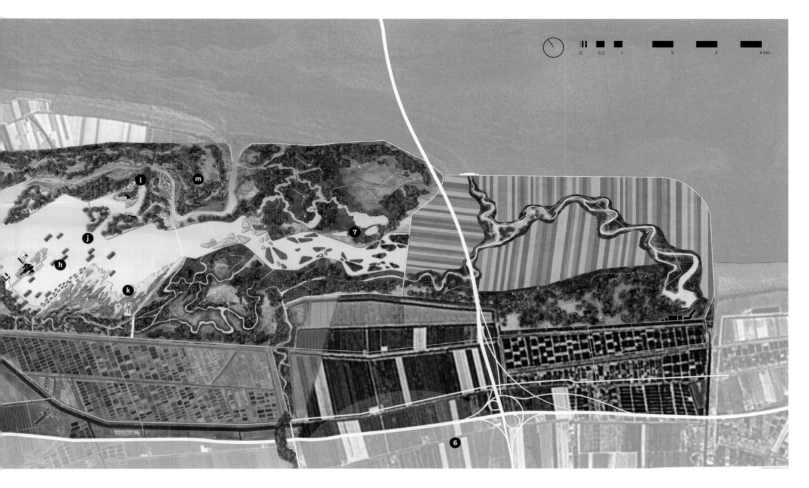

12

The utilization of wind farms became part of the development plan for the Dongtang Forest. The 20-turbine farm has the capacity to generate 15,000,000 kWh/year. These efforts, combined with the afforestation program, will contribute to harnessing global emissions and promote sustainability.

13

View looking out to the cultivated habitats and unique waterway edge produced through sediment accretion. Tourism is the final site strategy, helping to promote both the economy and education. Destinations on site will include a farm resort and agricultural research facilities, lake and spa resorts, wetland interpretive tours, trails, and a youth camp.

KYUNG-CHUN CLOSED RAILWAY RENOVATION

Repurposing a Post-Industrial Corridor

As the world's largest metropolitan area by population, Seoul has witnessed extensive development (and redevelopment) of its core urban centers and supporting infrastructure in recent years. With over half of the country's estimated 50 million people living within the Seoul capital area, issues of population density, housing, transit, and sustainability have arisen. As a reactive measure, the City of Seoul is actively assessing its urban and rural landscapes in search of opportunities to create open space for active and passive recreation. More than 70 percent of South Korea's terrain is classified as rugged, and thus finding accessible open space within walking distance is a challenge. With the advent of new technology, rail lines have been created to better serve the KTX high-speed train, leaving the obsolete tracks abandoned as brownfield sites, polluted with petrochemicals and heavy metals.

A design competition for one such rail line (east of Seoul) was held to demonstrate the potential for adaptive reuse of outmoded infrastructure as a connective open-space framework for community revitalization, water-quality enhancement, recreation, and wildlife. Set in varying terrain along 6.3 kilometers between Seoul and Chun-Cheon City, the rail corridor measures 22.7 hectares in size, with an average of 30 meters in width. It crosses the Han River and runs perpendicular to the drainage pattern, effectively intercepting and detaining runoff from a substantial urban watershed. Safety walls along each edge of the railway form additional barriers. The existing characteristics of the railway corridor present opportunities to incrementally build new recreational, cultural, and social programs into the rapidly changing context of metropolitan Seoul. Design for the rail line interprets the cultural landscape and establishes new destinations within the larger green network, through instilling a varied program of activities related to the adjacent neighborhoods and preserving pieces of the historic

rail structure. In contrast to the surrounding dynamic topography, the repurposed railway corridor acts as a level horizontal datum, generating a new kind of experience for bicyclists, pedestrians, runners, and tourists, which speaks to the notions of destination, education, and discovery. At a larger scale, the corridor addresses the urban watershed by utilizing various sectional configurations to hold and treat water in wetlands, gardens, and woodlands before diverting it to the river. As part of the design, safety walls were removed (fragments were maintained for exhibits and historical reference) and pedestrian crossings were placed at strategic connections between neighborhoods. Rail platforms become viewing stations along the continuous bicycle and pedestrian trails, while new activities (an art museum at the university campus, mixed-use commercial buildings near residential high-rises, and sports fields adjacent to schools) help to reinforce existing communities. A series of "green strings" connects wooded mountain slopes to the Han River, creating routes for wildlife and knitting the new open space into the larger landscape.

2a

2b

2c

2d

1 (opposite)

Aerial view of the existing site conditions. The abandoned rail line runs through the city's dense fabric as a forgotten and neglected relic. Where it is not elevated, much of the rail is fenced-in to prevent access and discourage use. Reenvisioning the site for public recreation and inhabitation involved a strategy for brownfield remediation and water treatment, but also provided precedent for the reuse of infrastructure to create open space.

2a – 2d

Rough sketches illustrate conditions along the railway and give a sense of site character, while depicting early design concepts. The drawings offer ideas for accessibility, program, and adaptive reuse of the rail corridor.

RAILWAY CORRIDORS

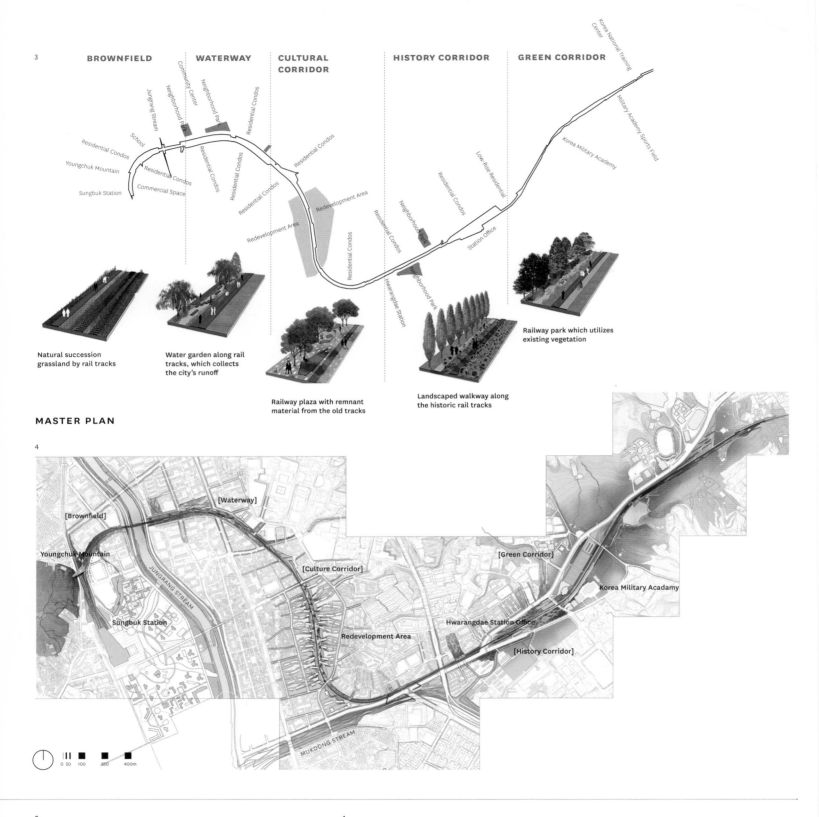

3

| BROWNFIELD | WATERWAY | CULTURAL CORRIDOR | HISTORY CORRIDOR | GREEN CORRIDOR |

Natural succession grassland by rail tracks

Water garden along rail tracks, which collects the city's runoff

Railway plaza with remnant material from the old tracks

Landscaped walkway along the historic rail tracks

Railway park which utilizes existing vegetation

MASTER PLAN

4

3

Outline of design implementations and experiences created through traversing the abandoned rail. The site is transformed from unused infrastructure into urban public park. Throughout the process, pieces of the old rail remain as a palimpsest. The tracks are kept in certain areas as a reminder of the network of transportation connecting city

and people. Pieces of the rail wall are also left to foster nostalgia and site memory. The landscape along the rail park transitions from land under natural succession, to vegetable gardens, to fields of flowers to urban forest. New infrastructure fills in around the remnant fragments and park land, providing integration and a sense of intimacy.

4

The master plan for the competition highlights connectivity. No longer just a linear track, the railway becomes a fully integrated park and living ecosystem. The project design creates a connective tissue between the mountains, the city, open space, surface water, and the river.

5

6

8

CONNECTIVE CORRIDORS

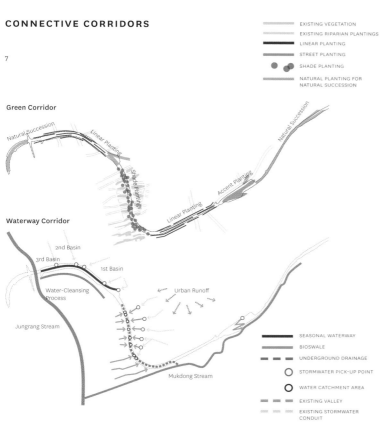

EXISTING VEGETATION
EXISTING RIPARIAN PLANTINGS
LINEAR PLANTING
STREET PLANTING
SHADE PLANTING
NATURAL PLANTING FOR
NATURAL SUCCESSION

7

Green Corridor

Natural Succession
Linear Planting
Shade Plantings
Linear Planting
Accent Plantings
Natural Succession
Natural Succession

Waterway Corridor

2nd Basin
3rd Basin
1st Basin
Water-Cleansing Process
Urban Runoff
Jungrang Stream
Mukdong Stream

SEASONAL WATERWAY
BIOSWALE
UNDERGROUND DRAINAGE
STORMWATER PICK-UP POINT
WATER CATCHMENT AREA
EXISTING VALLEY
EXISTING STORMWATER CONDUIT

5
Seasonal wetlands run parallel to the park. Varying topography allows for sloping steps down to the water and densely vegetated embankments. The waterways provide temporal change and promote ecological diversity, while serving to treat water runoff.

6
The overlapping pathways and integrated open space which provide opportunities of running, walking, and social gathering.

7
The diagram shows the two strategies operating along the railway park. The concept of "green strings" refers to the ecological and environmental treatments helping to remediate soil and cleanse water throughout the site. The planting strategy provides a visual "green string" that runs through the city, but also employs natural succession in areas where the land is disturbed or degraded. The treatment and management of water is the other strategy working on site. Seasonal wetlands are incorporated along the rail, to collect and cleanse water through biofiltration. In addition, a system of bioswales diverts runoff into underground drainage systems, helping to reclaim water.

8
A view of the park showing changes in the materiality of the different pathways and plazas. Pieces of the old rail tracks are also preserved as part of the site memory.

9

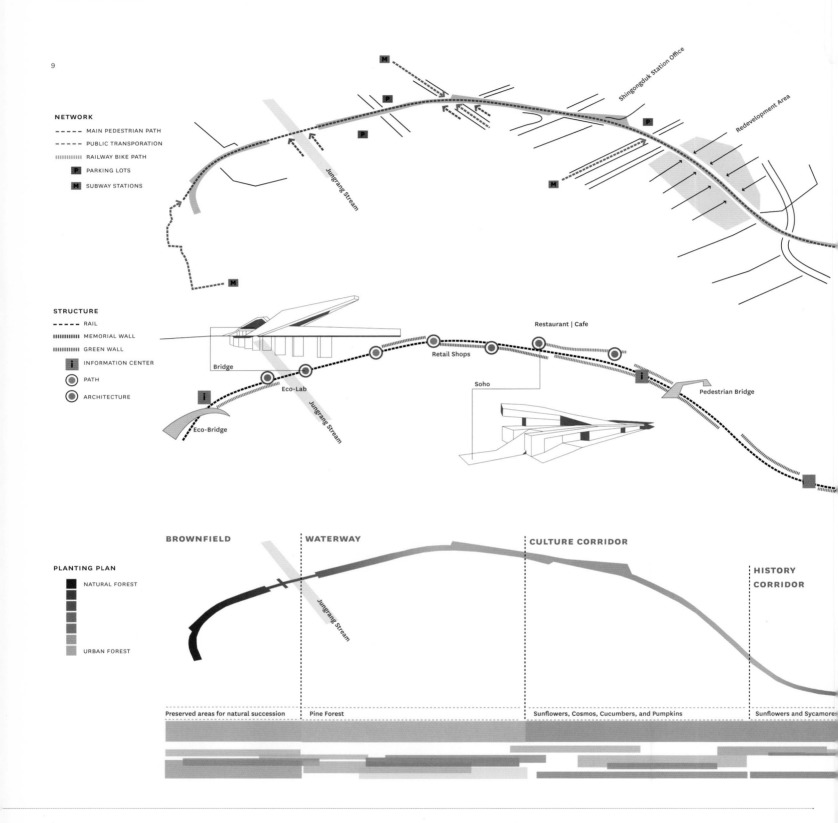

NETWORK

- - - - - MAIN PEDESTRIAN PATH
- - - - PUBLIC TRANSPORATION
||||||||| RAILWAY BIKE PATH
P PARKING LOTS
M SUBWAY STATIONS

Jungrang Stream

Shingongduk Station Office

Redevelopment Area

STRUCTURE

- - - - - RAIL
||||||||| MEMORIAL WALL
||||||||| GREEN WALL
i INFORMATION CENTER
⊙ PATH
⊙ ARCHITECTURE

Bridge

Eco-Lab

Eco-Bridge

Jungrang Stream

Retail Shops

Soho

Restaurant | Cafe

Pedestrian Bridge

PLANTING PLAN

■ NATURAL FOREST

URBAN FOREST

BROWNFIELD   **WATERWAY**   **CULTURE CORRIDOR**   **HISTORY CORRIDOR**

Jungrang Stream

Preserved areas for natural succession   Pine Forest   Sunflowers, Cosmos, Cucumbers, and Pumpkins   Sunflowers and Sycamore

9

This diagram disassembles the design into the three overlapping systems which integrate the urban, the public, and the natural. The network system maintains the rails' function of transportation, and provides pathways for overlapping programs with numerous points of access and routes to other areas of the city. New and old structures line the rail and add to the existing urban density. Cultural venues, restaurants, and information centers offer entertainment and educational opportunities, while bridges, platforms, and vertical wall fragments create experiential moments throughout the park. Finally, the planting plan incorporates natural succession, urban forest, and the cultivated gardens into a continuous corridor of green, which links into the surrounding regional ecosystems.

10

In the transformed rail line, the linear infrastructure remains, but the parallel walkways, access points, waterways, and plantings expand perpendicularly providing connectivity and linking city and park into a contiguous public space.

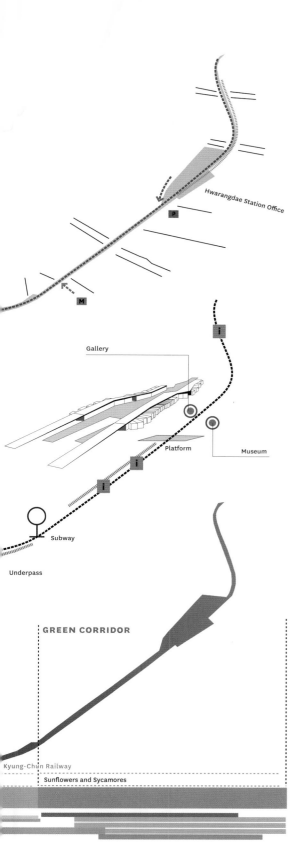

Hwarangdae Station Office

P

M

i

Gallery

Platform

i

Museum

i

Subway

Underpass

GREEN CORRIDOR

Kyung-Chun Railway

Sunflowers and Sycamores

PROJECT CREDITS

ANNING RIVER NEW SOUTH TOWN
Miyi County, Sichuan, China

OWNER/CLIENT:
Government Property Investment Ltd.
Miyi County, City of Panzhihua,
Sichuan Province, China

DATES: 2008–2010

SIZE: 330 hectares

SWA OFFICE/PEOPLE:
Los Angeles, California

Gerdo Aquino, Patrick Curran, Ying-Yu Hung,
Dawn Dyer, Alexander Robinson, Youngmin Kim,
Grace Qin Gao, Natalie Sandoval, Ying-Hu,
Michael Hee, Ryan Hsu, Hyun-Min Kim, Qiu Hong
Tang, Gary Garcia, Meng Yang

TEAM:
Studio Shift, *Architecture*
ARUP, *Sustainable Planning
and Engineering Consultants*
Shanghai Tongji Urban Planning
& Design, *Control Plan*
Biomatrix Water, *Ecological Engineering*
CBRE, *Economic Research Consultants*

BEIZHI RIVER WATERFRONT
Fuyang, China

CLIENT:
Fuyang Planning Bureau, City of Fuyang

DATE: 2010

SIZE: 56.7 hectares

SWA OFFICE/PEOPLE:
Los Angeles, California

Ying-Yu Hung, Gerdo Aquino, Michael Hee,
Carlos Hernandez, Dawn Dyer, Na Ra Park,
Woonghee Lee, Qin Gao, Qiu Hong Tang,
Oliver Seabolt, Huicheng Zhong

TEAM:
China Hanjia Design Group,
LDI (Local Design Institute, China)

BUFFALO BAYOU PROMENADE
Houston, Texas, USA

OWNER/CLIENT:
Buffalo Bayou Partnership

DATES: 2001–2006

SIZE: .9 kilometers (Phase 1);
     40 kilometers total

SWA OFFICE/PEOPLE:
Houston, Texas

Kevin Shanley, Nancy Fleming, Scott McCready, Mary
Edwards, Lance Lowry, John Cutler, Jennifer Kirton,
Timothy Peterson, Alaa Raslan, Rhett Rentrop, Ashley
Sutch

TEAM:
Fugro South, Inc.,
Geotechnical Engineering
United Engineers, Inc., *Civil Engineering*
Ken Tan and Associates,
Structural Engineering
Ferguson Consulting, Inc.,
Electrical Engineering
Mary L. Goldsby Associates,
Planting Design
Ellis Glueck and Associates,
Irrigation Design
L'Observatoire International, *Lighting Design*
Boyer, Inc., *Contractor*
Stephen Korns, *Artist*

CALIFORNIA ACADEMY OF SCIENCES
San Francisco, California, USA

OWNER/CLIENT:
California Academy of Sciences

DATES: 2002–2008

SIZE: 4.038-hectares; roof: 1.012 hectares

SWA OFFICE/PEOPLE:
Sausalito, California

John Loomis, Lawrence Reed, Zachary Davis, Michael
Odum, Sergio Lima, Masato Kametani, Rick Story,
Haven Kiers

TEAM:
Renzo Piano Building Workshop, *Architecture*
Stantec Architecture, *Architecture*
Chong + Partners, *Executive Architect
(prior to Stantec Architecture)*
ARUP, *Structural/MEP Engineering, Sustainability
Consulting*
Rana Creek Habitat Restoration, *Horticultural
Consultant*
Dickson Associates, *Irrigation*

CENTRAL OPEN SPACE IN MAC
Chungcheongnam-do Province, South Korea

OWNER/CLIENT:
Korea Institute of Landscape Architecture

DATE: 2007

SIZE: 72.9 square kilometers

SWA OFFICE/PEOPLE:
Los Angeles, California

Gerdo Aquino, Youngmin Kim,
Mio Watanabe, Lynn Kiang

TEAM:
Studio Shift, *Architecture*

GUBEI PEDESTRIAN PROMENADE
Shanghai, China

CLIENT:
Shanghai Gubei (Group) Co. Ltd./
City of Shanghai

DATES: 2005–2009

SIZE: 31.82 hectares

SWA OFFICE/PEOPLE:
Los Angeles, California

Ying-Yu Hung, Gerdo Aquino, Hyun-Min Kim, Leah
Broder, Kui-Chi Ma, Dawn Dyer, Yoonju Chang, Shuang
Yu, Ryan Hsu, Youngmin Kim

JEFFREY OPEN SPACE TRAIL
Irvine, California, USA

OWNER/CLIENT:
Irvine Community Development
Company, City of Irvine

DATES: 1999–

SIZE: 4.4 kilometers

SWA OFFICE/PEOPLE:
Laguna Beach, California

Richard Law, Jim Maloney, Sean O'Malley, Don Young,
Claudia Kath, Deni Ruggeri, Grace Zu, Trent Okumura,
Bingshan Wong

TEAM:
Hunsaker and Associates,
Engineering Services
dd Pagano, *Irrigation*

KATY TRAIL
Dallas, Texas, USA

CLIENT:
Friends of the Katy Trail,
City of Dallas

DATES: 1999–2007

SIZE: 7.2 kilometers

SWA OFFICE/PEOPLE:
Dallas, Texas

Chuck McDaniel, David Bickel, Shuyi Chang, Shawn
Luther, Todd Strawn

TEAM:
City of Dallas, *Trail Construction*
The Office of Christopher Miller,
Trail Entries, Trail Planting
David Rolston Landscape Architects,
Trail Planting
Brockette Davis Drake, *Structural Engineering*
Oracle Engineering, *Civil Engineering*
Robinette Associates, *Electrical Engineering*
Texas Irrigation Design, *Irrigation*
Hossley Lighting Associates,
Lighting Master Plan
James Richards, *Artist*

**KYUNG-CHUN CLOSED RAILWAY
RENOVATION**
Seoul, South Korea

OWNER/CLIENT:
City of Seoul

DATE: 2009

SIZE: 6.3 kilometers

SWA OFFICE/PEOPLE:
San Francisco, California

Jim Lee, Ji Hyun Yoo

TEAM:
CA Landscape Design,
Landscape Architecture

LEWIS AVENUE CORRIDOR
Las Vegas, Nevada, USA

CLIENT: City of Las Vegas

DATES: 2001–2002

SIZE: .4 kilometers

SWA OFFICE/PEOPLE:
Sausalito, California

Jim Lee, Lawrence Reed, Sergio Lima, Patrick Curran,
Rick Story, Aleksandra Dudukovic

TEAM:
City of Las Vegas, *Engineering Design*
Russ Mitchell and Associates, *Irrigation*
Poggemeyer Design Group,
Civil and Structural Engineering
JBA Consulting Engineers,
Electrical Engineering
The Fountain People, *Fountain Mechanics*
Xypex Chemical Corp,
Horticulture Consultants

**MASTER PLAN FOR THE NORTH LAKE
REGION OF CHONGMING ISLAND**
Shanghai, China

OWNER/CLIENT:
Shanghai Urban Planning
Administration

DATES: 2006–2007

SIZE: 34 square kilometers

SWA OFFICE/PEOPLE:
Los Angeles, California

Gerdo Aquino, Patrick Curran, Leah Broder, Hyun-Min
Kim, Youngmin Kim, Takako Tajima, Mio Watanabe,
Ying-Yu Hung, Lynn Kiang, Dawn Dyer, Pamela Barger,
Kui-Chi Ma

TEAM:
EOS Ecology, *Habitat Restoration*

MILTON STREET PARK
Los Angeles, California, USA

CLIENT:
Mountains Recreation and Conservation Authority,
City of Los Angeles

DATES: 2008–2011 (projected)

SIZE: 48 hectares

SWA OFFICE/PEOPLE:
Los Angeles, California

Ying-Yu Hung, Gerdo Aquino, Qin Gao,
Pamela Barger, Ryan Hsu, Youngmin Kim, Dawn Dyer,
Na Ra Park, Michael Hee

TEAM:
PSOMAS, *Environmental Engineering*
Soil and Plant Laboratories, *Soils Analysis*

NINGBO ECO-CORRIDOR
Ningbo City, China

CLIENT:
Ningbo Planning Bureau, City of Ningbo

DATES: 2006–2008

SIZE: 101.2 hectares

SWA OFFICE/PEOPLE:
Sausalito, California

Hui-Li Lee, Scott Chuang, Roy Imamura, Jack Wu,
Kathy Sun, Xun Li, Chih-wei Lin, Huiqing Kuang,
Chih-wei Chang

TEAM:
Ojanen_Chiou Architects, LLP, *Architecture*
Herrera Environmental Consultants, *Environmental
Consultants*
Biomatrix Water, *Ecological Engineering*

SHUNDE NEW CITY
Shunde, China

CLIENT:
Shunde Planning Bureau, City of Shunde

DATE: 2009

SIZE: 72 square kilometers

SWA OFFICE/PEOPLE:
Laguna Beach, California

Sean O'Malley, Xiao Zheng,
Scott Melbourne, Chunghwan Sung,
Qiuhong Tang

TEAM:
Gamble Associates, *Scenery Design*
Herrera Environmental Consultants,
Environmental Consultants

THE AUTHORS

GERDO AQUINO

Gerdo Aquino is the new president of SWA and adjunct associate professor of landscape architecture at the University of Southern California. He is a landscape architect and urban designer interested in issues of urbanism, landscape infrastructure, transit, and historic ecologies. Gerdo Aquino received his Master of Landscape Architecture degree in 1996 from Harvard University Graduate School of Design and his undergraduate degree from the University of Florida.

CHARLES WALDHEIM

Charles Waldheim is the John E. Irving Professor of Landscape Architecture, Chair of the Department of Landscape Architecture at Harvard University Graduate School of Design, and principal of Urban Agency, a multi-disciplinary consultancy in design and contemporary urbanism. His teaching and research examine the relationships between landscape and contemporary urbanism. Waldheim coined the term "landscape urbanism" to describe the recent emergence of landscape as a medium of urban order for the contemporary city. Waldheim has authored numerous articles and chapters on the topic, and edited *The Landscape Urbanism Reader* (2006).

YING-YU HUNG

Ying-Yu Hung is a principal of SWA Los Angeles, co-founder of the Infrastructure Research Initiative, and a Studio Professor at the University of Southern California. Her work focuses on interactions between complex urban systems, which argues that the potential of landscape can be maximized if examined within the context of infrastructure and urbanism. Hung was the recipient of multiple awards including the 2009 ASLA National Honor Award for Zobon City Sculpture Garden, and the 2008 ASLA National Honor Award for Chongming Island North Lake Region—both in Shanghai, China. Ying-Yu Hung received her Master of Landscape Architecture degree in 1994 from Harvard University Graduate School of Design.

JULIA CZERNIAK

Julia Czerniak is an Associate Professor of Architecture at Syracuse University and the inaugural Director of UPSTATE. She is also a registered landscape architect and founder of CLEAR, an interdisciplinary design practice. Czerniak's design work focuses on urban landscapes in the Rust-Belt cities of the United States, and it has been recognized with numerous awards. Czerniak is editor of *Large Parks* (2007) and *Case: Downsview Park Toronto* (2001), that focus on contemporary design approaches to public parks and the relationship between landscape and cities. Other writings include essays in *Landscape Alchemy: The Work of Hargreaves Associates* (2009); *Fertilizers: Olin Eisenman* (2006); *Landscape Urbanism* (2006); and *Assemblage 34* (1998).

ADRIAAN GEUZE

Adriaan Geuze, landscape architect and urban designer, is founder of West 8 urban design and landscape architecture, a team of architects, urban designers, landscape architects, and industrial designers with offices in Rotterdam, Brussels, Toronto, and New York. After winning the prestigious Prix-de-Rome, Geuze established a leading international reputation with his unique approach to planning and designing the public environment, relating contemporary culture, urban identity, architecture, public space, and environmental engineering. Geuze has authored numerous books and essays, including *Mosaics* (2007), *Polders!* (2005), *Colonizing the Void* (1996), *In Holland stat een huis* (1995), and *Accelerating Darwin* (1993).

MATTHEW SKJONSBERG

Matthew Skjonsberg, architect and urban designer, is a practitioner with strong roots in design theory and research, and works closely with Adriaan Geuze. He has obtained degrees from Taliesin and ETH Zurich, and has an active career in research and education, including recent lectures at the Berlage Institute, the Harvard University Graduate School of Design, and the University of Texas at Austin. He has authored a number of essays in the field of urban planning and his work has been published in various contexts, including *Explorations in Architecture: Teaching, Design, Research* (Reto Geiser, ed. 2008), and *Cities of Change: Addis Ababa* (Marc Angélil, ed. 2009).

ALEXANDER ROBINSON

Alexander Robinson, a graduate of Harvard University Graduate School of Design, is an Adjunct Professor of Landscape Architecture at the University of Southern California and an independent practitioner. He has worked on many large-scale landscape infrastructure projects, including a two-year master plan for the Los Angeles River. As an associate in the Los Angeles office of SWA, his focus was on advancing landscape practice through expertise and frameworks fostered in his book, *Living Systems: Innovative Technologies and Materials in Landscape Architecture* (2007)—a hybrid theoretical and practical exploration of the new potentials of landscape architecture materiality. Recent research is devoted to urban heat-island infrastructure and is exhibited at the Shanghai World Expo and Xi'an 2011 Horticultural Exhibit.

ILLUSTRATION CREDITS

All graphics courtesy of SWA unless otherwise noted.

GERDO AQUINO
Pages: 17a, 36-37, 46 (12), 57 (1abc), 59 (6), 71 (4c), 75 (9-10), 77 (13abc), 86-87, 105 (14b), 108 (20), 112 (32c), 113 (33), 115 (1ab), 118, 120-121, 137 (1b-2), 146-147

BOYER, INC.
Pages: 43 (8)

BUFFALO BAYOU PARTNERSHIP
Pages: 39 (1-2)

CALIFORNIA ACADEMY OF SCIENCES
Page: 67 (1)

CA LANDSCAPE DESIGN CO., LTD.
Page: 176 (1)

YOUNGJOON CHOI
Page: 88 (1-2)

KRISTEN ENGLISH
Page: 115 (2)

DAVID FLETCHER
Page: 31

TOM FOX
Pages: 15, 45 (10abc), 46 (13-15), 48 (18), 50 (19), 51 (21-22ab), 52-53, 54 (25-26), 55 (27), 68-69, 70 (3ab), 71 (4a), 74 (7), 75 (8), 76 (11), 77 (14), 82 (10), 88 (3), 92 (8), 93 (9ab-10), 94 (11-13ab), 95 (14), 96 (15abcd), 97 (16-18), 98 (19abcd-20), 99 (21ab-22), 102 (5), 103 (6-7ab), 104 (9, 11), 105 (12ab, 16), 106-107, 108 (19, 21), 109 (22abc), 110 (24, 25, 26a), 111 (28abcde), 112 (30-32ab), 113 (36ab), 129 (3), 130 (5), 131 (7ab), 132 (8-10), 133 (11-13), 134 (14-15), 135 (16ab-17), 157 (2), 160 (7), 161 (8-9), 162 (11-12), 163 (13ab), 164 (16bc), 165 (17abc)

YING-YU HUNG
Pages: 16, 17bc, 104 (10), 105 (14a), 110 (26b, 27a), 113 (34), 137 (1a)

KATY RAILROAD HISTORICAL SOCIETY
Page: 129 (1)

GORAN KOSANOVIC
Page: 85 (15a)

HUI-LI LEE
Page: 78 (1)

JOHN LOOMIS
Page: 71 (4b)

KUI-CHI MA
Page: 110 (27b)

SEAN O'MALLEY
Pages: 123 (1abc), 125 (3)

JIM MALONEY
Page: 157 (3)

GARY MORRIS
Page: 129 (2b)

RHETT RENTROP
Page: 40 (5ab)

DENISE RETALLACK
Pages: 161 (10), 163 (14), 164 (15ab-16a)

JIM RICHARDS
Page: 131 (6ab)

ALEXANDER ROBINSON
Pages: 32, 33, 34

IAN M. ROSENBERG
Page: 51 (23ab)

STUDIO SHIFT
Page: 63 (11)

ROBERT A. STAPLES
Page: 129 (2a)

BILL TATHAM
Pages: 18, 45 (11), 48 (17), 50 (20)

UPSTATE: A CENTER FOR DESIGN, RESEARCH, AND REAL ESTATE
AT THE SYRACUSE UNIVERSITY SCHOOL OF ARCHITECTURE
Pages: 20-23

WEST 8
Pages: 25, 26, 28

We are especially grateful to these image providers. Every reasonable attempt has been made to identify owners of copyright. Should unintentional mistakes or omissions have occurred, we sincerely apologise and ask for notice. Such mistakes will be corrected in the next edition of this publication.

ACKNOWLEDGEMENTS

SPECIAL THANKS TO:

Gerdo Aquino, Kinder Baumgardner, David Berkson, David Bickel, Rene Bihan, William Callaway, YoungJoon Choi, Scott Chuang, Scott Cooper, John Cutler, Julia Czerniak, Zachary Davis, Marco Esposito , Thomas Fox, Gary Garcia, Ron Heckmann, Adriaan Geuze, Cinda Gilliland, Carlos Hernandez, Lori Hjort, Ying-Yu Hung, Roy Imamura, Robert Jacob, Youngmin Kim, Elizabeth Lagedrost, Richard Law, Hui-Li Lee, James Lee, Margaret Leonard, John Loomis, Ye Luo, James Maloney, Chuck McDaniel, Ross Nadeau, Sean O'Malley, Na Ra Park, Timothy Peterson, Kalvin Platt, Lawrence Reed, Alex Robinson, Joe Runco, Natalie Sandoval, Kevin Shanley, Elizabeth Shreeve, Matthew Skjonsberg, Scott Slaney, Todd Strawn, Ria Stein, David Thompson, Corazon Unana, Melissa Vaughn, Amanda Walter, Charles Waldheim, John L. Wong, Danny Yee, Ji Hyun Yoo

MEMBERS OF SWA 2005-2010

Juanita Airo	Anthony Evon	Gloria Lau	Eric Perez	Karen Tautenhahn
Nayla Al Akl	Lauren Fasic	Eli Lechter	Dawn Perkins	Robert Taylor
Maribel Amador	Lei Feng	I-Hsien Lee	John Perry	Caroline Templeton
Kevin Arp	Nancy Fleming	Han Song Lee	Pavel Petrov	Travis Theobald
Melissa Aust	J. Shawn Freedberg	Kenneth Lee	Jamie Phillips	Cindy Thermidor
Michael Averitt	Robert Frisbie	Woonghee Lee	Paige Phillips	Jeffrey Thomas
Jessica Bacorn	Jennifer Gaines	Jinwook Lee	Laura Phipps	Leah Thompson
Allison Baker	David Gal	Jessica Leete	Michael Pon	Cary Thomsen
Pamela Barger	Qin Gao	Xun Li	Tanya Ponder	Andrew Trodler
Samuel Baucum	Elijah Gautney	Minhui Li	Christina Probst	Justin Trudeau
Matt Baumgarten	Mike Gilbert	Sergio Lima	Sol Rabin	Miao-Chi Tsai
Nathaniel Behrends	Ken Goodin	Chih-Wei Lin	Julianne Rader	Geoff Turnbull
Amy Benoit	Mary Gourlay	Conard Lindgren	Annabelle Reber	Maki Uchida
Jeremy Blad	Bing Gu	Huei-Lyn Liu	Karen Reeves	Chryssa Udvardy
John Brandt	Leah Hales	Joshua Lock	Jennifer Reisen	Carrie Van Valkenberg
Mary Breuer	Charleen Hansell	Jeffrey Longhenry	Rhett Rentrop	James Vick
Leah Broder	Andrew Harcar	Brent Longwell	Denise Retallack	Zachary Vieth
Timothy Brown	Brandon Hardison	Uriel Lopez	Matthew Reynolds	Bonita Wahl
Lauren Brown	Amber Harkey-Amadeus	Lance Lowrey	Bokyung Rhee	Sandeep Walia
Ellen Burke	Travis Hawkins	Ricardo Lozano	Rob Rider	Yan Wang
Meng Cai	Byron Hawley	Worasak Luangsuwan	Mary Anne Rinkin	Yunjia Wang
Megan Callaghan	Shuichiro Hayashi	Kui Chi Ma	Michael Robinson	Valerie Warner
Nathan Cameron	Xiongfei He	Zhen Ma	Felicity Rogers	Roger Warner
Micah Campbell	Michael Hee	Nora Machuca	Peter Rohan	Mio Watanabe
Marian Canicosa	Laura Henderson	Isabel Magdaleno	Steven Russell	Rachel West
Erin Cannon	Sean Henderson	Julia Mandell	Zachary Rutz	Sarah Wilkinson
Kelly Carmouche	Michael Herrin	Susan Martin	Timothy Ryan	Amity Winters
Ana Castaneda	Ryan Hsu	Margaret Masingill	Carrie Rybczynski	Justin Winters
Chih-Wei Chang	Ying Hu	Stephen McClain	Stephen Rydzon	Shan Wu
Shih-Ying Chuang	Myra Hyams	Scott McCready	Michael Samarripa	Zhaojie Wu
Jaewoo Chung	William Hynes	Yan Mei	Caleb Schultz	Zhiliang Xiao
Nancy Coulter	Cherry Intal	Scott Melbourne	Mark Schumacher	Peng Xu
Bradley Cowan	Akiko Ishii	Sheradyn Mikul	Shannon Scovell	Huaiche Yang
Xiaole Cui	Josselyn Ivanov	Geneva Miles	Oliver Seabolt	Wan-Chih Yin
Patrick Curran	Michaele Jaffe	Mehrdad Mohregi	Darren Sears	Seungjong Yoo
Elizabeth Curtis	Russ Jaycox	Allison Monroe	Holly Selvig	Donald Young
Kerri da Silva	Deanna Johnson	Christopher Morton	Raymond Senes	Shuang Yu
Shawn Dacy	Yoonju Kametani	Grey Moyed	Amirah Shahid	Peiwen Yu
Henry Dalton	Masato Kametani	Koichiro Nagamatsu	Wen Shang	Ding Yuan
Gerald De Dios	Sehgyung Kang	Jiyoung Nam	Stephen Sigler	Nanguo Yuan
Stephany Deddo	Pei-Ching Kao	Claire Napawan	Wendy Simon	Ying Zeng
Ning Deng	Claudia Kath	Jazibe Nash	Monica Simpson	Rui Zhang
Alfred DeWitt	Gary Karner	Joseph Newton	Kevin Slawson	Chaochao Zhao
Ying Dong	Candice Kelly	Darcy Nuffer	Alexander Song	Xiaodi Zheng
Deborah Drake	Lynn Kiang	Michael Odum	Lisa Spayde	Shuochen Zheng
Christiane Dreisbusch	Caroline Kim	Hyeon Oh	J. Lee Stickles	Xiao Zheng
Shaobo Du	Hyun-Min Kim	Trent Okumura	Rick Story	Huicheng Zhong
Aleksandra Dudukovic	Vira Klinetobe	Amy Oliver	Xiaoyan Sun	Xiao Zhou
Dawn Dyer	Benjamin Knoll	Jonathan Pal	Kathy Sun	Grace Zu
Lynn-Clar Elam	Goran Kosanovic	Stephanie Pankiewicz	Yige Sun	
Neil Emick	Stacey Krajewski	Shi Park	Chunghwan Sung	
Bonny Engler	Huiqing Kuang	Gyoung Park	Ricardo Supiciche	
Kristen English	Ashley Langworthy	Mandana Parvinian	Takako Tajima	
Carla Ernst	Todd Larudee	Larry Pearson	Qiuhong Tang	
Kanela Espinoza		Sarah Peck	William Tatham	